THE ESSENTIAL BHAGAVADGITA

A Study in Its Philosophy and Doctrine

By Jayaram V

Originally Published as Essays on the Bhagavadgita

Second Edition

Published by
Pure Life Vision LLC
New Albany, Ohio

The Essential Bhagavadgita: A Study in Its Philosophy and Doctrine
Copyright © 2012 by Jayaram V. All rights reserved.
Published and Distributed Worldwide by Pure Life Vision LLC., USA.
First edition 2012, Second Edition 2025

No part of this publication may be reproduced, stored in a retrieval system, or transmitted in any form or by any means, electronic, mechanical, photocopying, recording, scanning, or otherwise, now known or hereinafter invented, except for quotations in printed reviews, without the prior written, express permission of the publisher or the author. This strict copyright protection is meant to ensure the respect and integrity of the author's work. Requests to the publisher for permission to print portions of this book or for bulk purchase of the book should be addressed to Pure Life Vision LLC, PO Box 1003, 102 W Main St, New Albany, OH 43054.

NO AI TRAINING: Without in any way limiting the author's and publisher's exclusive rights under copyright, any use of this publication to "train" generative artificial intelligence (AI) technologies to generate text is expressly prohibited. The author reserves all rights to license uses of this work for generative AI training and development of machine learning language models.

Pure Life Vision LLC is a registered company in the U.S.A. Pure Life Vision books and E-Books are available through numerous bookstores, online websites, and our online store. For inquiries, please visit https://www.purelifevision.com.

Cover Design © Jayaram V, 2025

Library of Congress Publisher Cataloging-in-Publication Data

V, Jayaram, (Vemulapalli)
The Essential Bhagavadgita: A Study in Its Philosophy and Doctrine
       p. cm
       Includes bibliographical references
       LCCN: 2025936582
       ISBN-13: 978-1-935760-21-4
       ISBN-10: 1-935760-21-1
       1. Bhagavadgitā--Criticism, interpretation, etc. 2. Bhagavadgita--Philosophy. 3. Bhagavadgita--Ethics. 4. Bhagavadgita--Study and teaching.

Printed in the United States of America
10 9 8 7 6 5 4 3 2
Second Edition

About the Author

Jayaram V has authored over 3000 articles and 16 books, which include such notable works as Brahman, The Awakened Life, An Introduction to Hinduism, Bhagavadgita: Unveiling Gita's Secrets, Essays on the Bhagavadgita, Brahman, The Awakened Life, Hinduism, an Introduction, Selected Upanishads, Brihadaranyaka and Chandogya Upanishads, Shiva Sutras: Mystic Knowledge Explained, The Hindu Caste System, etc. His writings are appreciated all over the world for their originality and quality of information, and his analysis and interpretation of ancient texts. Jayaram V has studied Hinduism and related religions for over 40 years and writes regularly about various aspects of Hinduism, Buddhism, Jainism, spirituality, yoga, and self-improvement. Through his writings, he brings out the knowledge found in the ancient texts, their hidden symbolism, and the significance of various key concepts found in them, and interprets them objectively with modern insights and without sectarian biases. His scientific and spiritual background helps him examine the subjects analytically with an open mind and maintain objectivity in his writings and interpretations. He combines the mundane and finite aspects of life with the mystical and transcendental without losing sight of their spiritual and practical value in today's world. Inspired by Swami Vivekananda, Sri Aurobindo, and several other spiritual masters of the past and present, he founded Hinduwebsite.com in 2000 to counter negative propaganda and share authentic information about Hinduism and related religions. He believes in religious tolerance and the fundamental freedom of everyone to choose their faith or belief system according to their nature, needs, and preferences. He believes that atheism is also a part of one's spiritual journey. His efforts have helped make ancient Hindu texts more accessible to the world audience and appreciate the teachings found in them. His work has helped bring the wisdom of India's oldest religious and spiritual traditions to people around the world and educate and inspire them. You can explore more of his writings on Jayaramv.com and Hinduwebsite.com.

Books By Jayaram V

The Bhagavadgita: Unveiling the Gita's Secrets, 2024

Shiva Sutras: Mystic Knowledge Explained, 2024

The Awakened Life: Spiritual Knowledge from India's Sacred Traditions, 2024

Brihadaranyaka Upanishad, Revised 2024

Chandogya Upanishad, Revised 2024

The Bhagavadgita: A Simple Translation, Second Edition, 2024

Introduction to Hinduism, Second Edition, 2024

Brahman, Second Edition, 2025

The Essential Bhagavadgita, 2025

The Hindu Caste System, 2025

Sacred Numbers of Hinduism, 2025

The Bhagavadgita: A Complete Translation

Essays on the Bhagavadgita, 2012

Selected Upanishads

Think Success: Essays on Self-help

Being the Best: Practical Advice for Peace and Happiness

Thoughts and Quotations

Sadhana Panchakam - The Fivefold Spiritual Practice

Contents

Preface 11
Introduction 13
Bhagavadgita's Status in Hinduism 26
A Summary of the Bhagavadgita 33
Yoga According to Bhagavadgita 51
Five Lessons of the Bhagavadgita 55
Karma Yoga – the Path of (Selfless) Actions 65
References to Karmayoga in the Bhagavadgita 75
Jnanayoga – The Path of Knowledge 81
Knowledge as the Means and Goal 89
Buddhiyoga – Cultivating Discernment 93
Bhaktiyoga – The Yoga of Devotion 99
Types of Devotion and Devotees 105
Maya – The World as an Illusion 111
The True Meaning of Bhakti 125
Life's Lessons From the Bhagavadgita 130
Endearing Qualities of a Pure Devotee 139
Atma Samyama Yoga, Realizing the Self by the Self 146
Transforming the Physical Self 151
Stable Mind and Self-Realization 160
Purusha and Prakriti 170
Conquering the Ego, the False Self 177
Divine Qualities of Pure Souls 185
Demonic Qualities of the Wicked 191
The Body as a Vehicle of the Self 199
Making Sense of the Senses 206
Descriptions of the Pure Self 212
Seven Teachings of Bhagavadgita 222
The Triple Modes or Gunas 232
The Yoga of Sorrow 240
The Causes of Suffering 246
The Purpose of Sorrow 253
Resolving Sorrow and Suffering 257
Symbolism of Arjuna's Sorrow 262
The True Meaning of Renunciation 267
Symbolic themes from the Bhagavadgita 272
Bhagavadgita in Daily Life 289
Bibliography 299

Preface

The Bhagavadgita, one of the most revered and popular texts of Hinduism, continues to inspire and guide countless individuals on their spiritual journey. The first edition of this book, under the title "Essays on the Bhagavadgita," published in 2012, was well received by our readers worldwide. Now, after more than a decade, we are delighted to present the second edition, under the new title The Essential Bhagavadgita: A Study in Its Philosophy and Doctrine. This second edition, meticulously revised and updated by Jayaram V, contains many improvements. The new title appropriately reflects the central theme of the book: the essence of the Bhagavadgita and its core teachings and concepts.

Jayaram V, a distinguished author and scholar, has dedicated his life to the study and interpretation of the knowledge and wisdom contained in the Hindu scriptures. His knowledge and understanding of Hinduism, Buddhism, Jainism, spirituality, and transformational and inspirational wisdom are well reflected in his writings, which are known for their originality and depth. Jayaram V has written extensive commentary on the Bhagavadgita twice, making a unique contribution to our understanding of the scripture. He has also written hundreds of articles on the wisdom of the Bhagavadgita, which is still going on and can be found on our website: Hinduwebsite.com. In this revised edition, Jayaram V has not only corrected spelling and grammar errors but has also enhanced the layout, updated the cover page, adjusted font sizes, and reworked the line spacing and page numbers. Additionally, chapter titles and the book's title have been added to the headers on each page, and the text has been updated appropriately to improve the style or clarify certain points previously discussed.

The core content of the book remains unchanged, ensuring its reliability and authenticity. However, new information and a new chapter have been added, enriching the reader's experience and understanding of the Bhagavadgita. This edition also includes a preface, which was absent from the first edition, providing readers with a comprehensive overview of the book's significance and the author's intent.

The Bhagavadgita, with its timeless wisdom, offers profound insights into the nature of existence, the importance of duty, and the path to self-realization. Jayaram V's interpretation of this sacred text is both insightful and accessible, making it a valuable resource for scholars and spiritual seekers alike. His efforts have helped make ancient Hindu texts more accessible to a global audience, allowing readers to appreciate the teachings found in them. We hope that this revised edition of "The Essential Bhagavadgita" will continue to inspire and enlighten readers, making the wisdom of the Bhagavadgita more accessible and easier to understand. May this book serve as a guiding light on your spiritual journey, helping you navigate the complexities of life with clarity and purpose. May it inspire you, enlighten you, and help you in profound ways.

Publishers
July 7, 2025

Introduction

The Gita is not meant for anyone, or creed, or nation; it is meant for humanity. It speaks to a mind that has fought in life, a mind that is dissatisfied with constant want, a mind that is alert and thinking, and that has many conflicts. Swami Dayananda [1]

The Bhagavadgita is one of the most ancient religious scriptures of the world. It contains profound philosophical truths, representing "not any sect of Hinduism but Hinduism as a whole. [2]" Disparate traditions and paths of the ancient world are finely integrated into a harmonious and meaningful philosophy in the form of a lengthy discourse and a divine revelation. In many ways, the scripture reflects the internal reform and revival that took place within the Vedic tradition thousands of years ago, which contributed in no small measure to the survival and continuity of Hinduism later on. It is presented to us as a dialogue between Lord Krishna, the Supreme Self, and his dearest devotee in the person of Arjuna, a great warrior and one of the five Pandavas of the epic Mahabharata. The discourse was composed originally in Sanskrit, but today, its translations are available in almost every language. We do not know its exact antiquity. However, one of the popular opinions holds that its rendering in the current format was certainly pre-Christian, prior to the invasion of Alexander. Its religious and historical significance is intimately associated with the life and glory of Lord Krishna, who played a crucial role in the epic events of the Mahabharata and who is worshipped by millions of Hindus all over the world with love and devotion.

The historicity of Lord Krishna is uncertain. We have divergent opinions about His status as a divinity in our pantheon. In the Vedas, you do not find any hymns addressed to Him directly. However, ardent Hindus believe Him to be a historic person since many place names and popular pilgrimages in India are associated with Him. The Puranas affirm that Lord Vishnu, the Isvara of the manifested worlds, incarnated upon Earth in the form of Lord Krishna to root out evil and establish dharma or righteousness. However, some ardent devotees of Lord Krishna do not regard Him as an incarnation of Lord Vishnu, but as the Universal Lord, Isvara, Himself, who manifested on Earth to restore dharma. According to them, Lord Krishna represents Krishna consciousness, which is nothing but the universal consciousness from which all the worlds and the entire creation emerge. He is the universal Lord, with a universal form of infinite proportions. In his role as the preserver and upholder of dharma and as God Incarnate, he participated actively in the affairs of ancient India during the Mahabharata times and left behind a great legacy of his teachings in the form of the Bhagavadgita for the benefit of future generations. The scripture is truly a notable representation of the eternal religion (Sanatana Dharma), with a universal appeal, showing the way for people to live righteously in a world that is characterized by ignorance, materialism, delusion, and darkness, which comprehensively attempts to resolve their existential suffering through self-transformation and the help of God.

The teachings

The Bhagavadgita portrays in many ways the core beliefs and practices of Hinduism. It reflects its universality and the ideal vision of God as the center and circumference of all creation. If Hinduism is a way of life, the Bhagavadgita suggests how to live it. Its principles and doctrines are not easy to practice. They challenge to the core your resolve and commitment to follow a disciplined and virtuous life that guarantees freedom and bliss. Its message is simple: sacrifice your desires, but it is very difficult to practice because desires manifest numerously in our consciousness, and we are not always aware of them. It exhorts those who are curious and eagerly seek knowledge to live selflessly and virtuously with faith, knowledge, wisdom, devotion, surrender, and detachment, and perform their duties dispassionately as an offering to God. This is in contrast to the egocentric worldly life, with which we are familiar and in which we pursue our desires rather selfishly as part of our conditioning and self-promotion. The Bhagavadgita tells us how to attain peace and stability instead of strife and suffering, and live freely and fearlessly, without striving and without searching for happiness in worldly pursuits, and without suffering from desires and delusion induced by attraction or aversion to the pairs of opposites. The book is a discourse of immense spiritual value. It inspires those who are engaged in their daily battles and who want permanent solutions, like Arjuna himself, to resolve their problems and overcome their limitations without ignoring their duties and responsibilities and without compromising their core values and beliefs.

The scripture is not difficult to understand, but it has some complexity, which can be overcome with effort, with the help of an expert or enlightened guru. It has an infinite capacity to reveal itself to the extent you probe into its depths. With each reading, you learn more and develop newer insights. By studying it regularly, we can transcend our limitations and learn to live with humility, knowledge, wisdom, and discernment. We can learn to live responsibly and dutifully, performing our obligatory duties without losing our inner balance and without suffering from the consequences of our own actions. From its study, we realize how one can escape from the shackles of karma not by inaction, not by shunning one's responsibilities, not even by doing only the so-called good deeds, but by offering all actions to Isvara, as if one does not exist at all, attributing the doership and ownership to Him and renouncing the fruit of one's actions. In short, if you follow the scripture, you learn to live with real freedom as if your life is a great sacrifice with Isvara as the Sacrificer, the Sacrificed, and the Witness.

The Bhagavadgita is a book of self-discovery and an inward journey towards liberation and the Abode of God. It deals with the essential truths regarding life and reality, the nature of our existence, and our relationship with God. It explains how our desire-ridden actions cause suffering and bondage and how one may escape from the hold of Nature through knowledge, devotion, and selfless actions. It touches upon many subjects, such as the importance of discernment and detachment, the perils of desire-ridden actions, the nature of our existence, the triple gunas, the practice of yoga, the meaning and importance of true devotion, the right attitude one should cultivate towards the dualities of life, the meaning and purpose of maya or delusion and so on. It explains the difference between the body and the Self, between action and inaction, between knowledge and ignorance, between heavenly life and immortal life, and between divine and demonic qualities.

The scripture provides guidance to those who want to control their desires and achieve liberation through renunciation and detachment. In eighteen chapters, it covers a wide spectrum of spiritual subjects. In the second chapter, Lord Krishna explains how contact between the senses and sense objects leads to attachment and how, from attachment, delusion arises, resulting in bondage and suffering. He reminds Arjuna that the body is like a garment, which is destructible and discarded by the soul from time to time during its existence on earth under the control of Nature. He draws a clear distinction between the physical self (jiva) and the inner Self (atma), reminding him that he should not worry about the destruction that was about to happen in the war because the Self could neither be killed nor destroyed.

From the Gita, we learn that the source of karma lies not in actions but in the desire for the fruit of our actions. Therefore, one should not abandon actions but the desire for their result. Renunciation is not an escape from duty and responsibility but a means to overcome attachment and egocentric actions. Since one cannot remain free from actions even for a moment, one needs to perform them always, offering their result to God, who is the real Doer. When you do not live for yourself, God takes over your life and your responsibilities. When you live here as if you do not exist, your actions will not bind you. It is much better if you live here for the sake of others, as a service to God. It is part of a covenant between God and His devotees. It is a way out of the binding and deluding mechanism He creates with His Nature. When people live for themselves, God remains in the background as a Witness, letting them live according to their likes and dislikes. When they turn to Him, become passive witnesses to His Play, and live for Him, sacrificing their desires and interests, He reciprocates with unconditional love and takes care of their welfare and liberation. This is not like a king bestowing his favors upon a few loyal subjects. The scripture states clearly that God has no particular interest in favoring a few who show Him loyalty. His mercy (prasadam) is part of a set of rules (dharma) that govern our lives. What binds humans to this world is their very nature (svabhavam), characterized by the impurities of egoism, selfishness, desires, delusion, pride, lack of discernment, demonic qualities, and such that arise from the modes of sattva, rajas, and tamas. When they are gradually eliminated from one's character through austerities and the practice of yoga, one experiences peace, stability, equanimity, sameness, and inner harmony.

According to the Bhagavadgita, the external world is unreal not because it does not exist but because it is unstable and ever-changing. The reality that you perceive is a set of independent events, objects, and circumstances that create in you the illusion of continuity and meaningful experience. In reality, they are different perceptions and phenomena, which your mind tries to make sense of, just as it tries to connect dots on paper with its imagination and accumulated knowledge to create the illusion of some meaningful concept, form, or story. Since it is not true except as an illusion and keeps changing from moment to moment, you cannot live in it with peace and stability unless you cultivate discernment and deal with it with detachment and sameness. Our knowledge arising from our perceptions and our interactions with the objective world is imperfect and incomplete. It is not true wisdom (jnanam) that leads to liberation. It is worldly wisdom, practical knowledge, or ingenuity (vijnanam) that helps us think for ourselves and adapt to the ever-changing circumstances according to our desires and preferences. What we consider knowledge is, in truth, ignorance because it does not take us beyond the illusion of appearances; rather, it involves us with the world and its impermanence deeply and makes our escape even more difficult. We cannot truly rely on it to regulate our lives or find permanent solutions to the problems in our lives. We cannot also rely upon our perceptions or trust our senses fully because they are guided by our desires and inherent tendencies (prvrittis) rather than the reality of the world. They can only see the surface of things instead of what is hidden and imperceptible. The knowledge that we accumulate through them is a mental construct, or an illusory formation, colored by our desires and predominant gunas. The world that we perceive through them is also essentially an illusion of our minds. It does not necessarily correspond to the truth or reality of the world itself. In many ways, it is a product of our delusion and ignorance, whereby we mistake truth for falsehood, the body for the Self, impermanence for permanence, and bondage for freedom. The phenomenal world is subject to change and impermanence, and our likes and dislikes. It is always in a state of flux, just as our minds are. We cannot rely upon it to secure peace or happiness. We are bound to suffer if we cling to things that are impermanent and destructible. He who hankers after material things in search of happiness suffers from the duality of gain and loss and rarely experiences peace.

Therefore, the Bhagavadgita suggests that we should seek permanent solutions to the transience of life, not by changing the world but by withdrawing from it and changing ourselves, overcoming our self-seeking attitude and our attachment to it. To escape from the illusion of your worldly experiences, you must take refuge in your inner Self, which is eternal, permanent, and free from modifications. For that to happen, you must withdraw your mind and senses into your inner Self and escape from the illusions of the world. Through yoga, you have to remove the obstacles that stand between your physical Self and your spiritual Self and establish peace. Only when you silence your ego and your craving can you see your real Self through the prism of your pure consciousness beyond the chaos of your mind. The obstacles to peace and stability are ignorance, delusion, desires, and egoism. They are the impurities arising from the gunas to which we are all subject. To overcome them or suppress them, a seeker has to practice self-discipline and restrain his mind and body until he develops sattva. He should free his mind from past life impressions and arrest the continuing cycle of karma. When they come to rest, a yogi rests in the peace of his tranquil mind. In that stillness and self-absorption, he realizes that his life on earth has all along been a mental construction, and he is caught in an illusion of modifications and experiences.

The three secrets

In the eighteenth chapter of the scripture, Lord Krishna informs Arjuna that He taught him the most secret knowledge, which should not be imparted to those who were not austere, who lacked devotion, who had no interest in listening, and who habitually spoke ill of God. Hidden within the secret knowledge of the scripture are further secrets, discernible only to a few whose minds are pure and who are devoted to the knowledge of liberation. Among them, three are worth mentioning. They also constitute its core teachings.

Stick to your duty: The first one is that you must do your duty according to your inherent nature as determined by your gunas, not what you find convenient, profitable, or socially popular. Doing your duty is better than doing the duties of others (para dharma), however good they may be, because it is deeply connected to your past. Your past actions determine the nature of your obligatory duties (Dharma), and you cannot resolve the karma arising from them unless you fulfill your current obligations. Performing the duties that are expected of us and that have become part of our destinies, we must resolve the accumulated consequences of our past actions and pay off our past debts. Through desireless actions, we must also transcend the very gunas that induce desire-ridden actions and contribute to our bondage and suffering. According to the Bhagavadgita, a person's Dharma (obligatory duty) is neither a problem nor a burden but an opportunity to free oneself from the hold of Nature and attain liberation. While it is true that karma arises from actions, it is not actions but the desires that are hidden in actions that are responsible for one's karma and which lead to one's bondage and suffering. The desires are, in turn, induced by the gunas (modes). Therefore, the scripture says that to resolve the problem of karma, the gunas should be neutralized and silenced first. The gunas will come to rest if we perform our actions with detachment and dispassion, giving up the desire for their fruit. When we perform our actions in this manner, we arrest the accumulation of karma and the possibilities of the next birth. Free from attraction and aversion to things, we become equal to the dualities of life and experience peace and equanimity within ourselves.

You are an eternal Self: The second secret is about the presence of the inner Self. We are essentially spiritual beings. We have an eternal aspect beyond the physical aspect. This is because the Self exists in all. There are no exceptions. All living beings contain an individual Self (atman) hidden behind names and forms. Since it exists deep within the core of each being, as either a small dot or flame, beyond the mind and the senses, incomprehensible and imperceptible, it cannot be known through ordinary means. It can be known through transcendence only, in a state of unity that is similar to the state of deep sleep, but in which one is self-aware without the distinction of the knower and the known. We usually experience it in the advanced stages of yoga, when we practice samyama and combine the best techniques of concentration (dharana), meditation (dhyana), and self-absorption (samadhi). Because of ignorance, duality, and delusion, worldly people cannot discern the Self within them. Under the influence of their egos, they identify themselves with their names and forms. This delusion subjects them to the modifications of the mind and body, such as aging, death, and rebirth.

The Self is real, eternal, indestructible, immutable, and absolute. In its essence and essential nature, it is the same as Isvara, the Lord of the Universe, but in its embodied state, it is held in check by the modifications of Nature. The Gita says that to cultivate true wisdom and overcome our attachments, we must know the difference between our physical and spiritual selves. The Self is different from the physical being. It is distinct and different from the realities (tattvas) of Nature and entirely free from change and impermanence, even though it is held in bondage by it. Two opposite polarities exist in you, one pure and the other impure. To experience peace and balance, you must bridge the gap between the two and make them indistinguishable. The highest state of yoga is attained when these two are in perfect union and identical (samatvam). The Bhagavadgita declares that the physical self is a friend of the Self and its enemy. It means we achieve peace and liberation only when we subordinate the needs of the physical self to the liberation of the inner Self and subject it to necessary transformation so that it has divine qualities and reflects the purity and divinity of sattva. When you are in harmony with your inner Self, you achieve liberation; when you are in conflict with it, you increase your suffering, ignorance, and delusion. To establish inner harmony, one must not only sacrifice the interests of the lower nature for the sake of the higher nature but also integrate one's whole personality around the latter.

All this is for the habitation of God: The third secret is about the omnipresence of God. The world is filled with life because of the presence of God. Whatever moves here, whatever happens here is because of Him. The whole world is His manifestation. He is hidden in every aspect of it. He is both the cause and the effect. He is also the Creator and the created. He envelops all and pervades all. He inhabits the worlds He manifests, and He maintains them, even though He is complete in all respects and has no interest or desire whatsoever. Entirely free and independent and with no support for Himself, He supports everything. Timeless, there was no time when He was nonexistent, and there will never be a time when He will cease to exist. Ignorant people may not recognize His greatness or His manifestations, but His devotees know His diverse manifestations (vibhutis) and supreme perfections (siddhis). One may worship other divinities, but only by worshipping Him can one attain liberation. Therefore, says the Bhagavadgita, one should live in this world with the awareness that all that exists here is but Vasudeva. Since He is the real Doer and the Supreme Controller, one must perform one's duty with humility, surrender, devotion, and detachment, offering Him the fruit of one's actions. By performing actions in this manner and cultivating devotion, one earns the right to enter His Abode and live there eternally.

Thus, by understanding your purpose in this world, realizing your divine nature and spiritual identity, and acknowledging your inherent relationship with God, you should live on earth with the spirit of sacrifice as a responsible human being in the service of God. Knowing these three secrets, you can work for your liberation, practicing yoga with stability, balance, and sameness. These three secrets are known respectively as guhya (secret), guhyatara (more secret), and guhyatma (most secret). The first secret frees us from the cycle of karma, the second secret from delusion and ignorance, and the third from death and impermanence. The second, third, fourth, and fifth chapters, as well as the eighteenth chapter of the Bhagavadgita deal with the first secret; the second, sixth, and thirteenth to eighteenth chapters deal with the second secret; while the third, seventh, eighth, ninth, and tenth to eighteenth chapters deal with the third secret. Thus, one can see that while many scholars hold that the second chapter is central to its teachings, the eighteenth chapter also has great importance for the students of the scripture.

Prasthanatraya

If anyone asks you what the most important scriptures of Hinduism are, you can instantly reply that the Bhagavadgita is one of them. Historically, the scripture played a key role in shaping our philosophical thought and heralded the rise and popularity of several schools of Vaishnavism, which emphasized the importance of devotion (bhakti) in achieving liberation (mukti). It played a very significant role in the rise of devotional theism in Hinduism and contributed to its survival and continuity during the medieval period. Its teachings are used by scholars and devotees alike to widen their knowledge and delve deep into the depths of their own consciousness through devotion and meditation to understand the relationship between the individual Self and the universal Self and between the Ultimate Reality and the empirical reality with which we are familiar. Hence, it is considered one of the three most important scriptures (Prasthanatraya) of Hinduism (Sanatana Dharma), the other two being the Upanishads and the Brahmasutras. Followers of various schools of Vedic theism (Vedanta) have been relying upon these three since the earliest times to explain and justify their respective philosophies. If Shankaracharya found in them undeniable evidence to justify monism (Advaita), Ramanujacharya used the same scriptures to justify his philosophy of qualified monism (Vishistadvaita). In contrast, Madhava found ample justification in them to support his view that duality was inherent in the numerous forms and aspects of Isvara and His creation. Apart from them, there were others such as Nimbarka (A.D. 1162), the proponent of the dual but nondual doctrine (Dvaita Advaita), and Vallabha (A.D. 1479), the proponent of pure non-dualism (Suddha Advaita). They, too, relied upon the same scriptures to interpret the nature of Isvara and reality to justify their respective beliefs. Thus, the Bhagavadgita is a text of standard knowledge, which is useful to ascertain standard truths (sabda pramana), even though officially it is not given the same status as the Vedas, which constitute the revelatory scriptures (shruti) of Hinduism and which are used for the same purpose.

Statistical data

Originally written in Sanskrit, the Bhagavadgita has been translated into all the major languages and is now available to people all over the world. While it was composed a long time ago in a language that is no longer used in regular conversation, there is a certain pragmatic directness and timeless relevance to its teachings, which make it profoundly appealing and inspiring. People can relate to it even today. Its teachings are as relevant to the present-day world as they were two thousand years ago. They can be practiced and tested by anyone who has faith and devotion and is willing to make some sacrifices and adhere to austere self-discipline. There is also a certain plasticity and inclusiveness about its teachings and many expressions used in the verses. We can interpret them differently from different perspectives, just as we can do so with many universal truths. As a result, the more we read the Bhagavadgita, the greater the insight we gain into its hidden secrets. With the Bhagavadgita, the learning never stops. Even after studying for years, we may not be sure whether we have mastered it. Despite our understanding, a verse or a chapter may still elude our intellect and challenge our notions of duty, devotion, and sacrifice. The diverse philosophies and paths of liberation suggested in it are difficult to practice simultaneously. Hence, we may know part of it but seldom all of it.

According to Gita Karadinyasa [3], the presiding deity (devata) of the Bhagavadgita is Lord Krishna. Its seer is Vedavyasa. Its meter (chanda) is anushtup. Its seed (bija) mantra is the eleventh verse of the second chapter, which is as follows. It suggests that we should cultivate wisdom and not worry about things that are imperishable by nature.

The Supreme Lord said, "You are grieving for those who should not be grieved for. You have put forth wise arguments, but knowledgeable people do not grieve for the life that is gone or yet to be gone.

The 66th verse in the 18th chapter is its power (shakti) mantra, while the second part of the same verse serves as the axis or central aspect (keelakam) of it. It is as follows.

"Renouncing all obligatory duties, take shelter in Me alone. I will liberate you from all sins. Do not grieve.

The Bhagavadgita contains 18 chapters and 700 (or, according to some, 699) verses. It has four principal participants to whom the verses are attributed in the following manner.

- Dhritarashtra - 1
- Sanjaya - 41
- Arjuna - 84
- Lord Krishna - 574

Each verse in the scripture is considered a mantra. Many verses contain specific phrases that allude to major concepts and practices of Hinduism and serve as useful mental hooks for contemplation and concentration.

In the Bhagavadgita, Lord Krishna and Arjuna are addressed with several names. Lord Krishna is addressed with twenty-seven different names: Anantarupa, Achyuta, Arisudhana, Krishna, Kesava, Kesanishudana, Kamalapatraksha, Govinda, Jagadpatih, Jagannivasa, Janardhana, Devedeva, Devavarah, Purushottama, Bhagawan, Bhutabhavana, Bhutesah, Madhusudhana, Mahabahu, Madhavah, Yadava, Yogaviththama, Vasudeva, Varsheya, Vishnuh, Hrisikesa, and Harih. Arjuna is also addressed variously as Gudakesa, Kaunteya, Partha, Paramtapa, Bharata, Dhananjaya, Mahabahu, and so on. These names have symbolic significance and are associated with the glories, attributes, relationships, and achievements of Lord Krishna. They are used mostly to draw out a hidden purpose or meaning in the context of the intended teaching or to denote the mental state of the participants.

Historicity

It is difficult to determine the historicity and the antiquity of the Bhagavadgita. It is even more difficult to determine whether it was truly delivered in the middle of the battlefield, or the setting was chosen symbolically to signify the Field (body) where the three gunas and the thoughts of good and evil wage a relentless war between themselves for supremacy. We are also not certain how it evolved into its current form. The authorship is attributed to sage Veda Vyasa, who is also considered the author of the epic Mahabharata, of which the Gita is a part. The scripture appears in the epic from chapters 23 to 40 in the section on Bhishma (Bhishmaparva). The composition appears to be a work of the later Vedic period. It was probably integrated into the epic in its current form after the emergence of many principal Upanishads, as is evident from identical verses found in the Upanishads, such as the Katha and the Svetasvatara Upanishads.

Connection with yoga

The Bhagavadgita is essentially a scripture on yoga (yoga shastram). It presents various types of yoga practices and their significance in attaining liberation. It is, therefore, rightly referred to as a yoga Upanishad. In fact, it treats yoga more comprehensively than the

Yogasutras of Patanjali and broadens both its scope and purpose by integrating the various aspects of yoga into an integrated philosophy. Unlike the Yogasutras, it presents God in a dynamic role as the Creator and Sustainer. Each chapter in it deals with a specific type of yoga and bears the word yoga in its title.

The text might have been originally a later-day Upanishad and undergone some modifications over time to acquire the status of an independent scripture of great spiritual value. We have many Gitas (songs) in Hindu tradition, some long and some short, but the Bhagavadgita rules them all. Whatever its historicity or antiquity may be, it delivers a significant spiritual message to the spiritually advanced souls who want to transcend themselves and achieve liberation.

Footnotes

1. Swami Dayananda, the Teaching of the Bhagavadgita.
2. S. Radhakrishnan, Introductory Essay, the Bhagavadgita, Harper Collins, 1998.
3. Introduction to the practice of the Gita

Bhagavadgita's Status in Hinduism

Bhagavadgita occupies a unique position in the religious literature of Hinduism. It is not a revelatory scripture (shruti) like the Vedas, but it can be treated as one since its source is Lord Krishna. It has popular appeal because it is a part of the Mahabharata's epic narrative and is relevant to human life. Although Hinduism is not an organized religion, many regard it as the standard text of Hinduism and compare it with the principal texts of Christianity and Islam. Its title is defined, understood, and interpreted variously by scholars according to their knowledge, wisdom, and understanding. Bhagavadgita literally means the song of God. You may also interpret it as a divine song meant for the benefit of the bhagavatas, the servants of God. The scripture is a revelation by God about Himself and His numerous manifestations, in which He explains how we may find Him in creation, Nature, things, phenomena, beings, and within ourselves, and how we may relate to Him and worship Him for our liberation. We find a reference to the nature and status of the scripture in the scripture itself at the end of every chapter in the form of a chapter ending, which goes like this.

"Thus ends the ... chapter named ... in the Upanishad of the sacred Bhagavadgita, the knowledge of the Absolute Brahman, the scripture on yoga, and the debate between Lord Krishna and Arjuna."

This terse statement provides a valuable clue about the nature of the scripture and its status in our religion. It contains four important phrases, which are emphasized above in bold letters. Let us analyze them carefully to understand their meaning and significance.

The Bhagavadgita is an Upanishad

The Bhagavadgita is not just an ordinary religious text. It is prefixed with the title of 'srimad,' meaning sacred and auspicious. Besides, it is a Upanishad. Upanishad means sitting near. According to a long-established tradition, the Upanishads were taught in person by learned teachers to their students who were well-versed in the knowledge of the ritual part of the Vedas (karma kanda) and related subjects. Probably, there were exceptions to this rule, but it was the general practice. The Upanishads constitute the end part of the Vedas (Vedanta). In other words, they are taught to those who have the essential knowledge of the Vedas and related texts and have advanced far in their study and practice.

In the strictest sense of the word, the Bhagavadgita does not qualify as an Upanishad because it is part of an epic, not any Veda. However, the scripture has all the essential features of a Upanishad and serves the same purpose as the latter. Firstly, like in the Upanishads, it contains secret knowledge that is not known to everyone. Lord Krishna Himself declared the knowledge the utmost secret or the secret of the secrets (guhyatitam). Secondly, like the Upanishads, its knowledge is not meant for everyone but for a qualified few who should be chosen carefully and taught in person. In the scripture, Lord Krishna specifies clearly four types of people to whom it should never be taught: those who do not practice austerities, those who have no devotion, those who cannot render selfless service, and those who dislike God. As you can see, most people fall into this category and do not qualify for the knowledge. Thirdly, it should be taught in person and not revealed to everyone. Lord Krishna Himself taught this knowledge in person to Arjuna. At the other end, Sanjaya revealed it to Dhritarashtra again in person. In the olden days, the scripture was recited before people in person with the necessary explanation. Fourthly, the scripture is composed in the style of an Upanishad and contains a few themes and verses that are common to some of the oldest Upanishads. Like them, it deals with the knowledge and functions of Brahman, the individual Self, the nature of reality, divisions of Nature (tattvas), the means to attain salvation, descriptions of creation, time, manifestations of God, and so on. In many ways, it reflects the evolving vision of the Vedanta school and the unfolding of the bhakti movement. Finally, the scripture concurs with the Vedas in many respects and contains the same knowledge propounded by them. Technically, it is a synthesis of diverse Vedic traditions whose basis is the Vedas and whose inspiration is the Upanishads. Thus, although strictly it is not a Upanishad, it qualifies in many ways as a Upanishad.

The Bhagavadgita is a study of Brahman

Fundamentally, the Bhagavadgita is a study of Brahman

(brahmavidya), with particular emphasis on His duties, manifestations, creation, and relationship with humans, especially with His devotees and their liberation. It opens our eyes to the knowledge and glory of Brahman as the Lord and Controller of the whole manifestation. It clears our confusion about the nature of our existence and the role of God in our lives. It presents the Supreme Self in the most personal terms as our Teacher and Benefactor. It increases our opportunities to secure His grace and live in His protection. Unlike the Upanishads, it brings Brahman into our lives and hearts as a personal God to whom we can relate and in whom we can seek refuge.

A lot of sacred knowledge is hidden in the scripture, which can be used for spiritual advancement as well as liberation. Its source is Brahman. Its goal is Brahman; its subject is Brahman, and its purpose is Brahman. It describes the individual Self (Atman), the Supreme Self (Brahman), and the relationship between the two, apart from explaining their transcendental nature, their role in creation, the obstacles to their union, and the means to attain it. In every chapter, Brahman is its dominant theme and the fundamental goal. Those who study it sincerely find in it many opportunities to improve their knowledge of Him (brahmavidya) and overcome their ignorance and delusion. When we do not know Brahman, we suffer from ignorance and delusion and live our lives selfishly and egoistically, performing our actions out of desire and facing the consequences. When we know who He is, we open our eyes to the truths of our existence and try to transcend ourselves to reach His Abode.

The concept of Brahmavidya is well-known to the scholars of the Vedas. The Upanishads refer to several types of Brahmavidyas, numbering about 32, whose study and practice lead to knowledge and liberation, such as the science of breath (prana vidya) [1], the science of fire (panchagni vidya), the science of space (akasa vidya), and so on. Just like them, the Bhagavadgita provides information on Brahman, the Supreme Self, His essential nature, His manifestations, His functions as the creator, preserver, and destroyer, His universal form (visvarupam), and His role in our liberation. Entire chapters in it are dedicated to the study and understanding of Him. For example, the eighth chapter deals with the Imperishable (akshara) Brahman, who resides in the body as the Witness, the Enjoyer, and the imperishable

Self (adhyatma). In the ninth chapter, He is described as the sacrifice, the sacrificer, and the sacrificed, who is also the Father, Mother, Sustainer, and Grandfather of creation, the Supreme Goal, the Final Abode, Friend, Origin, and the End. The 10th chapter is dedicated to His manifestations, while the 11th chapter is dedicated to His universal form. In the 12th chapter, we realize that by fixing our minds upon Him and by devotion to Him, we can secure His mercy (prasadam) and attain liberation. Thus, the Bhagavadgita is rightly described as the science of Brahman (brahmavidya), a systematic study aimed at overcoming human suffering and attaining God through well-established, effective, and reliable spiritual methods, models, and practices that have withstood the test of time. It is a sacred scripture about Brahman by Brahman Himself in His incarnated form of Lord Krishna.

Bhagavadgita is a scripture on yoga

The Bhagavadgita is rightly described as a scripture on yoga (yoga shastram). It deals with the subject of yoga more comprehensively than any other scripture, including the Yogasutras. It also expands the scope and purpose of yoga by adding many new elements to its theory and practice that are not found in other scriptures on yoga. In fact, we can even call it a Song of Yoga (Yoga Gita) because its emphasis is on practicing various types of yoga and attaining sameness. It speaks about not one or two but a number of yoga disciplines. Every chapter in it contains the word yoga and deals with some particular practice of yoga or state of yoga. For the Bhagavadgita, yoga is not just a discipline. It stands for both the state to be attained and the means to attain it. In other words, you practice different types of yoga to attain different yogas (states), which may be equanimity, detachment, sameness, discernment, devotion, purity, and so on. The highest yoga is liberation or the state (bhava) of Brahman. The means are the yoga of action (karma yoga), the yoga of knowledge (jnana yoga or samkhya yoga), the yoga of renunciation (sannyasa yoga), the yoga of discretion (buddhiyoga), the yoga of the Self (atma yoga), the yoga of devotion (bhakti yoga), and the yoga of renunciation of the results (karmaphala sannyasa yoga).

The specific techniques to practice some of these yogas are the same as those mentioned in the Yogasutras, such as rules and restraints (yamas and niyamas), breath control (pranayama), restraint of the senses (pratyahara), concentration (dharana), meditation (dhyana), and self-absorption (samadhi). The other similarities include references to important concepts such as the Self as the lord of the body (Isvara), meditation upon Him as Aum, arresting the modifications of the mind by cultivating purity (sattva), controlling desires, practicing detachment, stabilizing the mind, purifying the intelligence, practicing samyama, arresting the afflictions, cultivating sameness, transcending the senses, and so on. It also defines yoga (2.48) as sameness (samatvam) and declares that in the early stages of yoga, work is the means, and in the later stages, equanimity. It means that in the early stages, one should focus on performing one's obligatory duties. When one has progressed sufficiently on the path of desireless actions, one should aim to stabilize the mind and experience equanimity. The highest form of yoga is the yoga of devotion. Unlike the Yogasutras, the Bhagavadgita recommends a more personal and intense form of devotional worship (Isvara pranidhana) in which not only the individual Self but also the Universal Self are revered as the objects of worship. Compared to the Yogasutras, it also has more theistic elements and emotional appeal. It regards Brahman more personally as the source and creator of all, and His worship and grace as vital to achieving liberation.

Bhagavadgita is a dialogue between God and His devotee

The Bhagavadgita is a dialogue (samvadam) between Lord Krishna and Arjuna. Symbolically, Lord Krishna represents the Supreme Self (Brahman), and Arjuna is the embodied self (jiva) who is caught in the phenomenal world of Samsara, subject to ignorance, duality, and delusion. They are also referred to as Narayana and Nara, respectively. Nara is the individual being made up of the waters of life (naara). Narayana is the Lord and the Supreme Self who pervades (ayana) all beings (naras) and the waters (naara) of creation. Their dialogue is a friendly conversation in which they exchange ideas and knowledge of profound philosophical and spiritual implications while appreciating their respective standings in life and their common goal, which is to protect and uphold Dharma. It is not a dispute (vivadam) in which the participants contest ideas with arguments to defend their egos or personal interests. It is also not a one-sided exposition (vadam) of a doctrine or philosophy in which one side prevails without letting the other side participate in it constructively or freely. It is a friendly debate or conversation (samvadam) between two close friends who have mutual love, respect, and admiration for each other, who understand and appreciate the urgency of the situation, and who share their thoughts and opinions without feeling dominated, slighted, or oppressed.

The Bhagavadgita is an outstanding example of how mutual love, faith and devotion can open communication channels between God and His devotees, regardless of location or context, facilitating the transmission of mystical knowledge from the highest heaven into the mortal world, without suppressing human thought or ignoring our spiritual and material needs or our limitations in comprehending transcendental truths. It represents a dialogue in which one has the freedom to ask questions, raise doubts and objections, and seek clarifications. Throughout the discourse, Lord Krishna did not force His ideas upon Arjuna. He gave him ample time and opportunities to comprehend the truths He revealed to Him. He allowed him to absorb the knowledge and draw his own conclusions. He even helped him understand it by bestowing His grace upon him and showing him His universal form. In the last chapter (18.63), He even told him that He revealed to him the secret of the secrets, upon which he should reflect and act according to his wish (iccha).

The purpose of this mutual conversation of extraordinary value is to resolve the problem of human suffering by providing spiritual solutions that do not add to our burdens further but only complement and augment our efforts, and simultaneously encourage us to persevere on the path of liberation without abandoning the world or our obligations. The solutions that emerge from that sacred dialogue address the root cause of our suffering, which is desire, and how we may neutralize it. The scripture is not a conversation between Lord Krishna and Arjuna alone. They symbolize the rather incongruous relationship between our human and divine nature and the conflicts we experience in crucial moments when we are tested by circumstances and difficult choices. Whoever reads it with sincerity and devotion can enter into a conversation with God and open their minds to His love and compassion. By reading the scripture and by assimilating the knowledge, one can earn His grace and work for one's liberation. Most scriptures deliver God's messages or communication indirectly through a medium or in the second person, but in the Bhagavadgita, the entire discourse is delivered by God Himself directly in the first person. That makes it personally relatable and impactful.

Reference

1. Some people may take objection to the use of the term science for religious subjects. However, we have used it since these subjects are systematic, well-structured, and based on observation and subjective experiences of countless yogis that indicate predictive outcomes for those who follow their established guidelines and empirical methods to realize the goals they promise to deliver.

A Summary of the Bhagavadgita

The Bhagavadgita teaches us how to live in this world, do our duties, and yet remain like lotus leaves in the waters of life, untainted by the laws of karma. The world in which we live is a world of illusion. Out of ignorance and egoism and through desires and selfish actions, we cling to this world, and not knowing our true nature and purpose, we indulge in desire-ridden actions. In the process, we become bound to the cycle of births and deaths and the forces of Nature until we wake up from our delusion and realize our mistake. The Bhagavadgita teaches us how to reach that austere goal, not by escaping from the burdens of the worldly life or avoiding our responsibilities, but by remaining amidst the distractions and afflictions of life and dealing with them squarely with dispassion, detachment, and stability, accepting God as the Doer and doing our ordained duties as an offering and a sacrifice.

According to the Bhagavadgita, salvation is not possible if we shun our responsibilities and indulge in desire-ridden actions. True renunciation is the renunciation of desires hidden in our thoughts and actions. Those who perform their obligatory duties without desire for their fruit are qualified for liberation. Those who live their lives with detachment in the contemplation of God earn His grace and qualify to enter His Abode. If liberation is the goal, first, it must begin in the mind as an idea and resolve. Then, it should be extended into our actions and relationships. The ideal state is freedom from the modifications of the mind. When the senses move among the objects, the mind should be still, and the perceiver should be indifferent. One must be free from delusion, ignorance, attraction and aversion, egoism, prejudices, opinions, dependencies, and desires.

Actions do not bind us. Desires bind us. Desire for the fruit of our actions creates our karma. Expectations bind us to our future. Selfishness binds us to our names and forms. When we perform actions with expectation and seek things avidly, we become responsible for their consequences. Thus, largely, the continuity of our existence on earth is in our hands (adhyatmikam), while our liberation depends upon our effort as well as the grace of God (adhidaivam). With detachment, we can suppress the impure gunas, arrest the formation of latent impressions (samskaras) in our consciousness, and thereby stop the cycle of births and deaths. When the mind becomes still like a placid lake, and the latent impressions are burnt away in the fire of selfless actions, we end the process of being and becoming.

The Bhagavadgita is for people like Arjuna and Sanjaya, who desire the company of God, who perform selfless service to His devotees, and who want to know answers to their suffering and perform their duties and obligations as an offering to God. If you want to know the perfect way to live on earth, the scripture is the right choice for you. If you want to live in the company of God and make your life a great sacrifice, the scripture is the right one to guide you. If you want to know the truths concerning your existence and your essential nature, the scripture is the perfect source of knowledge for you.

The first chapter in the Bhagavadgita begins with the despondency of Arjuna when he is suddenly overcome with profound sorrow in the middle of the battlefield at the thought of the bloodshed that was going to happen in his hands. Unable to bear the thought, he decided to renounce the world. His idea of renunciation was to abandon his duties as a warrior and live as an ascetic, seeking alms. In that state of depression, he forgot that he had a responsibility to help his brothers in their righteous cause against their evil cousins. His predicament stemmed from his egoistic thinking and mistaken belief that renunciation meant giving up actions to avoid their consequences. Lord Krishna, who agreed to act as his charioteer during the war, fittingly responded to his grief and opened his eyes to profound metaphysical truths concerning himself, his duty, and his equation with God. Out of extreme compassion and love, He taught him how to perform his ordained duties without incurring sin and how to work for his liberation by practicing renunciation and self-purification with the help of the yoga of action (karma), knowledge (jnana), and devotion (bhakti) without abandoning his duties or his obligations.

The following is a chapter-wise summary of the sacred text, with special emphasis on certain topics that are central to the doctrine propounded by Lord Krishna about liberation and the means to achieve it. It provides you with an overview of the entire teaching. This summary is useful if you want to familiarize yourself with important points without going through the whole scripture. For a complete understanding of the scripture, please go through my translation and commentary, "The Bhagavadgita: Unveiling the Gita's Secrets" or "The Bhagavadgita, a Simple Translation."

Chapter 1: Arjuna's Yoga of Sorrow

The chapter begins with a dialogue between Dhritarashtra and Sanjaya and introduces the principal characters involved in the war. Through the words of Duryodhana, we are introduced to the battle formations, the war strategy, and the names of a few renowned warriors on both sides. The principal characters, Lord Krishna and Arjuna, are introduced in the 14th verse. In the 21st verse, Arjuna asks Lord Krishna, who was acting as his charioteer, to take him into the middle of both armies. Lord Krishna complies with his request. Upon seeing his kith and kin arrayed on the battlefield, ready to fight and sacrifice their lives, Arjuna suffers from great sorrow. He is overwhelmed with the thought of waging a destructive war and killing his own relations and great souls like Bhishma and Drona. He begins to worry that his actions would lead to the destruction of many people in his hands, which in turn might lead to other unhappy consequences for him and his family. In a fit of depression, he lays down his bow and arrow and decides to renounce fighting to avoid causing suffering and destruction to others. The first chapter is rightly titled as the yoga of Arjuna's sorrow since it describes the sorrow and anxiety experienced by Arjuna at the thought of war and its consequences. The scripture begins earnestly with a chapter on sorrow because the teachings aim to resolve the problem of sorrow arising from our actions without us having to abandon them or escape from them. Arjuna's despondency also signifies the importance of sorrow in our lives. Sorrow is a rude awakener and a harsh teacher. It imparts valuable lessons by letting us know where we are wrong and what we should or should not do. It puts us on pause and forces us to review our priorities, choices, and actions. We usually turn to God in moments of crisis and great sorrow. As long as life goes on normally, we hardly pay attention to the larger issues of our lives, such as our spiritual welfare or the need for our liberation. When things go wrong and life takes an unexpected turn for the worse, we veer toward God and look for His guidance and help. In moments of despair, we realize the futility of finding peace and fulfillment in the dualities of life and the pairs of opposites. In many ways, Arjuna's sorrow symbolizes our inability to comprehend the truths or resolve the problems of our lives solely with our limited knowledge and intellect. It serves as a revelation for those who want to lead egocentric lives without acknowledging the role of God or His help in our spiritual transformation. It also reminds us of the need to work for our liberation and escape from the world of death and delusion.

Chapter 2: The Yoga of Knowledge and Practice

Lord Krishna, in his role as a divine teacher, responds to Arjuna's predicament with knowledge and wisdom, which He terms Samkhya yoga. Samkhya is about the nature of existence, and Yoga is about accomplishing inner transformation to become free from it and attain liberation. It is essentially the knowledge and practice of karma-sannyasa yoga with devotion, discernment, and self-control to achieve liberation. He reminds Arjuna that wise men do not grieve for the dead or living because they know that the Self, which is hidden in all and which is our true identity, cannot be slain or destroyed. The wise ones remain equal to both pleasure and pain because they know how the activity of the senses leads to attachment and duality towards the pairs of opposites. Those who remain equal to them become fit for immortality. One should also cultivate discernment to know what is perishable and what is imperishable. The body is perishable because it is like a garment worn by the Self, whereas the Self is imperishable and inexhaustible. It is unthinkable, invisible, and unborn. Therefore, it is not appropriate to grieve about the death of anyone. There is no sin in doing one's duty, especially when it is done for the sake of righteousness and without desire or expectation. Our right is to work only, not for its fruit. We should perform our actions with even-mindedness (samatvam), which means we should have sameness towards the pairs of opposites. Even-mindedness is called yoga because its practice leads to liberation. When actions are performed with equanimity, we call it skill in action or buddhiyoga. He who has equanimity, who renounces the fruit of his actions, is freed from the bonds of births and attains liberation.

Arjuna then wants to know the marks of a person whose mind is completely stable (sthithaprajna). Lord Krishna replies that he should be known as a stable person (sthitadhi) whose mind is stable, who is free from craving, contented in his mind, not perturbed by adversity or emotions, without affection everywhere, withdrawn and detached. He explains how we develop attachment because of the activity of the senses, how desires arise from attachment, and how one perishes as desires lead to anger, delusion, confusion of memory, and loss of discrimination. One should, therefore, control the senses and become free from likes and dislikes. When the mind is tranquil and steady, one becomes firmly established in Isvara. When desires are abandoned, one becomes free from attachment and egoism and attains the exalted state of Brahman (brahma-sthithi). He is no longer deluded or subject to the cycle of births and deaths or the suffering caused by attraction and aversion to worldly objects.

Chapter 3: The Yoga of Action

The second chapter is about the knowledge of the Self that leads to liberation and freedom from Nature. At the beginning of the third chapter, Arjuna wants to know if knowledge is so important, why was he asked to perform actions. Lord Krishna answers by saying that the path of knowledge is for men of contemplation, and the path of action is for those who are engaged in worldly actions. Liberation is not attained by abstaining from work but by doing it selflessly without seeking its fruit. Action is superior to inaction because we cannot keep our bodies alive by remaining inactive. Besides, the worlds exist because both gods and beings perform their duties. Actions performed with desires bind the beings to karma. One should, therefore, perform actions with a sacrificial attitude, without attachment, taking delight in the Self alone. Men should perform actions to foster gods, and gods should perform actions to foster men. Although He is free from desires, God Himself performs selfless actions to preserve the worlds He creates and sets an example to the people on earth. Actions are caused by the gunas, although people think they are doing them. We engage in actions because of desires induced by the gunas to seek objects in which they are present predominantly. Therefore, it is a delusion to think that we are responsible for our actions and that we are the doers. We should not take any credit for our actions because they stem from our inherent nature, with which we should not identify ourselves. To be free from the consequences of desire-ridden actions, people should surrender their actions to God, with their minds fixed upon Him, and perform them without attachment and hope. Attachment and aversion to objects are obstacles on the path of liberation since they keep the mind unsteady and distracted. One should not be swayed by them. A person becomes sinful when he acts under the influence of desires and passions caused by rajas. When wisdom is covered by the smoke of desires, one becomes deluded. To be free from it and conquer the enemy that exists in each of us in the form of desires, one should control one's senses with intellect and one's intellect with the knowledge of the Self.

Chapter 4: Jnana Karma Sannyasa Yoga

The fourth chapter begins with the assertion that the source of all knowledge is God, and He imparted the ancient knowledge of Yoga to the progenitors (Manus) of humankind. When Arjuna asks Him how He could teach the same knowledge to people of bygone eras, Krishna replies that although He was the immortal, unborn Lord of all beings, He manifests Himself from time to time whenever there is a decline of dharma and ascendance of evil. He does it as a duty to protect the virtuous, destroy the evil, and restore dharma. Those who know the divine nature and the absolute state of the Self through study and contemplation cultivate divine qualities, become free from attachment, and attain liberation. God is the source of creation, and He is responsible for the order and regularity (rta) of the universe. Actions do not taint him because He has no desire for their fruit. Those who are aware of this know how to perform their actions and remain free from their consequences.

Having explained how to perform actions with the right knowledge and remain free from evil, He explains to Arjuna the truth regarding action, inaction, and prohibited action. A yogi sees inaction in action and action in inaction because the fire of wisdom burns up his actions. Since he renounces attachment and does not depend upon anything, he does nothing and does not commit any sin, even though he engages in actions. With no expectations, his mind under control, giving up all possessions, ever contended, free from envy, balanced in success and failure, he, the karma yogi, is not bound by his actions. Actions should, therefore, be performed with a sense of sacrifice.

The Vedas prescribe many types of sacrifices that lead to the dissolution of sin. However, the sacrifices made with knowledge (jnana-yajna) are superior to the sacrifices performed with materials (dravya-yajna) to attain peace and prosperity. One should attain such knowledge by seeking the guidance of wise people and serving them variously. When actions are performed with knowledge, they are reduced to ashes, which means no sin is incurred. Knowledge is the best purifier of all. Knowledge comes with faith, control of the senses, and devoted service, and having attained it, one experiences supreme peace. When actions are performed with the right knowledge and even-mindedness, one is not bound by them.

Chapter 5: The Yoga of Renunciation of Action

The fifth chapter begins with a question from Arjuna, who wants to know which of the two, the yoga of renunciation and the yoga of action, is better. Lord Krishna replies that both lead to supreme bliss. However, the yoga of action is superior because he who performs actions without hatred and desires is a true practitioner of renunciation (sannyasi). Those who transcend the pairs of opposites attain liberation. Ignorant people think that the yoga of knowledge and the yoga of action are different, but both lead to the same goal. One can achieve liberation by practicing either of them. However, without renunciation, it is difficult to attain liberation, even with the yoga of action.

Renunciation of action does not mean one should give up all actions. Renunciation of the desire for the fruit of one's action is true renunciation of action. A person who practices it does not incur sin even though he is engaged in actions. God determines neither doership nor actions of the beings nor their consequences. Nor does he accept the merits or sins of anyone. It is nature that veils our knowledge and induces us to act in deluded ways so that we remain under its influence. Whoever possesses the right knowledge and whose sins have been washed away, the Supreme Being reveals Himself to them.

Such people view the world with equanimity and treat everyone with the same attitude. Unperturbed by the pairs of opposites, they live firmly established in Brahman. Having renounced all worldly attachments, a person who is established in that state of perfection does nothing even when he is engaged in actions. He lives untouched by sin like a lotus leaf by water. Offering the fruit of his actions to God, remaining unattached, finding happiness within, balanced and self-absorbed, he attains supreme peace and great bliss. In contrast, those who perform actions with selfish motives incur sin and remain bound. One should, therefore, practice the yoga of actions, renouncing desires and attachments, establishing oneself firmly in the contemplation of Brahman, and identifying oneself with Him. This is the yoga of renunciation of action.

Chapter 6: The Yoga of Self-control

The sixth chapter begins with the assertion that he is a true sannyasi who performs his actions without depending upon their fruit, not the one who gives up work or the sacred fire when he enters into the last phase of his life (sannyasashrama). Renunciation and yoga are the same because one becomes a yogi only by renouncing attachment to the world. Perfection in yoga comes only when one renounces all worldly desires. For this, one should practice self-control and conquer the lower self or the ego self. When the ego is disciplined, one abides in peace and remains equal to the pairs of opposites. He who remains dispassionate under all circumstances excels in it. A yogi should attain it by practicing yoga, meditation, and concentration in secluded places free from desire and possessions. He should practice yoga for self-purification, with his mind fixed upon God, practicing self-control and moderation.

In this chapter, Lord Krishna defines yoga as separation (viyogam) from union (samyogam) with suffering (dukham). In the mortal world, we are never free from suffering. Suffering is a constant factor in our lives, even when we are seemingly happy. We are separated from it only when we achieve perfection in performing actions with renunciation and detachment. By nature, the mind is very fickle. However, it can be controlled through practice and dispassion. Yoga becomes easier for one whose mind is subdued and who is established firmly in the thoughts of Brahman. Having heard the importance of subduing the mind, Arjuna then wants to know the fate of those who fail in their effort to control their minds and passions. Lord Krishna replies that there is no destruction for those who work for their spiritual well-being. Those who fall from yoga attain the ancestral world and, after exhausting their good karma, return to the earth to take birth in a family of enlightened yogis. There, he regains his knowledge and continues his practice. A yogi whose passions are subdued, whose mind is tranquil, and who performs actions without attachment and desire for the fruit of his actions is superior to an ascetic, to the wise ones who possess knowledge, and to those who engage in desire-ridden actions. Among them also, those who worship God and remain absorbed in Him are the best.

Chapter 7: The Yoga of Knowledge and Wisdom

In this chapter, Lord Krishna turns his attention from the individual Self to the Universal Self. He explains how to achieve God-realization by practicing devotion and yoga of action together, with the mind firmly established in the contemplation of Brahman, the highest God. Among thousands of people, only a few know Him in essence and the reality (tattvas) concerning His materiality. The Supreme Lord has a twofold nature, the lower and the higher, from which all beings arise. He is both the material and efficient cause of creation, and in the end, everything becomes dissolved in Him only. He is the highest of all. Nothing is above Him or remains independent of Him. He is omniscient and omnipresent. He is hidden in all. Everything evolves from Him and dissolves into Him. Deluded by His divine Maya (illusion) induced by the gunas, ignorant people, under the influence of demonic nature, do not recognize Him as the Supreme and Imperishable. Therefore, they do not worship Him. Virtuous people who worship Him are of four types: the distressed ones, seekers of knowledge, those who desire wealth, and the wise ones. Of them, Lord Krishna says that the last ones are dearer to Him as He is dearer to them. At the end of many births, people seek God, acknowledging Him as all. Others, out of desire and compelled by the modes (gunas), worship other gods and perform sacrificial rites to fulfill their desires. God does not interfere with their methods of worship or their object of worship. Whatever form they choose to worship, He stabilizes their faith in that. However limited is the fruit gained by those who worship gods. They go to them, while the devotees of Brahman go to Him only.

Chapter 8: The Yoga of Imperishable Brahman

This chapter describes the fate of those who die and depart from this world. It begins with a question on the meaning and significance of the following: Brahman, Adhyatma, karma, Adhibhuta, Adhidaiva, and Adhiyajna. Lord Krishna explains that the supreme and imperishable Being is Brahman. A person's essential nature (svabhavam) is (the reflection of) his pure Self (Adhyatma) in the field of Nature. It does not illuminate well if there are impurities. Karma is the creative and causative force that brings into existence all beings. All perishable things constitute the material self (Adhibhuta). Purusha is the individual Self (Adhidaiva) in the body, who acts as the inner witness. Isvara or Krishna is the Adhiyajna, the Supreme Self. Whoever remembers Him at the time of their death attains Him only, without doubt. Whatever a person thinks at the time of death, he attains that. One should, therefore, remember God always, even while performing mundane actions, and live with one's mind absorbed in His contemplation. Those who attain Him in this manner and reach His abode never take birth again. All words, including the world of Brahma, are subject to rebirth, but not those who have attained Him. The time at which a person dies is important because it determines the path by which the souls travel to the next world. Those who die during the first six months of the summer solstice go to the world of Brahman by the path of the sun, never to return to the earth. Those who die during the winter solstice travel by the path of the moon and attain the world of ancestors. After exhausting their karma there, they return to the earth and take birth again. Knowing these two paths, a wise person cultivates devotion and becomes steadfast in the practice of yoga.

Chapter 9: The Yoga of Sovereign Knowledge and Mystery

This chapter describes the supreme knowledge and supreme mystery concerning the Supreme Self. Knowing them, a person becomes free from impurities. God pervades the whole universe. All beings exist in

Him and depend upon Him for their support, but He does not depend upon any. During each cycle of creation, He brings forth all beings and withdraws them into Himself at the end of it. Actions do not bind Him because He remains unattached and indifferent while performing them. Under His control, Nature (Prakriti) manifests the whole creation. Deluded people who lack discrimination and who possess demonic natures do not recognize Him as the Creator. However, the great souls take refuge in Him, knowing that He is the primal and the original cause of creation, and worship Him with great devotion. He personally takes care of their welfare (yogakshema) since they surrender to Him and leave their welfare entirely to Him. Those who worship the gods instead of Brahman also worship Him, but it is an inferior form of worship that will not lead to liberation. Those who worship the gods, spirits, or the manes go to them, but those who worship Him attain Him only. Whatever is offered to God with devotion, He accepts it unconditionally, be it a fruit or a leaf, a flower or water. However, we should not be selective in what we offer to God. One should offer Him everything: whatever one does, whatever one eats, whatever one offers as an oblation, whatever gift one gives, and whatever penance one performs. Everything should be offered to Him without expectations. God is impartial. None is hateful or lovable to Him, but those who worship Him with devotion abide in Him and He in them. The devotees of God never perish. Even if a sinful person worships Him with pure devotion, He becomes saintly and righteous. One can, therefore, imagine how much merit will accrue if a pious person worships Him with devotion. Worship God with great devotion, with your mind fixed upon Him. Offer Him everything. Renounce all desires and attachments and put yourself into his care. If you do these, you will go to Him only.

Chapter 10: The Yoga of Divine Manifestations

The tenth chapter is about the manifestations (vibhutis) and greatness (mahimas) of the Supreme Self. Knowledge of the Supreme Self is useful in liberation. No one knows the secrets of His origin because He is the First among the gods and seers and the Source of all. Those who know Him as the unborn and without a beginning are freed from all sins. All the divine qualities and diverse feelings emanate from Him only. All are born out of Him only. Those who are free from delusion and know the reality worship Him with their minds fixed upon Him, surrendering to Him, speaking about His glory, and taking delight in His thoughts. To those who worship Him thus, Isvara gives the yoga of wisdom (buddhiyoga) by which they attain liberation. Having heard these words, Arjuna wants to know how to know Him through meditation (chintam) and in what states (bhavas) one should contemplate upon Him. In reply, Lord Krishna tells him about His prominent divine states (yogam) and manifestations (vibhutis). The Supreme Self abides in all and represents all known and unknown aspects of creation. Whatever in creation is resplendent, illuminated, reflects divine nature, beauty, symmetry, harmony, perfection, completeness, strength, valor, majesty, royalty, etc., is His manifestation only. Finally, He concludes that there is no use knowing these glories because they are but a little fraction of Him.

Chapter 11: The Yoga of the Vision of the Universal Form

In this chapter, Arjuna expresses his wish to see the Supreme Form of Lord Krishna. The Lord complies. He bestows upon him special vision and shows him His resplendent Universal Form (visvarupam), containing all the worlds, planets, gods, beings, colors, and shapes. In that Form, Arjuna sees everything, past, present, and future, and the fate of the war. He sees Him with countless arms, stomachs, faces, and eyes, without a beginning, middle, or end. He sees Him blazing as if thousands of suns are present in the sky at once. He sees His infinite vastness and His fierce and terrible form as Time (kala), the god of death and destruction. Showing him His fierce form, Lord Krishna asks him to slay his enemies, who are already slain by Him in His cosmic plan, and fulfill the duty and destiny for which he was born. The vision fills Arjuna with fear and trepidation. He praises Him profusely and, unable to see Him in that form, requests Him to revert to His peaceful and pleasant form. Krishna returns to his normal form and tells Arjuna that it is very difficult for anyone to see the universal form of God. Even the divinities do not see it. Then, He adds that He cannot be seen in this form or known in essence through the study of the Vedas, charity, or austerities, but only through single-minded devotion. He, who lives for

Him, without enmity towards others, performing all his actions for Him and acknowledging Him as the Supreme, goes to Him only.

Chapter 12: The Yoga of Devotion

The twelfth chapter is about the yoga of devotion. It begins with the question of which type of devotee is superior, those who worship Lord Krishna or those who worship the Imperishable. Krishna says that those who worship Him are considered perfect in yoga. However, those who worship the Imperishable and Indefinable with their minds and senses under control also come to Him only. Painful is the path of those who want to worship the Unmanifested Brahman, but those whose minds are set upon Him, who is manifested, He rescues them promptly. Therefore, He urges Arjuna to worship Him with utmost devotion. If he is unable to fix his mind upon Him, he should practice (abhyasa) devotion. If it is also not possible, he should perform selfless actions for His sake. If he cannot do even that, he should take refuge in Him and renounce the fruit of his actions because renunciation of the fruit of actions is better than every other form of devotional service. Lord Krishna then states that a devotee who is steady, firmly resolved, undisturbed, full of devotion, and equal to all is dear to Him.

Chapter 13: The Yoga of the Field and the Knower of the Field

The thirteenth chapter describes the Field, the Knower of the Field, and the meaning of true knowledge. The body is the Field (kshetra), the Self is its Knower (Kshetrajna), and the knowledge of both is considered real knowledge. The Self is the object of knowledge that leads to liberation. The Field is subject to modifications arising from the gunas, whereas the Self is imperishable and immutable. Beings manifest when the Self (Purusha), seated in Nature (Prakriti), experiences gunas born of Nature. Attachment to the gunas leads to rebirth in good and bad wombs. The Self does not participate in the modifications of the Field but remains as a Witness, the Support, and the Enjoyer. Those who know both the Self and Nature are not reborn. They attain liberation. The Self is attained by meditation, yoga of knowledge, and yoga actions. Some realize Him through worship. They are also liberated. Every being in this world is born from the union of the Self and the body. A man of knowledge knows that all actions arise from Nature and thereby becomes a non-doer (akarta). When he sees that all beings exist in One, he attains Brahman. The Self illuminates the Field just as the Sun illuminates the whole world. Although it resides in the body, it remains pure, untouched by Nature. Those who know the distinction between the Self and the Field and the liberation of beings from the hold of Nature attain the Supreme Brahman.

Chapter 14: The Yoga of the Division of the Triple Gunas

This chapter deals with the division of the gunas and their essential features. Isvara is the seed-giving Father. Nature is the womb. From their union, all beings are born. They manifest because of the gunas, which are three in number, namely sattva, rajas, and tamas. Sattva is pure and luminous. It manifests in us as divine qualities and binds us through attachment to pleasure, happiness, and knowledge. Rajas is born of passion and egoism. It binds us through attachment to actions. Tamas is born of ignorance, and it binds us through negligence, laziness, and sleep. The gunas try to dominate the Field (body), suppressing each other. Thus, sattva dominates by suppressing rajas and tamas. The mode of rajas dominates by suppressing sattva and tamas, and tamas dominates by suppressing sattva and rajas. When the mind is illuminated with knowledge, sattva predominates. When rajasic mode predominates, one indulges in selfish actions. When tamas prevails, one suffers from ignorance, inactivity, delusion, and carelessness. When a purely sattvic person dies, he attains the highest world and never returns. When a rajasic person dies, he attains the ancestral world. Upon his return to Earth, he is born into a family of hardworking people. When a tamasic person dies, he too goes to the ancestral world, but upon his return to earth, he is born to deluded parents. The fruit of sattva is purity, while the fruit of rajas is sorrow, and that of tamas is ignorance. From sattva arises knowledge, from rajas arises selfishness, and from tamas arises ignorance. When a seer perceives gunas as the real doer, he transcends them and reaches the Supreme. When a yogi transcends the gunas, he becomes free from births and deaths. He who transcends them remains free from delusion and attachment. Knowing that only gunas are responsible for actions, he remains indifferent and equal to the pairs of opposites. He attains Brahman, who is eternal and who upholds dharma for the welfare of all.

Chapter 15: The Yoga of the Supreme Person

This chapter is about the Supreme Purusha, the Cosmic Self. It begins with a description of the Tree of Creation (Asvattha tree), whose roots are in heaven and branches down below. A projection of Brahma, one can escape from it only through non-attachment. With liberation as a goal, one should seek refuge in Brahman from whom creation ensues and reach the Supreme Abode from where men do not return and where neither the sun nor the moon shines. The embodied Self is an aspect (amsah) of Brahman only. When he leaves the body, he goes, taking along with him the mind and the senses. Those who are ignorant, deluded, and impure do not perceive the Self in their bodies. Only those who have the eyes of wisdom (jnana-chakshu) see Him. The Universal Self who inhabits the whole creation is the highest of all. The sun and the moon shine because of Him. He pervades the earth and supports all beings with His vigor (Ojas). He remains seated in the body as the digestive fire and digests the fourfold food (solids, liquids, etc.). He alone resides in the hearts of beings and is responsible for their knowledge, memory, and wisdom. The transcendental Self is imperishable, while the lower Self is perishable. The Supreme Purusha (Purushottama) is distinct from both and superior to both—those who know Him as such and worship Him with devotion become accomplished in duty.

Chapter 16: The Division of the Divine and Demonic Properties

In this chapter, Lord Krishna enumerates the distinction between divine and demonic qualities. The divine qualities lead to liberation, while the demonic ones lead to bondage and delusion. Based upon them, the beings in the world are divided into divine and demonic. Because of their cruel, sinful, and demonic behavior, God casts them into worlds of darkness from where redemption is difficult to attain. One should, therefore, cultivate divine qualities, abandoning the three gates of hell, namely passion, anger, and greed, and attain the Supreme

State. Those who defy the scripture and the word of God attain neither happiness nor the Supreme Abode. Therefore, one should follow the scriptures to determine what should be done and what should be avoided, and act according to the guidelines prescribed in them.

Chapter 17: The Yoga of the Threefold Division of Qualities

In this chapter, Lord Krishna describes the threefold division of faith according to the predominant nature of beings. A person's faith is determined by that person's nature. Sattvic people worship gods, rajasic people worship celestial beings (yakshas and rakshasas), and Tamasic people worship ghosts and elemental spirits. Those who are deluded and filled with vanity and egoism and induced by lust and passions perform severe penances not approved by the scripture and subject their bodies to senseless torture. The food we eat is also of three types based on the gunas they represent. Sattvic people like sattvic food, which promotes purity and brilliance. Rajasic people prefer rajasic food, which promotes lust and passions; while tamasic people choose tamasic food, which promotes sloth and ignorance. Based on the gunas, sacrifices are also of three types. The sacrifices, which are performed according to the scriptures, without seeking their fruit as a duty, are sattvic in nature. Those that are performed with the desire for their fruit or vanity are rajasic in nature. Tamasic sacrifices are performed without faith and in total disregard of the scriptures and established traditions. Just as faith is of three types, the austerities (tapas) are also of three types. Sattvic austerities are performed gently and selflessly; rajasic austerities are practiced in a selfish and egoistic manner; and tamasic austerities are performed painfully and destructively. The rest of the chapter is devoted to describing the three types of gifts and the reason to commence sacrifices, charity, and penance always by uttering the sacred mantra, "Aum Tat Sat."

Chapter 18: The Yoga of Liberation by Renunciation

The last chapter begins with a question on renunciation (sannyasa) and sacrifice (tyaga). Lord Krishna explains that sannyasa means renunciation of desires hidden in actions, and tyaga means renunciation of the fruit of one's action. Actions such as sacrifice, charity, and austerities should not be given up. They should be performed by renouncing attachment to their fruit. Abandoning obligatory duties owing to delusion is declared tamasic. Abandoning them because they are troublesome or difficult to practice is declared rajasic, but performing them as a duty with detachment and a sacrificial attitude is called sattvic. A man of true renunciation has neither aversion to disagreeable work nor attraction towards agreeable work. Free from doubt, he attains purity. Deluded jivas cannot give up work completely, but through practice and detachment, they can renounce desires and offer the fruit of their actions to God. All actions, whether they are right or wrong, arise from five causes, namely the body, the doer, the sense organs, the organs of action, and divine providence. He who has no ego, whose intelligence is free from attachment, is not bound by his actions. He remains free even though he performs them. Every action is induced by knowledge, the knower, and the object of knowledge, and every action involves one or more causes, the mechanism of action, and the doer. These three are again of three types according to the gunas. By sattvic knowledge, we see everything as part of Brahman. By rajasic knowledge, we see everything as separate and distinct. By tamasic knowledge, one sees nothing beyond oneself or one's actions. Sattvic actions are performed without desire and attachment as obligatory duties. Rajasic actions are performed strenuously with desire and egoism. Tamasic actions are performed delusionally without consideration for truth or reality. Similarly, we can classify the doers (kartas) into sattvic, rajasic, and tamasic based on their attitude and conduct. Based upon the triple gunas, intelligence (buddhi), firmness (dhriti), and happiness (sukham) are also of three types. Thus, the gunas pervade everything. There is nothing in the manifested worlds that is free from them. Based upon them, the scripture prescribes different duties for different categories of people. By performing them according to one's nature, with detachment and devotion, one attains peace and perfection in action. Having attained perfection in the yoga of action, he attains Brahman. Attaining Brahman, he neither grieves nor desires. Equal to all beings, He experiences supreme devotion to God. Through devotion, he realizes the truths about Him and finds a place in the

Supreme Abode.

Having explained the division of the gunas and their manifestations, Lord Krishna advises Arjuna to perform actions with his mind fixed upon Him, without egoism, mentally renouncing all actions to Him. Even if he decides to act otherwise, the gunas in him propel him to perform actions. Finally, in the end, having explained the importance of duty, actions, renunciation, and detachment, Lord Krishna tells Arjuna that He revealed to him the most secretive teaching because he was dear to Him. He advises Him that it should be taught only to those who are qualified and who have faith and devotion. He who teaches the knowledge of the Bhagavadgita is the dearest to Lord Krishna. Next are those who study it, and then come those who listen to the discourse through others. Having heard the discourse, Arjuna experiences great joy and declares that his delusion has gone, and he is now ready to fight. Hearing their conversation from afar, Sanjaya, who has been narrating the discourse to Dhritarashtra, expresses great joy and thanks sage Vyasa for giving him an opportunity to act as a messenger to the king.

Devotees believe that the Bhagavadgita scripture is incomplete without the knowledge of the greatness of the Bhagavadgita (Gita Mahatyam) and the benefits of studying and understanding its essential teachings. The text may also contain information about its seer (rishi), presiding deity (devata), seed mantra (bija), main Shakti, and other details to internalize its knowledge and invoke its energies both ritually and contemplatively for self-purification through a practice called Gitakaradinyasa.

Thus ends the Bhagavadgita, the divine teaching of Lord Krishna, the great Upanishad, and the scripture of Yoga, containing the knowledge of the Absolute and the debate between Arjuna and Lord Krishna.

Yoga According to Bhagavadgita

It is difficult to understand the meaning and significance of yoga from the teachings of the Bhagavadgita if you are accustomed to the traditional definition of yoga as a union, practice, type of knowledge, discipline, or collection of techniques. The scripture uses the word in a broader sense to denote not only these but also state or mode. The latter definition carries greater significance in the Bhagavadgita, and unless we understand this clearly, we cannot grasp its teachings correctly.

For many people, yoga means practicing some highly formalized and even commercialized techniques of breathing, postures, meditation, and concentration. In truth, they represent only one aspect of yoga. They are the means to attain a state of well-being (yogakshema) or a pristine state of mind that is completely free from modifications (vrittis) and impurities. Even Patanjali declares yoga as a state that is free from modifications (yoga chittavritti nirodhah). Some scholars also interpret it as its purpose. The Bhagavadgita uses the word yoga to denote a state as well as a means, method, practice, or approach. One may also use a specific mental or physical state to practice yoga to reach another state or mode. Thus, yoga (practice, technique, or method) leads to yoga (state). Everything in the world exists in some state. Literally speaking, everything is in some yoga. However, these are relative and imperfect states, and they subject us to modifications.

Yoga as a state or a method

The scripture interprets yoga in terms of techniques and practices such as selfless service, self-study, practice of rules and restraints, restraint of the senses, breath control, meditation, concentration, and devotion. It also uses it to denote any state or condition. Its purpose is self-transformation or purification that eventually leads to the highest yoga (state), which is variously described as the state of self-absorption (samadhi), becoming established in the Self through self-control (atma-samyama), union with the Supreme Self (brahma-sparsa), aloneness (kaivalya), and supreme bliss. In this journey, whatever mental or physical states one cultivates, or the actions one performs to attain the transcendental states, are also considered yogas. Hence, we have different yogas, such as the yoga of action, the yoga of renunciation of desires in action, the yoga of knowledge, the yoga of devotion, and so on.

This concept is not peculiar to the Bhagavadgita alone. We find references to it in other scriptures also. They use yoga to refer to both material and spiritual states found in creation. For example, brahmayogam means the state of Brahman. One may attain it by the grace of God or by effort. Mahayogam means the supreme state, which may be any extraordinary situation in which one experiences greatness or abundance of something. Vishadayogam means the state of sorrow that Arjuna experienced at the beginning of the discourse. All human beings experience sorrow (vishadam) whenever they are overwhelmed with difficulties or adversity. In some cases, it heralds a new beginning, a new understanding of life, or a new insight into its meaning and purpose. Subhayogam means the state of auspiciousness, which arises from good works, sacrificial actions, or the blessings of gods. Vivahayogam is obtained by marriage. Putrayogam arises from the birth of a son. Rajayogam arises from gaining a kingdom. Dhanayogam arises from attaining wealth. These yogas refer to different states of attainment and have little relevance to the discipline of yoga or the philosophy of yoga. The opposite of yogam is viyogam, which means separation or loss. When you attain something, it is yoga, and when you lose something, it is viyoga. Even inanimate objects have a state, the state of inertia (jadayogam).

Today, many people practice yoga for health reasons, as some form of physical or mental exercise. No doubt, it is an auspicious goal and better than living a sedentary life. However, one should practice yoga for its original purpose, which is to attain overall physical, mental, and spiritual well-being – in other words, not only good health but also peace, balance, and equanimity. In a broader sense, we go through various yogas as we experience union and separation from things. Every experience (anubhava) and state of being (bhava) through which we pass or with which we become involved mentally or physically is a kind of yoga only. Some of them are ordinary yogas, even impure ones, which arise naturally in the field (kshetra) of experience, while some are very extraordinary ones experienced rarely. At some point, these experiences eventually culminate in the highest yoga, which is the state of liberation or bliss.

The whole universe exists in a state of union (yoga) between the Supreme Self and the Primal Nature. It has many intermediary states, some of which are eternal and some temporary. Creation is yoga. Divinity is yoga. Existence is yoga. Ignorance is yoga. Knowledge is yoga. Wisdom is yoga. In the course of our lives, we go through many different states (yogas), both positive and negative. Some of them arise in us naturally, and some through effort.

The Bhagavadgita interprets yoga both as a state and a means to attain it. It touches upon several yogas, such as karma yoga, jnana yoga, sannyasa yoga, buddhi yoga, karmaphala-sannyasa yoga, atma-samyama yoga, and bhakti yoga. They are complementary yogas. You practice them by cultivating specific states of purity, thinking, and attitude. At the same time, it also recommends some techniques of Classical Yoga, such as the practice of rules and restraints (yamas and niyamas), breathing (pranayama), restraint of the senses (pratyahara), concentration (dharana), meditation (dhyana), and self-absorption (samadhi). These techniques help us purify our minds and bodies so that they can sustain and experience higher states (yogas) of awareness and intelligence.

Cultivating yoga states

You practice yoga by following certain methods or techniques that are traditionally approved to attain specific goals or states. They may be positive states of peace and happiness, or well-being, or transcendental states of self-absorption. The ultimate purpose of all spiritual yogas is to attain the highest state of union with Brahman. Since one cannot reach it directly, one has to practice different means and cultivate the required purity to qualify for it. The scripture recommends karma yoga as the most basic yoga to perform actions with a state of detachment and selflessness. In this state (yoga), you do not shun your obligations. You appreciate your obligatory duties as a means to overcome desires and express your devotion to God by offering them to Him. You enter into this state by cultivating detachment, acknowledging God as the real Doer. Jnana yoga is another important state the scripture recommends. You practice this yoga by cultivating a state of knowledge and awareness whereby you realize that you are an eternal soul rather than a mere physical being. The practice of jnana yoga leads to the knowledge of the Self and Brahman, whereby you experience oneness with them. In buddhi yoga, you enter into a state of wisdom whereby you know the right from wrong and the good from evil. You learn to use your discretion, choose wisely, and avoid negative consequences. In sannyasa yoga, you resort to a state of renunciation, whereby you renounce desires and the fruit of your actions. You do not renounce work but the desire that is hidden in it.

You may interpret the other yogas mentioned in the scripture similarly, as states that are essential for one's transformation. You cultivate these states with resolve until they become part of your awareness. You focus on them and cultivate the required attitudes and thinking modes until they become firmly established in you. These states are the means to your transformation and liberation. They lead you from the state of sorrow (vishada yoga) to the state of final liberation (moksha). With their help, you bring God into your life and stabilize your mind in Him. Eventually, you reach the state of God and experience peace, equanimity, stability, sameness, devotion, and oneness with Him.

Reaching the highest yoga

If you want to pursue liberation, you must integrate the various aspects of your personality (mind and body) into a harmonious whole. You must balance and harmonize your lower nature with your higher one and align them so that you can work for the same goal without being conflicted or confused, while your consciousness stabilizes in the serene state of sameness (samatvam) in which nothing can disturb or distract you. This knowledge has immense practical value. If you understand yoga as a state and know that certain states (yogas) are inauspicious and lead to bondage and suffering, and certain states are auspicious and lead to peace and equanimity, you can use such knowledge to your advantage. With practice, you can cultivate certain modes of thinking and remain in particular states to stay free from desires and passions. By entering into certain mental states that facilitate desireless actions, knowledge, wisdom, renunciation, devotion, purity, and sameness, you can gradually move towards the highest Yoga, which is union with God Himself.

Five Lessons of the Bhagavadgita

The Bhagavadgita is a book of learning, knowledge, and guidance. A practical philosophy studded with the gems of ancient wisdom, it has the power to sharpen our intelligence and refine and transform your character and conduct. It has a purifying effect on all those who read it and assimilate its teachings. It leaves a strong impression upon all those who are pure in their hearts and who contemplate upon its wisdom and integrate its philosophy into their daily living. To be exposed to its light and brilliance is a blessing, and to practice its wisdom is to change your destiny forever. Every living being on earth ekes out an existence, but living responsibly and dutifully with knowledge and intelligence is what sets humans apart from other beings. Many people live in the darkness of their minds, unmindful of their spiritual obligations, surrounded by ignorance and delusion, and prefer to live that way even if it causes them pain and suffering. From the Bhagavadgita, we learn that we do not have to live in darkness, and there are ways and means to break the inertia that consumes our minds to achieve liberation.

Lord Krishna also leaves a stern warning to those who succumb to dark passions and demonic qualities, stating that they will descend to the darkest hells from where redemption will be very difficult. The God of the Bhagavadgita is not a God of vengeance. He is indifferent and dispassionate. However, He insists upon austere discipline and commitment to virtuous living as an obligatory duty. He sets in motion several laws to regulate the worlds and beings of His creation. To disregard them means inviting punishment and destruction, not from God but from your own actions. Thus, according to the scripture, your life and destiny are mostly in your hands, although the hand of God shapes them every moment. You are safe if you live with humility and the spirit of surrender, claiming neither the doership nor the ownership of your actions and transferring the responsibility and the consequences of your actions to the One who is the source of all. Your liberation from this world is ensured if you follow His immutable laws dutifully and sincerely and do your part in ensuring the order and regularity of the world and society without developing attachments to the things with which you may come into contact in the course of your existence. If you hanker after them or strive to make them your own, you will attract punishment and cast yourself into the deepest and darkest hells. In other words, if you ignore the warnings found in the scriptures, whether they are revelations or otherwise, and jump willfully into the turbulent waters of life against the wisdom of the ages, you have none but yourself to blame and accept responsibility for the actions you perform and the consequences you reap from them.

The Bhagavadgita contains transformative wisdom. If you are serious about liberation, you do not need any guru. You must accept Lord Krishna as your teacher and follow His teachings. You will be rescued from the world of impermanence. Many verses in the scripture contain seed thoughts, fragments of profound wisdom, and flashes of immense brilliance, which you can use for concentration and contemplation and find great comfort in the possibility of securing liberation and divine grace. With the Bhagavadgita in your hands, you are in the company of Lord Krishna Himself. By thinking about it, you invite Him into your life. By practicing it, you open yourself to the secret knowledge that shows you the way to the Abode of Brahman. In the eighteenth chapter, Lord Krishna identifies three types of people who are dearest to Him. First are those who preach the scripture to others and take the message of the Bhagavadgita to the devotees of the Lord. Next are those who study the Scripture with devotion and sincerity. In the third category are those who hear the knowledge from others and assimilate it. Thus, having even a little interest in the scripture's divine teachings has its own beneficial effect.

The scripture is not meant for proselytizing people or forcing its knowledge and wisdom upon unwilling and unprepared minds. Lord Krishna clearly amplifies that His teachings constitute secret knowledge, and they should be imparted only to a qualified few who deserve it and are ready for it. He says that under no circumstances should one teach his philosophy to those who are not austere, do not have devotion, envy God, and have no desire or inclination to learn from it. The following are a few important concepts we find in the Scripture that are useful for contemplation, spiritual growth, and self-transformation.

1. Know that you are an eternal Self

One of the important lessons we learn from the Bhagavadgita is that having the right awareness about oneself and becoming centered in the eternal Self can transform our lives, behavior, and outlook. Ordinary people identify with their physical or egoistic selves as distinguished by their names and forms or their possessions, but Bhagavadgita teaches us that we are immortal, indestructible, and transcendental selves and that we embody divinity. In other words, our death is temporary, but our existence is continuous. It also means we are different from our physical selves (minds and bodies) that we think we are, or the names and forms that represent us. If you think carefully, you will realize that the problems we face in our lives arise mostly because we regard ourselves as mortal beings and fail to acknowledge our eternal existence. Fear, anxiety, worry, and insecurity arise when you think you have but one life, and you are vulnerable to death and destruction.

The Bhagavadgita states clearly that the body is unreal. It is like a garment worn by the Self. It is a temporary construct, subject to modifications. If you are attached to it, you will experience sorrow and suffering, as happened in Arjuna's case. If you think that you are an eternal being, you will take things in your stride and look at your problems and your existence from a broader perspective. Such awareness makes you more responsible and dutiful in your thinking and actions since you know that your actions may leave impressions that may last for several lives and seriously hamper your chances of liberation.

We should, therefore, regard ourselves as spiritual entities and bring a paradigm shift in our thinking and attitude. We should identify ourselves with our divine nature and consider ourselves pure, eternal, immutable, indestructible, and real. The inner Self is an aspect of the Supreme Self. It is beyond the grasp of the mind and the senses. We are truly free only when we are free from Nature's control, overcoming our ignorance and delusion.

2. Learn to control your desires

Our minds are storehouses of memories, thoughts, desires, impulses, habitual thought patterns, and latent impressions (samskaras), which ensure our continuity as embodied selves in a world of change and impermanence. They act as reservoirs of our perceptions and seats of our ignorance, delusion, and duality. Our wandering senses keep them restless and unsteady, as they are constantly flooded with wave upon wave of sensory information, demanding our attention and provoking our responses. As we constantly interact with the world outside, our senses (jnanendriyas) and organs of action (karmendriyas) create in us desires and attachments to various kinds for worldly objects. In turn, they subject our minds to various modifications (vrittis) and conflicting emotions. Thereby, we experience attraction and aversion to the pairs of opposites.

An unstable mind that is subject to duality and delusion is not conducive to peace or stability. It is vulnerable to suffering and mental afflictions arising from egoism and desire-ridden actions. Those who are attached to things through attraction and aversion are not truly free. Nature holds them in control through the modes for the purpose of ensuring the continuation of creation and existence. As long as they are restless and unstable due to insatiable cravings, they are not fit for salvation. With their minds scattered and senses wandering among sense objects, they remain entangled in the impermanence of the phenomenal world. The mind's instability, therefore, is a serious problem. The various forms of yoga are meant to resolve it to establish a solid foundation of character and conduct that leads the initiates to liberation. They instill strength and fortitude in them to practice austerities (tapas), duty (dharma), renunciation (sannyasa), firmness (dhriti), rules and restraints (yamas and niyamas), breath control (pranayama), withdrawal of the senses, concentration, contemplation and self-absorption (samadhi), which strengthen divine qualities and righteous conduct without which success in any yoga is difficult.

The mind is fickle by nature. It is difficult to control its movements, inclinations, or propensities even after years of practicing yoga. It is even more difficult to rectify the logical distortions or weaknesses to which it is prone, which makes it even more difficult to perceive things as they are or comprehend the truths that are hidden in our scriptures. We need an intense and sustained effort, with unyielding resolve, to achieve progress and experience balance, sameness, and stability in our thinking and attitude. The Bhagavadgita suggests that through selfless actions, knowledge of the Self, and devotion to God, a devotee should control his senses, develop detachment from the sense objects, and achieve freedom from karma, tranquility, and sameness (samatvam). When the mind is tranquil and the senses are resting, we remain the same to both pleasures and pain, and we stop reacting to the situations arising in our lives. With peace ruling our minds, we experience love and devotion to God. When our desires rest in the silence of our minds, we rest in the bliss of the Self. We become free from the delusion and ignorance to which we are subject. We journey to the world of immortals by the sunlit path, which is reserved for those who attain liberation.

3. Know what true renunciation means

One may achieve mental stability by living in secluded places, renouncing all duties and responsibilities, and avoiding public contact. This was the tradition of renunciation practiced in ancient India at one time. After a certain age, householders gave up their worldly possessions and retired to forests to practice asceticism and achieve true loneliness. To silence their cravings, they stopped the use of fire for bathing, warming their bodies, protection against wild animals, or cooking food, and subsisted on as little food as they could manage until their bodies wasted away. The Ajivakas, an ancient Indian sect that thrived in the 6th century B.C.E., believed in fatalism. They gave up struggling against Nature or the ways of the world, shunned their duties and responsibilities, and led passive lives, as they believed in the fatalistic notion that everything was predetermined and no one had real control over their lives or destinies. For them, what was destined to happen would happen, and no one could alter that. They also did not believe in supernatural powers or beings. Therefore, they resigned themselves to their fate.

The doctrine of karma suggested, on the other hand, that human beings possessed the knowledge and intelligence to change their lives and destinies by indulging in righteous actions and avoiding evil actions. The Bhagavadgita added another layer of complexity to the practice of renunciation, suggesting that karma was determined not by actions but by the desires hidden in them. Therefore, the focus should not be on actions but on the desires hidden in them, and one should practice renunciation of desires rather than actions. It is better accomplished when one engages in actions without desire for their fruit. This approach would ensure the preservation and orderliness of the world and, at the same time, our liberation from the world of births and deaths.

According to the Bhagavadgita, inaction is also not a solution to the problem of karma because, firstly, inaction is impractical, and secondly, inaction has consequences, which may lead to bondage and delusion. Actions are imperative for our survival and the continuity of the world. Even God engages in them for the sake of order and regularity of His creation. None can ever remain free from engaging in action. The gunas make sure that we remain helplessly active, performing actions and pursuing our desires. The wise ones know this, and therefore, they renounce the desire for the fruit of their actions and offer them to God. An ignorant person acts with attachment, thinking, "I am the doer," whereas the wise one acts without attachment, desiring the welfare of the world order. He does not depend upon anything to achieve anything and remains disinterested or indifferent to what has been done or not done by him or others. In this respect, says the Gita, God Himself is a great example. Actions do not taint Him, even though He is engaged in actions, because He has no desire for their fruit. A wise man follows His example upon earth and becomes free. He acquires the knowledge of actions and the various ways in which sacrifices are performed. Knowing thus, through knowledge, he becomes free from the bondage of action. He burns up his actions in the fire of wisdom. Thus, through knowledge, he attains peace by performing actions with discernment, without desire and doership.

Bhagavadgita says that better than the renunciation of action is the renunciation of ownership, doership, and the desire for the fruit of one's actions. A knower of truth, while performing actions, knows that he does nothing at all because he renounces ownership and doership of his actions and their fruit. Therefore, he attains freedom from karma or the consequences of his actions. He acts selflessly and dispassionately, offering his actions to God without desires and attachments. Detached and unbound, he remains untouched by sin like the lotus leaf by water. A karmayogi performs actions with his senses, mind, intellect, and body for his purification, without becoming involved with them and without desires and attachments. He offers the fruit of his actions to God as a sacrifice. Renouncing the desires in his actions and remaining self-controlled and mentally stable while performing them, he lives in his body happily, neither acting nor making others act. Offering the fruit of his actions to God, he attains peace in the form of Self-realization. He becomes one with God and attains liberation.

The Gita further declares that a true sanyasi ceases to entertain any attachment to the sense objects or actions and renounces all thoughts about the world and worldly things. He conquers his ego-self with his real Self. He becomes established in God and remains the same in heat and cold, pleasure and pain, honor and dishonor. For him, a piece of earth or a piece of gold is the same. Equal-minded among friends and foes, among the partial and impartial, and among saints and sinners alike, he remains firmly established in the contemplation of God or the Self, indifferent to what happens or does not happen.

4. Make your life a devotional offering to God

The Supreme Brahman is universal, eternal, imperishable, and immutable. At the beginning of every cycle of creation, He creates a multitude of beings with His divine Maya (yogamaya) and keeps them under its influence. Therefore, according to the Bhagavadgita, He is both the material and the efficient cause of creation. Actions do not bind Him because He is unattached and indifferent to them. In the body, He dwells as the divine Self (adhidaivam) and the inner Witness (sakshi). While He is untouched by the activities and modifications of Nature, the Self is bound to the world until it is liberated. The God of Bhagavadgita is the all-powerful, all-pervading, and all-controlling Supreme Lord. Nothing happens without His will or involvement, even though He remains indifferent to all that happens. Even the liberation of mortals happens with His grace only,

The Bhagavadgita states that all knowledge emanates from God, and He is the original teacher and primal source. Those who know the truths about Him become absorbed in steadfast yoga. Since He is the source of everything, we must look to Him only for our liberation. To achieve that auspicious goal, we must consecrate our lives and actions to Him, remaining contented and happy, with the spirit of surrender and humility, acknowledging Him as the Supreme. To those who are absorbed in devotional service with love, He gives them knowledge and wisdom by which they come to Him only. Out of mercy for them, He removes their darkness, residing in them as their own Self, and shines upon them the lamp of knowledge. One should, therefore, take refuge in that Primal Being (Adi Purusha), who is seated in the heart of all and who is responsible not only for memory and knowledge in all but also for their loss. By practicing the yoga of action, with their minds fixed upon Him, giving up all attachments, the yogis attain the Supreme Self. His very thoughts are so purifying that whoever remembers Him only at the time of death attains immortality.

In the Bhagavadgita, we find an assurance that those who surrender to God in devotion and offer their lives to Him, He takes care of their lives and responsibilities. Fools do not recognize His greatness and disregard Him, but the wise ones know His true nature and worship Him with unwavering devotion. Thus says the scripture, those devotees who worship Him only, always thinking of Him, and ever united, God takes care of their wants and needs and looks after their welfare. Even those who worship other gods also, in a way, worship Him because He is the Lord of all offerings. In whatever way people worship Him, He strengthens their faith in that. Those who worship the gods go to them, but those who worship Him attain Him only. Therefore, while one may worship any divinity, it is always better to worship the Supreme Self because He alone ensures our liberation and a place in His eternal Abode.

The Gita says that God accepts whatever is offered to Him by those who have faith and devotion. He accepts our offerings unconditionally because He has no expectations and nothing that would complete Him or complement Him. However, He is merciful. Although He is complete and perfect and does not require anything, out of mercy, He is always willing to help His devotees. He bestows His grace upon those who approach Him with faith and devotion. Therefore, offer Him whatever you have, whatever you do, and whatever you sacrifice. Give Him all, keeping nothing for you. When you selflessly offer Him your actions, possession, ownership, and doership with a pure heart and exclusive devotion, you earn His grace and His infinite love. Through pure devotion, by constantly thinking of Him and worshipping him, doing actions for His sake, taking refuge in him, and renouncing the fruits of actions, with desires subdued, with no expectations, and steady of mind, one can easily attain God.

5. Self-purification is self-transformation

The body is the field of activity, and God dwells in the body as the Knower of the Field. The body is made up of several tattvas or realities of Nature: the five elements (mahabhutas), intelligence, ego, the mind, the ten senses, and the five subtle senses. It is also the seat of all desires, feelings, emotions, and mental energy. Being a creation of Prakriti and made up of her parts, it is an aspect of Her, subject to modifications caused by the triple modes (gunas), namely sattva, rajas, and tamas. The gunas tend to suppress each other to prevail and predominate over the fate of jivas, inducing desire-ridden actions and influencing their essential nature. All actions arise from this internal strife waged by them. By pervading the mind and body and promoting desires and attachments through attraction to objects of a similar nature and aversion for those of dissimilar nature, they bind the imperishable soul to the body and keep it in bondage. Sattva is pure and luminous. It binds the soul through attachment to happiness and knowledge. Rajas is born of passion. It binds the soul through selfish actions and attachment to the fruits of actions. Tamas is the mode born of ignorance, delusion, and indolence. It binds the soul through negligence, inertia, sloth, and sleep. We cannot escape from the influence of the gunas altogether. However, we can practice virtues, austerities, and yoga to remove the impurities of rajas and tamas from our minds and bodies. At the same time, we can increase the mode of sattva, which leads to purity, illumination, and liberation.

Conclusion

According to the Bhagavadgita, true renunciation means renunciation of desire and attachment. One may live in secluded places to practice yoga, but one should not abandon one's obligatory duties or indulge in inaction to avoid the consequences of karma. Instead, one should perform one's obligatory duties with devotion and as a sacrifice, without attachment, ownership, doership, and egoism. Restraining his mind and senses, controlling his desires, and practicing self-purification, he should keep his mind focused upon God with faith and devotion, offering Him the fruit of his actions and accepting life as it happens. Actions performed in this manner or life lived selflessly do not bind us. They lead to knowledge, equanimity, illumination, devotion, and liberation. We can learn many lessons from the Bhagavadgita. We can interpret its teachings in various ways and apply them to various disciplines, professions, and pursuits. The lessons or teachings we have discussed above are a few important ones. There are many others that an astute reader or student can discern. By following them, devotees can experience peace and balance in their lives.

Karma Yoga – the Path of (Selfless) Actions

Karmayoga is the most suitable form of spiritual activity for worldly people, especially householders who pursue the four aims of human life and engage in worldly actions or obligatory duties because of desires and detachments, devotion to God, or to uphold Dharma. The simplest form of karma yoga involves performing actions as ordained by the scriptures to fulfill one's obligations and desires to the extent possible and obtain a better life in the next birth. In the higher variations of karma yoga, one transcends selfishness and desires, cultivates knowledge and desires, and engages in selfless actions, consecrating them to God as a sacrifice, taking no credit for oneself, and offering the result to God. The former is simple karmayoga, which will not liberate you but will give you a chance to improve your life, destiny, and circumstances in the next birth. The latter is karma sannyasa yoga, or the renunciation of desire-ridden actions and their fruit. Karma sannyasa does not mean that you renounce actions, but only the desires in your actions. This form of karma yoga is difficult to practice for anyone engaged in worldly actions. However, it resolves the problem of karma and frees you from bondage and suffering permanently. In this essay, I may often use karmayoga to refer to both because of their common features, and request the readers to interpret the word according to the context.

In a very broad sense, karmayoga (also spelled karma yoga) means doing your part in God's creation and fulfilling the obligation that He entrusts to humans for their welfare as well as for the welfare of gods, humans, ancestors, and others. If you perform those duties, you will fulfill your promise to God and earn His support to live on earth under his protection for as long as you are stuck in samsara. If you want liberation, you must transform it into karma sannyasa yoga by renouncing desire-ridden actions and performing actions and obligatory duties, and offering their fruit to God with a sacrificial attitude. Karma sannyasa is a state of mind with which a devout Hindu householder engages in selfless actions without desiring their fruit (results), without assuming ownership and doership, and offers them to God as a sacrifice. In a very narrow sense, it is performing obligatory duties as an offering to God. The state of mind (yoga) or the thinking required to practice this yoga must be steeped in an attitude of duty, sincerity, detachment, dispassion, and absence of desires. All the other yogas invariably contain an element of karma yoga since pursuing knowledge, practicing meditation, worshipping God, etc., are actions that will produce karma if performed with desires. Hence, karmayoga is foundational to all spiritual practices, and its importance in achieving liberation should not be ignored. However, in the context of the Bhagavadgita, we must understand karmayoga as performing obligatory duties for one's material and spiritual well-being, for the order and regularity of the world, and in service to God, the Creator. In Karma sannyasa yoga, one must perform actions without desires, ownership, doership, and expectations. One may desire to engage in actions for righteous purposes. However, the fruit of such actions must be offered to God with devotion.

Karmayoga is appropriate for all classes and ages of people, more so for those who lead worldly lives as householders. In the world of God, every living being participates in actions in one form or another. The highest of all karma yogis is God Himself, who exemplifies karma sannyasa through His actions. Although He is complete and perfect in all respects and has no desires, He engages in actions to set an example and ensure that the worlds are preserved until the end of the time cycle. He performs His obligatory duties of creation, preservation, and destruction indifferently, helps His devotees according to their nature and devotion, protects them from evil, imparts knowledge through seers and sages, and uplifts those who want to escape from the hold of Nature by granting them liberation. While performing these actions, He upholds Dharma and maintains the order and regularity of the world, rewarding the pious and punishing the evildoers. Whenever the order is disturbed and worlds fall into confusion and disorder due to actions of evildoers, He incarnates upon earth to destroy them, restore order, protect the weak, and promote balance, order, and the welfare (yogakshema) of all. He also rescues his devotees who worship Him with exclusive devotion from samsara and grants them the immortal life.

The Karma doctrine stipulates that our actions are responsible for our bondage and suffering. The karma arising from our actions produces consequences that bind us to the world of death and rebirth. Karmayoga is an antidote to the recurring and ongoing problem of karma and the suffering and bondage that arise from it. In karmayoga, we use the very actions that produce them as the means to achieve a better life in the next birth or eternal liberation. In other words, we transform our actions into stepping stones to build a bridge or a path to peace and happiness, or eternal freedom. By converting the problem into a solution and by performing actions in such a manner that they do not bind us, we improve our chances of overcoming mortality and escaping from here. Hence, karmayoga is a perfect solution for those who want to uphold their obligatory duties and personal responsibilities in the pursuit of Dharma, Artha, and Kama, without ignoring the ultimate purpose of Moksha, liberation.

Actions are of various types and produce different types of consequences. Since we live in a world of duality, we can divide actions into good and bad, divine and demonic, moral and immoral, dharma and adharma, etc. However, the Bhagavadgita says that this division is superfluous. Actions, by themselves, are neither good nor bad and produce neither karma, akarma, nor vikarma. What gives them these characteristics is the nature of desire or intention hidden in them. Good actions may be performed with bad intentions, while bad actions may be performed with good intentions. When this happens, the consequences arising from them will also be different from what society expects. A soldier on the battlefield killing an enemy in combat is not the same as a criminal killing an innocent bystander. They do not produce the same results, although the act of killing is common to both. However, they both produce karma of different types. Therefore, Lord Krishna says that a yogi on the path of liberation should not be interested in performing either good or bad actions or their consequences because they both prolong our liberation. He must aim to be free from all consequences arising from his actions. He can accomplish it only when he performs them without desire and without desiring any result or outcome. His practice of karmayoga becomes more effective when he offers them to God as a sacrificial offering without seeking their fruit.

Karmayoga of the superior kind is thus a way of sanctifying our lives and actions and consecrating them to God as the means to self-purification and inner transformation. It is bringing God into the center of our lives and making Him the owner and doer of our lives and actions. It is transferring our responsibilities to Him and making Him the caretaker of our destinies. When actions are performed sincerely and dutifully as an offering to God, He assumes responsibility for our lives and takes care of our needs. In the Bhagavadgita, we find this assurance from Lord Krishna clearly and loudly. Continued and regular practice of karmayoga by renouncing desires and attachments leads to self-realization. Even a little practice has its rewards. Those who fail on this path do not lose anything. Upon their death, they go to the ancestral world. Once their karmas are exhausted, they return to the earth and attain a new birth in a good family to continue their journey further.

In the context of the Bhagavadgita, "sannyasa" means renunciation of desire-ridden actions, and "tyaga" means giving up the fruit of such actions. However, it is not uncommon to use both words interchangeably. A karmayogi must practice both to achieve peace and perfection on the path. In other words, one should not renounce actions but only the desire for their fruit. According to the scripture, a true sannyasi does not hanker after results while performing actions. He worships God. He serves others, especially those who are devotees of God. He upholds Dharma by performing his obligatory duties (daily and occasional sacrifices) and, thereby, fulfills his commitments towards his family, ancestors, gods, spirit beings, and other living beings. He does all these as a part of his covenant with God, the Creator. Lord Krishna says that a person of such merit is a true sanyasi, not the one who gives up actions or the sacred fire (6.1).

Significance of karmayoga

Karmayoga is the simplest and most straightforward approach to resolving the problem of suffering and bondage. Anyone and everyone can practice it by bringing spirituality and selflessness into their actions. Having the right knowledge is the greatest aid to practicing karma yoga, which is why the fourth chapter of the Bhagavadgita has the title Jnana Karma Sannyasa Yoga, meaning practicing karma sannyasa with the right knowledge. With discernment, detachment, devotion, and renunciation, which arise from knowledge, karmayoga becomes a powerful transformative tool to stabilize the mind and body. Knowledge is essential to understanding the underlying causes of any action and the way they bind us to the world. Discretion enables us to discern things correctly and remain centered in the divine rather than the demonic nature. Detachment helps us control our minds and senses. Devotion helps us earn God's grace and protection. Renunciation helps us cleanse our minds of latent impressions and burn away the seeds of our future through selfless actions.

While desires are the root cause of our suffering, they are, in turn, caused by the triple gunas: sattva, rajas, and tamas. The three gunas tend to compete with each other for predominance and, in the process, induce jivas to indulge in desire-ridden actions and seek things that agree with them. They are responsible for our experience of attraction and aversion to things and the pairs of opposites. Since they are inherent in us, no one can escape performing actions. They drive all beings ceaselessly into performing actions of one kind or the other since, through actions alone, they acquire strength and become predominant. Therefore, the Bhagavadgita rightly states that freedom from action cannot be achieved by avoiding actions or by renouncing them. He, who indulges in mere meditative practices, restraining his organs of actions, neglecting his obligations, is but a deluded soul and a hypocrite. By refraining from action, it is not possible to maintain even one's own body. Dynamism (chaitanyam) is the fundamental characteristic of life. Even in inanimate objects, unseen activity happens at the atomic and subatomic levels. Therefore, it is a delusion to believe that one can escape from the consequences of actions by not doing anything. Even the Imperishable Supreme Brahman does His work dutifully, although He has no desire either to perform them or seek their fruit. There is nothing in the three worlds for Him to do or yet to attain. Still, He engages in actions because, says Lord Krishna, if He does not perform His duties, men will follow His example and neglect their own.

Therefore, those who want to attain liberation should follow God's supreme example of karma sannyasa and do their obligatory work without attachments and without any interest whatsoever in what is being done or not done, knowing that their right is to work only, but not to the fruit thereof. They must live dutifully and be even-minded in both success and failure, surrendering to God, offering the fruit of their actions to Him, and partaking of only that which has been offered to Him.

Actions bind people when they are performed with egoism, thinking that one is the doer, with a desire to enjoy their fruit. Whoever thinks that he is the doer of his actions is but a deluded soul who does not know the truth about the influence of the gunas and how they are responsible for all binding actions. Performing actions out of desires and attachment, with an intention to enjoy their fruit, a deluded soul becomes bound to their consequences, whether they are good or bad. Depending upon the nature of his activities, he may gain either sorrow or happiness in this world or other worlds.

An enlightened karmayogi, on the other hand, knows action in inaction and inaction in action (Ch . 4.17). He knows who the real doer is, how the gunas drive jivas to perform actions, and how they bind them to sorrow and suffering. When a karma sannyasi performs actions, he remains indifferent to the consequences (karma) that may arise from them because he is aware that it is only the senses that are occupied with the object of his senses, and his mind and body are engaged in actions, and he is not in them. Thus, he actually becomes inactive even while performing actions and remains untouched by the fruit of his actions, like a lotus leaf by water.

A karmayogi who aims for liberation (moksha) while pursuing Dharma, Artha, and Kama ought to be aware of the nature of the gunas and their influence on his behavior. All actions arise from gunas only, and whether they are sattvic, rajasic, or tamasic, they all bind people and beings. Therefore, while karmayogis may perform actions that are ordained for them or not prohibited for them and produce positive karma, those who practice karma sannyasa should not refrain from any actions that they are fated to perform by providence, whether they are related to their obligatory duties or not. They should perform all types of actions without exception and expectations since they renounce all types of willful actions while remaining duty-bound.

On the path of self-transformation and liberation, sattva is the preferable mode. However, there is no cause for concern if the other two modes predominate, since one can never rule out the influence of past life karmas and the intervention of divine causes (adhidaivika). The modes cannot be wished away or suppressed easily. They persist in us despite our best efforts and intentions since we accumulate them over several lifetimes. A karma sannyasa yogi should focus on performing his actions selflessly in harmony with his gunas rather than against them. He should adhere to his essential nature (svabhava) and the obligatory duties (svadharma) that arise from it, however inferior they may be, rather than adopt the nature and duties of another (para dharma). When actions are performed with the spirit of renunciation in accordance with one's gunas, it will eventually lead to the predominance of sattva and the strengthening of divine qualities.

Karmayoga is the highest form of sacrificial action (yajna) when performed as an offering to God. It disciplines the mind and purifies the body, strengthens devotion, establishes a firm foundation for one's liberation, and leads to sameness (samsiddhi) and freedom from karma (naishkarmya siddhi). It is the simplest form of physical austerity, although not everyone can practice it with utmost perfection. Even the animals and lower life forms practice karmayoga of some sort. No special knowledge is required to practice this yoga. However, sincerity and attitude are very important to control one's desires and expectations in performing actions. The persistent practice of karmayoga with even-mindedness and exclusive devotion leads to knowledge, wisdom, and devotion, stabilizing the mind and leading to equanimity and sameness.

Karmayoga in daily life

Karmayoga encompasses every aspect of life. For a human being, the very process of living is indeed an inevitable outcome of engaging in actions, whether they are driven by desires, ulterior motives, or higher wisdom. No one can escape from being a karmayogi, even if they are unaware of the fact. All beings who perform actions for any reason are karmayogis only. Ascetic people also perform karmayoga. However, they perform actions that are primarily related to their bodily functions or to keep their minds and bodies actively engaged in contemplation and other ascetic practices. Karma sannyasa (renunciation of desire-ridden actions and their fruit) becomes a natural part of their initiatory vows of sannyasa. Therefore, they do not consider it a separate practice. On the other hand, householders must fulfill many obligations and responsibilities, which keep changing as they progress from one phase of life (ashrama) to another, from student to householder to being a retiree and recluse. Therefore, they have many opportunities to practice karmayoga, following the principles and techniques suggested in the Bhagavadgita, and test its real value in self-transformation. They can rely upon karmayoga, as true servants of God, to overcome their desires, selfishness, and other impurities and impure modes and experience dispassion, detachment, equanimity, and sameness. By practicing karma yoga as a way of life, they can bring God into the center of their lives and sanctify their actions with His presence.

A devotee can practice karmayoga in many different ways according to his duties and obligations. He can perform actions holding the thought that he does nothing, but every action is performed by God only with him as the witness and the instrument, and God as the ultimate doer. He can remember Him constantly while engaged in actions, holding Him as the real Doer and their true owner, acknowledging the energy and the inspiration as blessings from heaven. While performing his actions, he may even step into the role of God and identify himself fully with Him or believe that he is doing them for the sake of God and with His help and guidance. Knowing the omnipresence and omniscience of God, he can acknowledge that the actor (karta), the action (karma), and the offering of the action (kriya) are God only. Most importantly, he should consecrate his actions to Him and take no credit whatsoever for them. A karmayogi makes himself invisible. He lives and acts as if he does not exist. He replaces himself with God in thought and deed and lets Him rule his mind and body. He lets Him control his life and shape his destiny while not taking credit for his actions. He does not call attention to himself. He neither projects himself nor defends himself with the assured feeling that he will be protected. He keeps his ego under check and refuses to participate in egocentric clashes. He may fight the battles of life or even fight with others, as Arjuna did. However, he will not do it for himself or his benefit but for the sake of God to fulfill his obligations to him, society, or his Dharma (religion).

One simple and direct method to practice karmayoga is to remember God in everything one does and make Him the real Doer without claiming the credit or discredit for one's actions. If you do it sincerely and unassumingly, you will transform karmayoga into karma sannyasa yoga and improve your chances of spiritual progress and self-purification. Remembering and thanking God after you complete a task, successfully or otherwise, is also a part of karma sannyasa yoga. If you remember God constantly, you are already on the path of karmayoga. If you keep God always in the back of your mind, your life becomes one continuous sacrifice on the path of karmayoga. If you focus your mind on the result, your performance will suffer, and your sacrifice will become tainted with impurities. If you focus your attention on your performance rather than its fruit, most likely, you will become skillful in your actions. Therefore, it makes sense to focus on the action or the technique rather than the result and perform them with devotion and concentration. When you concentrate on actions rather than their outcome, results will take care of themselves. It is not true that karmayogis do not plan their actions or foresee possibilities. Planning is essential for any undertaking, especially if it involves time, effort, and skill. Karmayogis may also plan actions or draw plans of action to complete their tasks. However, they would not take credit for them or their results. Instead, they would regard their plans also as the work of God and give Him the credit.

Karmayoga is a very practical and suitable solution to bring God directly into the center of our awareness and use every available opportunity in our lives to remember Him and express our love and devotion to Him. In today's competitive world, you can use it to raise your efficiency and skill in action without suffering from stress and anxiety. You can face the challenges of your life with God on your side rather than against you. By saturating your mind with the thoughts of God, you can elevate your own consciousness and discern things clearly. You can use your actions to transform and elevate yourself mentally and spiritually rather than indulging in desire-ridden actions and binding yourself to egoism, ignorance, and delusion.

With karmayoga, you can experience peace and stability and become free from the modifications and afflictions of your mind. A karmayogi accepts responsibility for his life and actions, but he would not take pride in his achievements. With great humility, he attributes his successes and failures to fate or God. He is troubled by neither his past nor his future. He feels no anxiety. He does not suffer from insecurity. He does not feel the compulsion to outsmart others or belittle them to feel important. He does not use aggression or anger to intimidate others or coerce them into submission. He does not lie or cheat to impress others or mislead them. He is not ashamed of his failures or his weaknesses. He reposes complete trust in God and lets Him rule his life and dictate his actions, reactions, and responses. He lives in the present and performs his actions with detachment and dispassion. He plans his work with precision and executes it with utmost sincerity without being consumed by the fear of failure or passion for success. Keeping his emotions firmly under control and accepting God as the real Doer, he takes things in his stride without being disturbed by their consequences. Since he is duty-bound, he would not hesitate to make unpleasant decisions or express his opinions frankly. At the same time, he would treat others with dignity and respect, acknowledging their divine nature and their identity as immortal souls. Even if you do not possess all or most of these qualities, you can still spiritualize your actions and your consciousness by becoming a karmayogi with a change in your thinking and attitude, by bringing God into the center of your life, and performing your actions with devotion and humility.

References to Karmayoga in the Bhagavadgita

The yoga of action (karmayoga) proposed in the Bhagavadgita teaches devotees how to perform their obligatory duties and qualify for liberation without being tainted by their actions. It is the first discipline they must practice on the path of liberation. Without perfection in it, one cannot progress far in other yogas, such as the yoga of knowledge (jnanayoga) or the yoga of devotion (bhaktiyoga), become skillful (yukta) in them, or experience peace and equanimity. Karmayoga encompasses the whole of life. The worlds exist because of actions. Everyone must engage in actions. Even God and the various divinities of the pantheon practice karmayoga. They are duty-bound and must perform actions according to their ordained duties to keep the worlds in good order and ensure that the wheels of Dharma, karma, and creation progress as intended. Human beings must practice it in all the four phases (ashramas) of their lives to honor their obligatory duties (ashrama dharmas) and achieve the four aims of human life. They must practice karma yoga, even when they renounce worldly life and retire to secluded places to maintain their bodies, practice self-control, or achieve perfection and liberation.

Karmayoga is a state (yoga) of the mind in which you perform actions with sameness, indifference, and disinterest. It is characterized by dispassion, detachment, and commitment to selfless and desireless works. According to the Bhagavadgita, actions arising from desires bind humans to their consequences and subject them to their karmic consequences. However, this does not mean you can resolve the problem of karma by intentional inaction or selective actions. Both are troublesome and binding because they are driven by desires and produce consequences. As the Bhagavadgita declares, no one can attain freedom by abstaining from work or renouncing it (3.4) to avoid the consequences. It is delusional to believe that if karma arises from actions, we can prevent it by doing nothing. None can remain inactive even for a moment. The gunas drive everyone hopelessly to perform actions (3.5). Actions keep us alive. They are necessary to fulfill our obligations toward ourselves and others, and to participate in God's creation to play our part. Without actions, we cannot maintain our bodies or keep them in good health (3.8). The autonomous functions of our bodies, such as breathing and digestion, are not under our control. Whatever we may resolve, we cannot stop or renounce those involuntary actions. Therefore, the Bhagavadgita concludes that actions are superior to inaction and should not be renounced under any circumstances.

In life, we receive many things from the universe and incur many debts. We have to repay them in some form. Whatever we receive from God as a blessing should be returned to Him as an offering. The offering may be a simple acknowledgment or a dedication. It does not matter how you express it. What matters most is the attitude with which you receive and reciprocate the many blessings of your life. Of the many gifts we receive from God, food is the most important one because the universe is sustained by it. Our bodies need food for survival. The gods need food for their survival. The universe needs food (energy) to sustain creation. The objects need food (energy) to function according to their nature. The nourishment for all comes from Isvara only. He is the ultimate nourisher. He created food before He created beings because He knew that the beings would need food to remain alive and perform sacrificial duties to keep others alive. Thus, according to the scripture, the virtuous ones who know this show humility and gratitude. They eat only that which has been offered to God as a sacrifice and do it sincerely for the sake of nourishing their bodies alone. In this manner, they do not incur any sin (3.13).

Lord Krishna affirms in the Bhagavadgita that on the path of action (karmayoga), there is no loss or any adverse consequence. Even a little practice safeguards one from the fear of birth and death (2.40). One's right is to work only, but not to the fruits of their actions or inaction (2.47). True karmayoga consists of performing one's duty without attachment and remaining even-minded in both success and failure (2.48). This can be accomplished by controlling the senses (2.64-65) and desires (2.71). A true karmayogi knows that controlling the senses is important (3.6) because desires and attachments stem from them. He, therefore, engages in actions by restraining his mind and senses, unattached, directing his organs (karmendriyas) to work. (3.7). He overcomes in this way his desires and remains contented, taking delight in the Self alone (3.17). For him, there is no interest whatsoever in performing actions or in not performing them, nor does he depend upon anyone for anything (3.18). He performs his duty without attachment, with his mind and body under firm control. He lives his life as a sacrifice and an offering. He lives his life as if he is guided by God every step of the way. He lives by the word of God as revealed by Him in the scriptures.

The scripture further declares that even the Lord Supreme is a true Karmayogi. He also engages in actions, although there is nothing left in the three worlds for Him to do or attain (3.22). He performs actions so that men would follow His example (3.23), and the worlds that depend upon humans for sacrificial food could be saved from disorder and confusion (3.24). The ignorant act with selfish motives, with attachments, while the wise act without attachments, for the greater good of the world (3.25). They follow in His footsteps and exemplify His attitude towards duty.

The sense of doership is another area of personal reform. A knower of the triple gunas knows that all actions are caused by them (3.27) and, therefore, remains detached (3.28). He surrenders his actions to Isvara, with his mind fixed upon Him, free from expectations, attachment, and mental agitations (3.29). In performing selfless actions, restraint of the senses is more important than restraint of actions (3.34). The merit does not lie in performing right or wrong actions but in performing them with the right mental attitude and the spirit of surrender and devotion. The Bhagavadgita declares that desire is an eternal enemy of the wise upon earth, the insatiable fire (3.39), which deludes the soul by overpowering the senses, the mind, and the intellect (3.40). A true karmayogi, therefore, controls his senses and desires with wisdom and discipline and performs desireless actions. He performs his duty and never abandons it even if it is imperfect because, as the Bhagavadgita declares, real fulfillment arises from performing one's duty rather than that of another, however perfect it may be.

Renunciation of actions with knowledge is described in the fourth chapter. Lord Krishna affirms that he taught the supreme knowledge of renouncing actions to many great people in the past, but over time, it was forgotten (4.2). Therefore, He revealed it once again to Arjuna, his beloved devotee, to revive the practice and redeem the world.

Renunciation of action through knowledge means becoming free from the bondage of actions by renouncing the desires that are hidden in them and by knowing the truth concerning action, inaction, and prohibited action (4.17). By knowing them and by cultivating detachment, a karmayogi learns to see inaction in action and action in inaction. God Himself follows this ideal in His actions concerning creation, preservation, and dissolution of the created worlds. Although He is unborn and everlasting, He incarnates upon the earth from time to time to restore order, protect the pious, and destroy the wicked (4.8).

For a karma yogi who has dedicated himself to performing actions, the knowledge of Isvara is in itself liberating and uplifting. The Bhagavadgita assures us that those who know the divine birth and actions of God are freed from the cycle of births and deaths (Ch.4.9). By the fire of knowledge of the Divine, they attain His being (Ch.4.10). The fourfold order was created by Him (Ch.4.13), with no particular desire, but with a view to establish order and regularity in the world. The ancient seers knew that actions would not taint Him, as He had no desire for the fruits of His actions. By that knowledge alone, they attained perfection. No wonder our sacrificial ceremonies are modeled on the Great Sacrifice performed by Brahman at the beginning of creation to create the worlds and beings using Himself as the sacrificer and the sacrificed.

The scripture suggests that after knowing the truth about actions and using that knowledge, a man of wisdom engages himself in actions that do not bind him. How does he achieve this? The answer is provided in the fourth chapter. He does it by renouncing attachment to actions and remaining ever contented, without any shelter (4.20) and expectations, with his mind and body under his firm control, giving up all possessions and performing only body-related functions (4.21). He remains contended in that state with whatever comes to him on its own, free from jealousy, beyond dualities, and equal in success and failure (4.22). With his attachments gone and his mind purified and established in wisdom, his actions become elevated as sacrificial actions, and he is completely liberated from the bondage of actions.

The Bhagavadgita also makes it clear that renunciation of actions through knowledge alone is very difficult to achieve. Still, it can be achieved in conjunction with the yoga of action by performing one's actions dutifully and selflessly (4.6). However, one should know how to renounce actions by performing them rather than avoiding them. Who is a true sanyasi, according to the Bhagavadgita? He who does his work without depending upon the fruit of his actions should be considered the true renunciant, not the one who gives up actions and the sacred fire (6.1).

According to the Bhagavadgita, true renunciation is the renunciation of doership, ownership, and desire for its fruit, not the action itself. A karmayogi accomplishes this by offering his actions to God, shaking off his attachments (4.10. He performs them with his body only for the sake of self-transformation and inner purification (4.11) and offers the fruit of such actions to God alone since all actions arise from Him. By that self-sacrifice, he attains Supreme Peace (4.12). The scripture also describes the qualities of a true sanyasi in the fifth chapter as stated below.

- A true practitioner of renunciation (sanyasi) renounces all actions mentally and rests happily in the city of nine gates (5.13).
- He looks with the same eye upon everything, remaining intelligent, humble, and unassuming (5.18) in his approach.
- He does not rejoice upon getting what is pleasant, nor does he feel depressed when he gets what is unpleasant (Ch . 5.19).
- He is unattached to the external world, always engaged in the contemplation of Brahman, identifying himself with Him (4.21).
- He is self-disciplined, having the ability and discernment to control his desires and anger whilst still in the body (4.23).
- He is delighted in himself and illuminated within (4.24).
- He does not engage in selfish actions but in such actions that promote the welfare of the world (4.25).

How should one attain such an exalted and perfect state? The Bhagavadgita says that it can be done by withdrawing the senses from the external world, with one's gaze fixed firmly between the eyebrows, and by regulating the flow of prana and apana. Controlling his senses, mind, and intelligence and overcoming his desires and anger, he attains the highest freedom. This is the higher path of karma yoga, with karma sannyasa or action with renunciation as its central theme, as suggested by Lord Krishna in the Bhagavadgita.

Jnanayoga – The Path of Knowledge

'Jnana' means knowledge. Yoga means a method, state, or union. In jnanayoga, you use the right knowledge as the means to know your divine nature (Self or Brahman) and attain the highest state, the state of the all-knowing, infinite, self-existent, and eternal pure consciousness. In this quest for knowledge and liberation, you may resort to many practices and approaches. Initially, you may study the scriptures to understand the truths concerning the world and yourself. You may serve an enlightened master to purify yourself and spiritualize your thought process so that you can intuitively comprehend transcendental truths that are imperceptible and incomprehensible to ordinary minds. Knowing them, you overcome your delusion about yourself and the world and attain the mystic states (yogas) of balance, harmony, stability, and sameness.

Knowledge (jnana) opens our eyes to the truths beyond the apparent reality and dispels our mental darkness and inner chaos. It serves as a bridge that rests on the pillars of faith, devotion, sacrifice, and resolve, by which a devotee can safely cross the river of delusion and ignorance and connect with Isvara in a transcendental state. Hence, jnanayoga is an important approach in Hindu spirituality to know yourself and free yourself from the limitations that life and your nature impose upon you.

In Hinduism, the word "jnana" has many meanings. In a broader sense, it means any knowledge, and in a spiritual sense, it means the knowledge of the pure Self. For the mystics, knowledge can be both liberating and binding, depending upon which knowledge one pursues and for what purpose one uses it. In life, we use knowledge as a means to achieve certain ends. We may use it to fulfill our desires, such as passing an examination or obtaining employment, or we may use it to overcome our ignorance and delusion and liberate ourselves. We may use it to know the truth or to cover it up. Nature conceals the knowledge of the Self. Using the senses, the mind, and the elements, She deludes us and keeps us bound to our natural functions and limitations. We can use the right knowledge to overcome these obstacles and see the truth hidden behind the perceptible reality. We can also use it to know how to perform actions with the right attitude to overcome the problems of karma and rebirth.

Hence, Hindu scriptures identify two types of knowledge, the lower and the higher. Both are essential for material and spiritual progress on earth, but at some stage, one must know the difference and choose between the two. The knowledge that leads to the fulfillment of obligatory duties (Dharma), attaining material wealth (artha), and enjoying worldly life (kama) is considered lower knowledge. Sometimes, it is also termed avidya or ignorance because it perpetuates ignorance of the Self rather than revealing it. This knowledge is good, but it does not liberate people. The knowledge that leads to the truths of the Self and liberation is considered the higher knowledge or the real knowledge (vidya). Real knowledge liberates us from the three delusions of our existence, namely the delusion that the ego is the real self, the delusion that through desire-ridden actions, we can experience happiness and fulfillment, and the delusion that we are distinct and different from the rest of creation. It also liberates us from the three impurities of Nature, namely sattva, rajas, and tamas. Right knowledge also frees us from the afflictions created by the disturbances in our consciousness (chitta) and from the dualities of life and the pairs of opposites.

Jnanayoga is the pursuit of true knowledge on the path of self-realization and liberation. It is ideal for those who are driven by curiosity to know themselves, the world, and God. With its help, we can understand our true nature, the nature of the Self, the distinction between knowledge and ignorance, and the essentials of self-transformation that eventually lead to sameness, equanimity, and self-absorption.

Types of knowledge

In the practice of jnanayoga, a yogi relies upon different types of knowledge in his progress to achieve self-realization. These are listed below.

1. Knowledge of the Field (kshetra jnanam): This knowledge helps us understand the truths concerning our minds and

bodies, how modifications arise, and how we become bound to the world through our desires and actions.

2. Knowledge of Nature's divisions (tattva jnanam): This knowledge helps us understand how constituent aspects of Nature contribute to our bondage and delusion. From this knowledge, we realize how the activity of the senses leads to attachment, how the gunas induce desire-ridden actions, how the elements cause modification, and how the internal organ (antahkarana) creates mental fluctuations (vrittis) and prevents us from knowing the truth concerning ourselves.

3. Knowledge of scriptures (shastra jnanam): This is acquired through study or listening to others. By studying the scriptures, we open our eyes to the reality concerning our existence. Scriptural knowledge may not help us directly in achieving self-realization, but it helps us sharpen our intellect and discern things rightly. The widely recommended method to obtain scriptural knowledge is self-study (svadhyaya).

4. Knowledge of sacrifices and other obligatory duties: This knowledge helps us to perform our duties selflessly and achieve perfection in the practice of karmayoga. We acquire this knowledge from others, teachers, scriptures, and our elders.

5. Knowledge of the Self (atma jnanam): This is the knowledge concerning the individual Self and its essential, eternal nature as an aspect (amsa) of God and its bondage to Nature in the mortal body. This knowledge helps us stabilize our minds in the contemplation of the Self and experience equanimity, stability, and sameness.

6. Knowledge of God (brahma jnanam): This is the knowledge concerning the Supreme Self and our relationship with Him. This knowledge helps us know about Him and the means to secure His mercy (prasadam) through sacrifices, desireless actions, devotion, and surrender.

7. Knowledge of gods, divinities, and other beings (dharma jnanam): This knowledge helps us perform sacrifices and nourish the gods, ancestors, spirit beings, and other creatures. With this knowledge, we can practice religious duties (dharma) and contribute to the order and regularity of the world and

beings.

8. Knowledge of the means to liberation (moksha jnanam): This knowledge helps us understand the significance of liberation, the various means that are available to us to achieve it, and the path that may be most suitable for our specific needs.

Knowledge vs. ignorance

True knowledge is the knowledge of your essential nature, and ignorance is the absence of it. Knowledge is knowing that you are an eternal and indestructible Self, and ignorance is identifying yourself with your physical self and accepting your individuality, name, and form, or your egoism, as your true Self. When your divine nature is enveloped by the impurities of darkness and delusion, you will consider the phenomenal world as real and fail to discern the truth hidden beyond the surface reality. Knowledge is becoming aware of your hidden Self in a state of self-absorption, and ignorance is experiencing the distinction between the knower and the known in a state of duality. Knowledge is overcoming our desires and attachment and treating everything with an equal eye, and ignorance is pursuing our desires and suffering from attraction and aversion to the pairs of opposites. With knowledge, we know what binds us to the world and make the necessary effort to liberate ourselves from the mortal world. With ignorance, we acknowledge truth as falsehood and falsehood as truth and allow demonic nature to take root in our consciousness. Knowledge liberates us, while ignorance binds us. We come to know about the distinction between the two with the help of intelligence (buddhi), which is considered the highest faculty of Nature. The various limbs of yoga and types of yoga help us to cleanse our minds and intelligence and develop the right knowledge and awareness about God, our existence, and our essential nature.

Worldly knowledge vs. spiritual knowledge

Knowledge is also classified in our scriptures as worldly knowledge (vijnanam) and spiritual knowledge (jnanam). Some people also classify them as knowledge and wisdom. In a broader sense, vijnanam is the knowledge of the material world or universe consisting of things and beings. It is the immediate and direct knowledge of the objective reality we experience regularly in our wakeful state (jagrt). It helps us pursue our chief aims, fulfill our desires, and perform our obligatory duties. Hence, it is essential for our survival and well-being. We acquire it through study, observation, perceptions, analysis, intellectual deliberation, direct experience, and learning. In a narrow sense, worldly knowledge is the knowledge of sacrificial ceremonies and scriptural knowledge, which helps us perform our obligatory duties and nourish the gods, ancestors, and other beings, whereby we earn good merit and seek peace and happiness in our lives.

True knowledge (jnanam) is the knowledge of the individual Self and the Supreme Self and their relationship. It is transcendental knowledge, which cannot be acquired through the senses, mind, or intelligence but only through direct contact with the inner Self or the Supreme Self (brahma sparsah). True knowledge is beyond the mind and the senses. However, in a state of purity, true knowledge is reflected in the brilliance of our intelligence (buddhi) since the intelligence in us is illuminated by the Self only. True knowledge is neither lost nor gained. It is always present in our consciousness, hidden in our divine nature, and distinct from our surface consciousness and from all the commotion and turbulence we experience in our daily lives. Because of ignorance and delusion, we cannot discern it. When delusion is removed, it reveals itself as the knowledge of the Self. Ignorant people do not have transcendental knowledge. Therefore, what is knowledge to them is ignorance for the wise ones. For them, true knowledge is that which is eternal, unchanging, independent, liberating, and enlightening. Through the practice of jnanayoga, they receive this knowledge and remain centered on it.

The importance of Jnanayoga

In jnanayoga, we advance from one state of knowledge to another. We progress from ignorance to knowledge and from delusion to wisdom through a gradual enfoldment of consciousness arising from the purity of our intention and clarity of thought, and purpose. In this yoga, knowledge is the means, and knowledge is the goal. The purer the knowledge and intention, the greater our progress. Through the practice of jnanayoga, we come to know how desire-ridden actions bind us to the cycle of births and deaths and how we may find freedom from it. We learn to control our minds and senses and remain focused on the pure Self so that we can gradually distance ourselves from the phenomenal world and our attachment to it. Jnanayoga also helps us draw a clear distinction between the Field (kshetra) and the knower of the Field and know the cause of rebirth, existential suffering, the means to liberation, and the interplay of the gunas.

The Bhagavadgita identifies jnanayoga as one of the important paths to liberation, which may directly lead to liberation or advanced states of self-absorption and devotion. It is superior to the path of action and complementary to the paths of desire-less or sacrificial actions and devotion. Its practice eventually leads to inner perfection, sameness, freedom from karma, and pure devotion. The practice of jnanayoga may take years to yield positive results. In the first stage, you become aware of the truths concerning your existence and the means to escape from it. In the second phase, you put into practice the knowledge you gain from your study and observation, and with its help, you achieve perfection on the path of yoga. As your mind and body are filled with the brilliance of sattvic knowledge, your devotion to God increases, and your mind becomes stabilized in His contemplation. While the path of devotion is described as superior to the other two, one cannot practice pure devotion right away. Karma yoga opens the path. Karma sannyasa widens it. Jnanayoga sets the milestones for the cultivation of exclusive devotion, and exclusive devotion eventually earns you God's grace and liberation. Jnanayoga is especially suitable for those who are inherently curious, drawn to study and learning, deeply intellectual, and not easily satisfied with simple answers or the superficial aspects of religious practices and observances.

Jnanayoga is rooted in the knowledge of the individual Self, the Universal Self, and Nature as stated in the Vedas, Tantras, and other scriptures. It is also espoused in the traditional Samkhya philosophy as well as in the Samkhyayoga of the Bhagavadgita. In many ways, Bhagavadgita's Samkhyayoga is a purely theistic interpretation of the relationship between God and Nature (Purusha and Prakriti) and is different in many respects from the Classical Samkhya. However, the concepts and practices it suggests bear a close resemblance to those of the Yogasutras of Patanjali, which is traditionally associated with the

Classical Samkhya. In many ways, the Bhagavadgita elaborates the themes presented in the Yogasutras, with special emphasis not just on the essential practices of yoga but on its practical value to those who practice Dharma and aim for liberation. Rightly, therefore, the Bhagavadgita is described as a yoga scripture (yoga shastram).

The second chapter of the Bhagavadgita, known as Samkhyayoga, is translated by many as jnanayoga. It is one of the most comprehensive chapters in the scripture. In terms of its importance, perhaps it is the most important one because it contains a summary of all the teachings and covers all the important concepts and ideas presented by Him. An astute reader will notice that the first part of the chapter contains the knowledge of the Self (Samkhya), and the second part contains the methods to realize it (Yoga). Therefore, it is appropriate to equate it with jnanayoga only. In this chapter, Lord Krishna explains how beings become deluded by the modes (gunas) and remain bound to Nature and samsara. The following are its salient teachings.

- One must know the distinction between the Self and the not-self (the body), and between action and inaction.
- The Self is eternal and distinct from the body, the physical self, which is destructible and regularly discarded by the Self like a garment.
- Desires are the root cause of our suffering. Through attraction and aversion, induced by the gunas, they bind us to the consequences of our actions.
- Renunciation of desire is more important than renunciation of actions because it alone leads to sameness to dualities (samsiddhi) and freedom from karma (naishkarmya siddhi).
- Attachment, anger, and delusion arise from the activity of the senses and lead to delusion and bondage. They must be withdrawn and restrained to overcome desires and attachments.
- Actions by themselves are not the cause of karma. Desires that are hidden in actions are responsible for it. Hence, actions should be performed without desires, and their fruit must be offered to God as a sacrifice to resolve karma and attain liberation.
- The triple modes (sattva, rajas, and tamas) induce desire-ridden actions and prolong our bondage to the cycle of births and deaths

and our suffering. They are the root cause of our suffering and bondage. One must transcend them to attain the ultimate freedom.
- The mind remains restless and unstable due to desires and the outgoing nature of the senses in their purpose. Therefore, yogis must cultivate equanimity and sameness by controlling their senses, stabilizing their minds, and withdrawing them from the sense objects.
- The wise ones (munis) differ from the mundane ones because they restrain their minds, senses, and speech, abandon their desires, and remain free from egoism, delusion, craving, and attachment. Through persistent practice, they attain the highest wisdom.
- The right knowledge helps us practice karma yoga with the spirit of renunciation and bhakti yoga with exclusive devotion, with the awareness that those who worship the lower gods go to them while those who worship the Supreme Lord attain Him alone.

Knowledge as the Means and Goal

The mind is an obstacle to attaining the highest state of yoga. It is also the doorway to knowledge and liberation. Knowledge is also helpful up to a certain point in spiritual practice. Then, it becomes an obstacle if one clings to it and relies upon it. The idea is that at a certain stage, one must renounce and let go of all desires and attachments to achieve true and complete liberation. Whatever you rely upon binds you and limits you.

You are unique because, with your mind, you can perform many tasks and manage your life and actions according to your life's essential purpose. You can think, reason, feel, know, remember, and discern things from one another to navigate your way through the labyrinth of life. The course of your life depends largely upon how creatively and intelligently you use your mind and determine your priorities and your life's central purpose. Your life offers you many choices. You may not acknowledge them, limited by your fears and circumstances. You may fill your mind with knowledge or ignorance; you may fill it with the light of the Self or the darkness of evil; and you may use it to serve God or fulfill your selfish desires. They are your fundamental choices, which decide the direction of your life. He who does not know how to use his mind is ignorant; he who does not know how to use his mind correctly delays his liberation, but he who uses it for evil purposes falls into the darkest hell. We learn this from the Bhagavadgita.

You can transform your mind. You can elevate your character and bring light and wisdom into it with your actions, knowledge, sense-restraint, intelligence, purity, renunciation, devotion, concentration, meditation, and self-absorption. These purificatory processes transform the mind of an ignorant, deluded, and restless person into a resting mind, a seeking mind, a stable and self-absorbed mind, and an enlightened mind. They lead the seeker to stability, sameness, detachment, equanimity, balance, harmony, surrender, knowledge, wisdom, compassion, devotion, contentment, and discernment. Knowledge plays an important role in this enduring process. With knowledge and the practice of yoga, you transform your mind and experience peace and equanimity even if your mind and senses are actively engaged with the external world.

Thus, with knowledge and effort, we can transcend our limitations. We can overcome ignorance and delusion and become aware of the causes of our suffering and the means to overcome it. As we light up the dark corners of our minds, in that illumination, we see the hidden presence of the Self and realize that as eternal souls, we have a destiny beyond the mortal life to which we are presently bound. The purpose of jnanayoga is to guide us on this path of self-discovery. It leads us from untruth (asat) to truth (sat), darkness (tamas) to light (jyotih), and death (mrtyu) to immortality (amrit) by helping us learn to master the very forces that prevent us from knowing the truth about our existence.

Knowledge is of different kinds. Ignorance is also a form of knowledge since it can arise from the absence of the right knowledge or having the wrong knowledge. We can pursue any of them, but we have to pay the price if the knowledge that we acquire does not lead to liberation but to delusion and bondage. The highest knowledge is the knowledge of the Self or the Supreme Self. This supreme knowledge arises in us at the end of a great journey stretching over several lives. Material knowledge leads to bondage and suffering, while spiritual knowledge leads to enlightenment and liberation. You cannot gain spiritual knowledge unless you purify yourself with sattva and keep your mind and senses under firm control. To accomplish it, you have to practice detachment, stability, and self-control. You have to recognize the factors that disturb you, and you have to deal with them firmly.

From the Bhagavadgita, we learn that self-transformation is a comprehensive process. You cannot focus on just one aspect of your life and expect liberation or purification. You must deal with all your vulnerabilities through a detailed set of yogic practices and use your daily experiences and obligatory duties to practice the highest ideals of Dharma. Your liberation must happen here and now, in the midst of life, facing the ordinary and the mundane challenges where your faith and beliefs are tested severely and where you are vulnerable to the forces of Nature and the temptations of life.

On the path of liberation, ignorance is a major problem for everyone. We are not only ignorant but also ignorant of our ignorance, which makes our transformation even more difficult. The knowledge that we acquire through self-study (svadhyaya) is helpful, but it does not take us far unless we awaken the knowledge that is inherent in us. Mental knowledge puts us on the path of liberation, but at some stage in our progress, we have to silence our minds to experience equanimity and sameness, which arise only when we are silent in every sense of the word. To see your hidden Self, you have to step aside, withdrawing your senses and silencing your mind. In other words, we may rely upon our minds and senses to cultivate certain attitudes and states of mind that are essential for our transformation, but later on, we have to keep them under control to transcend ourselves and see the truth hidden deep within ourselves.

Right knowledge leads to liberation. Jnanayoga is the use and pursuit of the right knowledge for the right cause. If liberation is your aim, you must know what right knowledge means and how it manifests in your consciousness. The scripture says there is no failure on this path. Even a little practice in its pursuit has a beneficial effect. Even if you fail to secure the right knowledge, you will have opportunities in the future to redeem yourself. It is not easy to suppress the gunas or shut down the mind completely. However, in moments of deep meditation, you will experience the cessation of all mental activity for a very brief time. You will also enter this state when you land in the silence that is hidden in your mind between one thought and another. In those moments, you will experience a great awakening. Such moments may not last long or recur frequently, but if you keep your resolve and persist in your practice, they begin to linger and take root in your consciousness.

In today's world, we have access to a wealth of information on spiritual subjects, which was hitherto unavailable to people except through a guru unless they were born into families of pious and wise elders and parents. Today, we can also reach out to many gurus directly by visiting them or indirectly by reading their writings and discourses. With the knowledge thus gained and with the firm resolve of the sattvic type, we can bring transformation within ourselves and become God-centric by cultivating virtues and divine qualities and transcending our base nature. With faith and perseverance, we can perfect our practice of various yogas, apply the principles we learn from the Bhagavadgita, and experience peace and stability. That journey begins with karma yoga and gains momentum with jnana and sannyasa yogas. For some, bhakti yoga may also help if exclusive devotion arises in them naturally. The practice of jnanayoga and the transformation of the mind and body lead to the following developments.

- Self-knowledge
- Freedom from ignorance and delusion
- Knowledge concerning the phenomenal world
- Detachment
- Divine qualities
- Devotional services
- Sacrificial attitude
- Discerning wisdom
- Predominance of sattva
- Suppression of rajas and tamas
- Devotion
- Grace of God
- Strengthening of faith and devotion
- Peace and equanimity
- Freedom duality
- Sameness
- Skill in yoga

On the path of knowledge, to stabilize the mind, one may pursue knowledge by various means. To reach this goal, one must engage in self-study (svadhyaya), listening to the words of wise ones (sravanam), recollecting the name of God or the knowledge already gained (smaranam), and contemplating (dhyanam) on the inner Self and the Supreme Self. Their repeated practice (abhyasam) and the grace of an enlightened guru or God (Isvara prasadam) also lead to enlightenment. Knowledge is effective when it is free from egoism, delusion, desires, and attachments. Therefore, yogis should not be proud of their knowledge and must practice detachment even from the knowledge they acquire through these methods.

Buddhiyoga – Cultivating Discernment

Buddhiyoga helps us find direction in the darkness of the world and confusing dualities with discernment and awakened intelligence. It leads us to clarity, understanding, and certainty of purposes and resolve without the distortions to which the mind is subject due to desires and attachments. When you enter the pure state of your intelligence through buddhi yoga, you are no longer deluded by the duality of your perceptual experience or the turbulence of the mind. Buddhi means the faculty or the organ that is responsible for thinking, reasoning, and intelligence. Some call it the higher mind or the thinking mind, in contrast to the memorial mind known as manas. In other words, Hindu scriptures distinguish between these two aspects of the human mind, unlike modern science, which regards the mind as one unity with different faculties and abilities. Because of the buddhi, we are able to think and act rationally and make sense of things. Intuition, insight, common sense, reasoning, and analytical ability arise from intelligence (buddhi) only. It is also the highest aspect of Nature present in us. When it is pure, it reflects the brilliance of the Self and reveals to us the transcendental nature of our existence. It is responsible for our discernment and our ability to make rational decisions and perform self-willed actions. When it is pure and filled with sattva, we discern things clearly with equanimity and without being judgmental. In the macrocosm, it is known as the Great One (Mahat), which is responsible for the intelligent design hidden in creation.

In buddhiyoga, you purify and sharpen your intelligence to the point where you can think, reason, and know clearly right from wrong and truth from falsehood. You learn to avoid actions that lead to suffering, bondage, ignorance, delusion, and demonic nature. You learn to adapt to situations and circumstances and improve your chances of survival and success. According to our scriptures, the mind (manas) and the intelligence (buddhi) are separate entities. Intelligence draws information from the senses and the lower mind to perform its functions. You may even refer to it as the higher or the rational mind.

The lower mind is a repository of memories and perceptions of the objective world, which constitute mental knowledge, lower knowledge, or ignorance (avidya), while intelligence is that which dissects it and uses it to discern causes, make right decisions, and solve problems. Both are aspects (tattvas) of Nature and form part of the internal organ (antahkarana). Awareness that arises from the right thinking and discernment of the Self that leads to liberation (Moksha) is called true knowledge (jnanam), while the understanding arising from observation of the world that helps us in the pursuit of Dharma, Artha, and Kama is called worldly wisdom (vijnanam).

In Buddhiyoga, you remain undisturbed by external events as you develop the intelligence and the fortitude to be equal in all situations. According to the Bhagavadgita, even-mindedness is called Buddhiyoga (2.48). It arises from staying free from both attraction and aversion to things, which is difficult to achieve because of the conditions in which we live. Our minds remain disturbed and preoccupied mostly with some problem or the other because of desires and our attitude towards the pairs of opposites. The Bhagavadgita says that equanimity, detachment, and sameness towards all should be cultivated by controlling the mind, the body, and the senses, practicing inner discipline, and renunciation of desires. The mind and the senses tend to run in all directions. They must be withdrawn and restrained for even-mindedness, which, through sustained practice (abhyasa), culminates in the state of self-absorption (samadhi). In that state, a yogi transcends his mind, senses, and duality. He becomes completely immersed in himself, unaware of the world outside and detached from it. Thus, through constant practice and dispassion (vairagya), he finally accomplishes the supreme goal of disconnecting himself from the union with pain and suffering - *dukkha samyoga viyogam* (6.23).

"Buddhi," pure intelligence, is different from "chitta," consciousness formed out of the accumulated knowledge stored in the memorial mind. From the Bhagavadgita, we learn that intelligence gives us the discriminating power to make choices and stay on course in the pursuit of our liberation or any goal we may choose. It is the source of our discerning wisdom and analytical knowledge. A man of lesser buddhi does not discriminate well and does not make the right decisions. Most likely, he remains deluded and even perverted, with increased tamas in his thinking and actions. He is constantly driven by his senses and the desire for sense objects, whereby he remains disturbed or distressed as he experiences union and separation from sense objects and attraction and aversion to them.

Buddhiyoga is the use of intelligence and wisdom to overcome the weaknesses of our minds and achieve a state of equanimity so that we remain alike in pleasure and pain, gain and loss, victory and defeat (2.38). When we make the right decisions and know the truth concerning our existence, we achieve freedom from the bondage caused by our desire-ridden actions (2.39). The Bhagavadgita declares that performing disinterested actions through cultivated intelligence (vyavasayātmika buddhi) is the aim of buddhiyoga. It gives us the ability to see through things and phenomena and remain indifferent to them. The scripture affirms that the practice of Buddhiyoga leads to many rewards.

It further states that in this yoga, there is no loss of effort or progress. Even a little practice protects one from the fear of birth and death (2.40). A practitioner can always return to the path if, by chance, he abandons it and begins from where he left off. However, sincere effort is required to achieve correct results. Perfection in this yoga cannot be achieved by the mere study of the Vedas or by engaging oneself in flowery speeches and intellectual discussions (2.42). There should be a sincere effort to control one's desires and detach oneself from the things of the world, including one's thoughts, beliefs, and opinions. One must balance and transcend the triple gunas and withdraw the mind and senses into oneself to reach perfection. It is by overcoming the gunas, conquering the duality and distinction, and establishing oneself in purity (sattva) that one obtains enlightenment (2.45). By developing even-mindedness in success and failure, renouncing the fruit of actions, and becoming detached, says the Bhagavadgita, a buddhi yogi becomes free from the bondage of mortal life. (2.48-51).

However, how to know whether we have achieved perfection on this path? What are the marks of the one who truly excels in mental stability (sthithaprajna)? The scripture provides the answers. A stable-minded yogi gives up all cravings arising from his mind and remains withdrawn and satisfied (2.55) to be equal to all situations and dualities. He is not afraid of adversity or suffering, nor does he crave prosperity or happiness. He should rightly be called a stabilized sage (sthithadhir muni) who is free from passion, fear, and anger (2.56). Without friends or relations (anabhisneha), equal to auspicious and inauspicious events and situations, he remains detached, unconcerned, and absorbed in himself (2.57).

The senses are responsible for the mind's delusion and instability. They make us restless and keep us ignorant of the truths they cannot grasp. By establishing contact with the outside world, by constantly dwelling upon the sense objects, they subject the mind to experience attraction and aversion to them. This is but the state of bondage or attachment in which one remains limited by his own volition. When we are attached, we are not free. Out of this attachment, the desire for material things and sense objects is born. From that desire arise passions, delusion, anger, loss of memory, confusion, and finally, loss of Buddhi or intelligence (2.62&63). This leads to karma, births, and rebirths.

Knowing this truth, a Buddhiyogi tries to achieve mental stability, withdrawing his mind from the objects he perceives, the way a tortoise withdraws its limbs (2.58). He stops enjoying the objects to end his sorrows. Controlling his senses, devoting himself, heart, and soul to Isvara, he becomes firmly established in Him (2.65). He becomes an awakened Yogi, who remains fully awake with wisdom and discernment when others are asleep with ignorance and delusion. He is asleep to ignorance and delusion when all beings are awake to them in the world of desires (2.69) and impermanence. He becomes the ocean itself, undisturbed by the rivers of knowledge that keep flowing into him from all sides (2.70).

To achieve such a Supreme State of pure consciousness through buddhiyoga and remain detached from Nature, one has to practice the yoga of self-discipline (atmasamyama yoga), which is described in the sixth chapter (10-19). Atma means the Self. Samyama means the simultaneous practice of concentration, meditation, and self-absorption. When you practice it upon the Self, it becomes atmasamyama-yoga. It leads to the highest state of self-absorption and oneness with the Self.

The scripture says that a yogi should concentrate his mind constantly upon his Self, leading a solitary life, controlling his mind, free from desires and possessiveness. Placing his seat firmly in a clean place, neither too low nor too high, covering it with a soft cloth, deerskin, and kusa grass, he should practice yoga for his purification, keeping his mind, senses, and activities under firm control. Holding his body, neck, and head erect in a straight line, concentrating his gaze on the tip of his nose, undistracted, with a peaceful and fearless mind, practicing celibacy, subdued in passions, he should become established in Isvara and attain the highest peace and nirvana (6.10-15).

The scripture cautions us not to resort to extreme measures to sharpen our intellect. Discretion is the hallmark of buddhiyoga. There is no place for extremities in it (6.16-18). This yoga is neither for the voracious eater nor for the non-eater. It is neither for the constant sleeper nor for the one who does not sleep well. A buddhi-yogi, who is regulated in eating and relaxation, in sleeping and waking, becomes impervious to the dualities of life, resting in the Self only. Freed from all desires, he becomes established in the yoga of equanimity. In that state, he realizes his essential nature, becomes satisfied in the Self (6.20), finds unlimited happiness, develops an understanding of the transcendental state through his intellect, and remains unmoved by all sorrows. He enjoys extreme bliss from his union with Brahman. Envisioning Him in his own heart, he experiences the Self in all and all in the Self (6.21-29).

Buddhiyoga is the foundation for success and perfection in all walks of life, including the practice of other yogas. It is an adjunct to the practice of both jnanayoga and karmayoga and is the foundation to perfect the practice of bhaktiyoga. Without discernment and the right knowledge, it is difficult to overcome desires and attachments and attain perfection in other yogas. A true karmayogi has to subdue his mind, restrain his senses, control his desires, and develop detachment from the world to practice true renunciation, offering the fruit of his actions to God with a sacrificial attitude (3.7&5.3). A true devotee of God must control his mind and his desires by detaching himself from all the objects with which he develops attachment and remains devoted to God only so that he can concentrate his mind upon Him and become fully absorbed in Him (Chapters 9 and 12). Buddhiyoga makes a human being a truly rational and intelligent being. It brings out his humanity, frees him from the clutches of his social conditioning, and elevates him mentally and intellectually to think freely and fearlessly with a clear mind, clear goals, wisdom, and discernment.

Bhaktiyoga – The Yoga of Devotion

In terms of both the intensity and the object of one's veneration, we may classify devotion into many types. Of them, devotion to God, a deity, or some supreme power through direct worship and exclusive devotion (ananya bhakti) is considered the highest. It is sustained by purity, faith, concentration, conviction, and, according to our scriptures, the grace of God Himself. When devotion is divided, it loses its intensity. Hence, the Bhagavadgita particularly emphasizes exclusive devotion to the highest Supreme Being as the best and quickest path to liberation. Devotion may be sattvic, rajasic, or tamasic in nature. Rajasic devotion is passionate and demanding. Tamasic devotion is deluded and even perverted. Sattvic devotion is pure and free from delusion and attachment. When we are not free from desires, we seek fulfillment of our desires through devotion. When we are not pure, we cling to the objects of our devotion. In their lives, people become devoted to many things, depending upon their knowledge, awareness, and predominant qualities.

If we do not have discernment, we may mistake passion for devotion or worship many gods. In its purer aspect, devotion is a form of spiritual love, the longing of the individual Self for the Supreme Self. Sometimes, it may also degrade into a kind of attachment, especially when it is induced by desires and worldly concerns. Devotion may also manifest in us in various ways. Some become devoted to their work, some to a cause, and some to material things, concepts, ideas, relationships, and institutions. Some people worship wealth, and some power, or those who wield power. In these cases, devotion arises from the activity of the senses in a state of duality between the knower and the known. In these instances, one can physically grasp the object of one's devotion. It is difficult to experience the same in the case of devotion to God, who is invisible and transcendental. Hindu tradition recognizes this problem and permits the worship of idols so that people may see God in them and express their devotion to Him physically. The idols are deemed living symbols or direct manifestations (arkas) of God so that we can treat them as His living embodiment in image form. Idol worship may not be the ideal practice for spiritually advanced souls who are inclined to worship God in other ways. However, it has its place and value in one's spiritual progress and inner transformation.

The Bhagavadgita lays great emphasis on devotion and its importance in liberation. It advises people to cultivate devotion to God, fixing their minds upon Him constantly, cultivating virtues and knowledge, and offering their actions to Him with an attitude of sacrifice without seeking their fruit. Lord Krishna promises to deliver those who are devoted to Him and who worship Him wholeheartedly. He also declares that worshipping other deities is also worthy, but worshipping Him directly alone delivers one from the mortal world. We learn from the scripture that single-minded devotion to Vasudeva is the surest path to self-realization. Perfection in this practice leads to union with Brahman (brahmasparsha) and a sure place in the Highest Abode.

However, bhaktiyoga is not easy to practice. Going to temples, praying to God, performing occasional ceremonial worship (poojas), and temple rituals (archanas) are considered obligatory duties (Dharma) rather than acts of true devotion unless they are performed with exceptional purity and without expectations. Such devotional services may strengthen your faith and earn you a place in heaven, but they do not lead to liberation. In true devotion, the object of worship alone remains, and the devotee disappears. Such self-effacement is not possible unless one's mind is completely absorbed in the contemplation of God, and one's own identity is lost in His thoughts.

True devotion arises after years of practice, after one has achieved perfection in the yoga of action, renunciation, and knowledge. When the mind and body are purified and filled with sattva, feelings of selflessness and surrender intensify, and true devotion arises. True devotion is free from attachment and selfishness. It is characterized by intense aspiration to be with God and experience oneness with Him, with no ulterior motive. True devotion is not practiced for personal gains or worldly benefits. A true devotee does not look to God in times of distress, only when there are difficult problems. The Bhagavadgita affirms clearly that closeness to Isvara is achieved through love and devotion. In whatever way a devotee approaches Him, says Lord Krishna, He accepts them because men approach Him from all directions (4.11), and what draws them closer to Him is not the path they choose but their love for Him.

People who are completely devoted to God and who devote their lives to Him unconditionally are difficult to find in today's world. Such people are born only after earning great merit in their previous lives. Great souls (mahatmas), who are born thus, know how to worship God with undivided minds. They know Him to be Imperishable and the true cause of all beings (9.13). Always singing His glories, says the Gita, striving to attain Him, with firm determination, prostrating fully before Him, ever established in Him, they worship Him (9.14). A true devotee is never lost to God. He lives in His constant gaze and under His continuous protection. The Lord always takes care of the needs of a pure devotee who is totally lost in his devotion to him (9.22). Pure devotion is the highest form of love to which God responds with unconditional love and immediate attention.

The Vishistadvaita (qualified monism) school holds the view that when a liberated devotee departs from here, God eagerly awaits his arrival. He sends many messengers and close attendants in advance to make sure that he receives a grand reception. When he finally arrives at His Doors, He Himself comes forward to meet him. The essence of this is that God is as eager to meet His devotee as the devotee is. He is as fond of the company of His devotees as they are. The Abode of God (Vaikuntha) is a happy place because everyone, from the Supreme Self to the last of His devotees, is filled with unlimited love and rapturous bliss.

The Gita assures us that those who worship Vasudeva Krishna with single-minded devotion (ekanta bhakti) are speedily rescued from the ocean of mortal existence (12.7). Upon their death, they travel by the sunlit path of immortality and reach Him directly. The Bhagavadgita says that to attain liberation, devotees must practice contemplation with their minds and intelligence fixed on God (12.8). Those who cannot practice devotion with unwavering attention should practice concentration (12.9), restraining themselves, until their minds are trained and stabilized. If they cannot practice concentration also, they should take refuge in God, renounce desires and attachments, and perform actions without desiring their fruits (12.11).

God is omniscient, omnipresent, and omnipotent. All living beings are created by Him, and they exist in Him. He is their source and support, but deluded by the threefold modes of nature, many do not recognize Him, nor do they acknowledge His supremacy and greatness. The deluded persons of illusory hopes and actions follow the way of the demons (asuras) and do not give Him their due respect (9.12. However, the noble and the virtuous, who are pure and possess a divine nature, knowing Him as the prime cause of creation and imperishable, worship Him and identify with Him unconditionally in a complete state of surrender and egolessness. By that, they become extremely dearer to Him.

In the scripture, Lord Krishna assures His devotees that they will never perish. Even if a sinful person worships Him with complete devotion, he will be regarded as a saint because he has made the right decision to work for his liberation, choosing Him as his support and goal. By the grace of the Supreme Lord, he speedily becomes a righteous soul (dharmatma) (9.31). Redemption is, therefore, possible for those who undergo a change of heart and surrender to God with faith and humility. However, those who act with hatred and envy towards Him and give themselves to demonic thoughts and actions will perish. They will fall into the lowest hells.

There are, however, a few important conditions to earn God's grace. First, devotees must worship the Supreme Self alone, who is the Highest and the Lord (Isvara) of the Universe. Second, they must worship Him with single-minded devotion. Devotees of the Supreme Lord stand far above those who worship lesser divinities with desires. Lord Krishna says that those who perform sacrifices (9.20) and those who worship other gods (9.23) worship in a way Brahman only. However, they do not attain Him because they take refuge in others or material things. Only those who take refuge in Him and worship Him with unflinching devotion qualify for liberation. However, they may worship other divinities regarding them as Brahman or the Supreme Lord. Then, they would be deemed God's exclusive devotees and rescued.

Thus, the path to liberation is through the heart of the Supreme Lord. He reciprocates the love and devotion of His devotees with abiding compassion. They are never lost to Him. Even though He is indifferent and treats all equally, He rescues His devotees from samsara by reciprocating their love and giving them an exalted place in His eternal heaven. Death and destruction do not taint those who reach the Supreme Abode (parandhama). They are forever free from samsara. We do not know exactly what happens to them after liberation, whether they continue to exist individually or merge into the Supreme Self. According to Dvaita and Vishistadvaita, God's devotees who are liberated (muktas) will remain in God's highest heaven either in His company or connected to Him internally through their pure consciousness. They will not perish even during the dissolution of the worlds, while everything else around them perishes. However, others do not have that privilege.

The fate of the ignorant ones who succumb to desires is somewhat different. The knowers of the Vedas who worship Him through sacrifices to fulfill their desires and those whose wisdom has been carried away by desires and delusion and worship other gods ascend to the temporary heaven of the ancestors upon their death, where they will enjoy celestial pleasures. After exhausting their karma partially, they return to the earth to take another birth again (9.20 & 21). This does not mean that God is partial to His exclusive devotees. He treats them all equally according to their nature. If they love Him, He loves them back. If they ignore Him, He remains indifferent. He lets the mortals live according to their karma (actions) and does not interfere with their destinies unless they approach Him and seek His intervention.

Rewards and punishments in this world arise from our karma. Our lives and destinies are shaped by our essential nature and the universal laws (Dharma) He establishes for the order and regularity of life on earth. He does not condemn the sinners to an eternal hell, nor does he compel anyone to worship Him against their will. He does not confuse the deluded ones with knowledge and wisdom they cannot comprehend, nor does He ignore those who are ready for liberation. He gives them the freedom to live according to their nature and pursue their own paths. He lets people progress and manifest their will in the direction of their thoughts and desires. He does the same in the case of devotion. In the Bhagavadgita, He assures everyone that in whatever form devotees worship Him with faith, He stabilizes their faith in that form and, through those forms, helps them obtain their desired enjoyment (9.21 & 22). However, He cautions us that the fruit gained by men of lesser wisdom is limited and inferior. Those who worship gods go to them, but His devotees attain Him only (9.23).

Types of Devotion and Devotees

The Bhagavadgita declares that a person is essentially made of his faith. As is his nature, so is his devotion. In this, the gunas play an important role. Some people are devoted to worldly pleasures and material things such as wealth, name, fame, etc. Some people are devoted to themselves, some to their families or communities, and some to God or a higher cause. Some people devote their lives to worshiping gods for success and enjoyment, and some to a higher cause or purpose that outlasts them. Devotion is an aspect of one's personality, essential nature, past life karma, upbringing, spiritual evolution, fate, and even circumstances. In this chapter, we will focus on types of devotion and devotee, how they are connected to other factors, and how they may result in different outcomes for the people involved. Hinduism recognizes this fundamental aspect of human nature. Hence, it accommodates different perspectives on the metaphysical aspects of our existence. They are known as Darshanas or points of view.

Types of devotees

Even among those who worship God, there are categories. The scripture identifies four types of devotees: those who are in distress (arta), the inquisitive types (jignasu), seekers of material wealth (artharhti), and the wise beings (7.16). Of them, declares Lord Krishna, a wise person who is established in single-minded and uninterrupted devotion, is extremely dearer to Him (7.17). According to Lord Krishna, all devotees are noble, but He regards a man of wisdom as His very Self in perfect union with Him (7.18). It is only at the end of many births that a person is able to achieve such a supreme state of devotion (7.19). We find an irrevocable assurance in the scripture that those who are fully absorbed in Him (8.14 &10.10) with utmost devotion are assured of immortality and a permanent place in the world of God. Lord Krishna declares that to a constantly busy devotee who remembers Him always without diverting his attention elsewhere, He is very easy to attain. He further adds that those who worship Him always with loving devotion, to them He gives real wisdom.

From the Bhagavadgita, we can deduce other classes of devotees: those who worship many gods, demigods, and spirits, those who perform sacrifices and make offerings to gods to fulfill their desires, and those who transcend desires and worship God with exclusive devotion. Lord Krishna says the first kind goes to the worlds of gods or spirits, etc., whom they worship. They do not attain liberation. The second kind goes to the ancestral world and returns after exhausting some of their karma to obtain another birth. The third kind of devotees earn God's grace and reach His abode. As they attain final liberation, they remain in Brahman's immortal heaven forever.

In the Bhagavadgita, we find another classification of devotees according to their faith: sattvic, rajasic, and tamasic. The devotion of sattvic ones is pure. They are duty-bound, abide in the scriptural injunctions, perform their obligatory duties, pursue knowledge, and strive diligently to attain freedom from suffering and karma. The devotion of rajasic ones is impure since they are driven by passions and desires. They also perform their duties as ordained by the scriptures to enjoy worldly pleasures, name, fame, etc., through the triple aims of Dharma, Artha, and Kama. Hence, they accumulate meritorious karma but do not attain liberation. Tamasic devotees engage in deluded and unconventional methods and entertain false expectations. They try to control the gods or draw their attention by force. Some may resort to extreme methods and torture their minds and bodies to attain their goals. They may impress the gods they worship and obtain boons, or they may indulge in harmful and evil practices to harm others or control them. Each of these types of devotion leads to different results. In some cases, it produces mixed results and, in some, leads to continued bondage and suffering. These modes of devotion bind people to samsara by inducing in them different types of desires. Hence, the scriptures advise people to transcend the gunas and remain indifferent to the desires and attachments they induce.

Types of devotion

As already stated, we can classify devotion into three types, namely sattvic, rajasic, and tamasic types of devotion. Sattvic devotion manifests in those who have the predominance of sattva and are inclined to the pursuit of liberation as their most important aim. They practice austerities, sacrifices, charity, and penances as obligatory duties to promote dharma and establish peace and harmony. They seek oneness with God through devotion, practicing virtue, adhering to righteousness (dharma), and offering their actions to Him without egoism and attachment. Rajasic people practice devotion to fulfill their worldly desires and gain material things, such as name, fame, wealth, and power. They approach God expecting Him to help them resolve their problems and achieve their goals. Their devotion is induced by egoism, delusion, desires, and attachments. Tamasic people practice devotion for all the wrong reasons. They practice false methods and pursue deluded goals. Due to ignorance and delusion, they disregard traditional and established methods and practices and resort to unconventional methods disapproved by scriptures or tradition. They may also practice devotion out of vanity, anger, pride (mada), or envy, with an aim to impress the world, show off their power and prestige, increase destructive powers and evil strength, or control and coerce others.

Sattvic devotion arises from knowledge and purity; rajasic devotion from greed; and tamasic devotion from delusion and ignorance. Of the three, sattvic devotion is the best. Sattvic devotion results in inner purification and transformation, which hastens one's progress on the path of liberation. Rajasic devotion is tinged with desires and passions and leads to sorrow and bondage. Tamasic devotion is tinged with ignorance and delusion and may lead to self-destruction and spiritual downfall unless one exercises restraint and acts with knowledge and awareness. Sattvic people go to the higher worlds, rajasic people go to the middle worlds, and tamasic people go to the lower worlds (14.18).

However, for a yogi on the path of liberation, sattvic devotion is not an end but the only means. Higher than all this is the devotion of the one who transcends the gunas. When devotion arises from the soul's aspiration rather than from the gunas, it is the highest and purest form of devotion. The soul is always in love with God. One cannot feel it unless one is free from the influence of the gunas. For God, the love of His devotees, which stirs from their pure hearts, is irresistible. He swiftly rescues those who let their devotion express through them without desires and any interference from their gunas. For human beings, this state is not easy to attain, unless they become adept in their practice of yoga.

Those who transcend the gunas seek the company of God and derive their happiness solely from their thoughts of Him. When they are engaged in actions, they know that only their gunas are engaged in actions, and they do not become involved with them. They spend their lives in His contemplation, seeing Him in all and all in Him, offering Him whatever they have, and expecting nothing in return. They remain unconcerned, unmoved by the gunas, staying alike in pleasure and pain, censure and praise, honor and dishonor, and treat everything with stability and sameness. They remain contented with what is obtained by the will of God and live freely and fearlessly with detachment, dispassion, sameness, and equanimity. Yogis and devotees reach this supreme state of devotion after reaching perfection in their practice of the yoga of action, the yoga of knowledge, and the yoga of renunciation, and after suppressing the impurities of rajas and tamas. Devotion is the soul's intense yearning for oneness with God and return to its pristine state of perfection and completeness as the free Self. It arises in a yogi whose mind and body are pure and whose heart is clean. True devotion is possible only when the mind is free from cravings, and the ego is completely in submission to God. It is the highest and most sublime form of emotion.

In the sixteenth chapter, Lord Krishna also speaks of the devotion that manifests in humans due to demonic nature, such as vanity, arrogance, self-pride, anger, harshness, and ignorance, qualities that lead to bondage and suffering. He says such people do not know what should be done or what should not be done, and do not know the importance of cleanliness or approved methods and practices to perform any task. "Self-conceited, stubborn, and filled with pride and the arrogance of having wealth, they perform sacrifices in name only, out of vanity and against established practices." Lord Krishna says he casts these worshippers of the unclean, who envy Him and are filled with evil passions, into inauspicious and demonic hells. Demonic people are subject to the triple evils of "lust, anger, and greed, the triple doors to hell." Therefore, seekers of liberation must abandon these qualities, follow scriptural injunctions, and perform their duties with devotion.

The essentials of true devotion

Purity of heart and devotion are supremely important in practicing the yoga of devotion. It does not matter what you offer, but with what attitude you do it. The Gita says that whatever is offered to Isvara with pure devotion, be it a leaf, a flower, some fruit, or water, He readily accepts that sacred offering of the pure soul with unconditional love (9.26). One can even make an offering of one's whole life and actions. A true devotee offers everything to God without conditions and expectations. He stands before God selflessly offering Him whatever he does, whatever he eats, whatever he accepts or gives away, and whatever penances he observes. He does it with a clean heart, out of love, and without expectations. He worships Him, remembering that everything in this world is for the Lord's habitation, and nothing belongs to us. Relinquishing the ownership and doership, he performs his actions selflessly. Living with such a sacrificial attitude, He earns His love and attention (9.27).

God is impartial. He has no desires. He has no personal need or purpose to do or not to do any action. We may quarrel among ourselves about His names and forms, but for Him, everything is a part of Him and inhabited by Him. The individual souls are his aspects (amsah) only. For God, none is hateful or dearer. He is equal to all and is present in all. However, He does respond to pure devotion. He listens to our prayers and helps those who win Him over with their devotion. The scripture states clearly that those who worship Him with devotion are forever closer to Him and earn His grace. They are in Him, and He is in them (9.29). The power of devotion is such that by remembering God at the time of death, a devotee would easily attain the Highest Goal (8.13). However, remembering God at the time of death is not easy, especially for those who spend their lives pursuing material goals and craving worldly pleasures. In order to remember Him all the time and even at the time of death, a devotee must be steadfast in yoga (*nityauktaysa yoginah*), with his heart and mind filled with devotion, remembering Him always and thinking of him alone (8.14).

While no restrictions are imposed on which Supreme Lord we should worship or how we should worship, Lord Krishna advises people against worshipping the Unmanifested Brahman. He states that worshipping the formless and Unmanifested Being is not only difficult but painful (12.5). However, by worshipping the Manifested Brahman with single-minded devotion as Isvara or Lord Krishna, one can easily attain the Highest Abode, never to return to the mortal world.

Maya – The World as an Illusion

In the great epic Mahabharata, when Duryodhana enters the hall of illusion (Maya Sabha), he loses his way as he cannot make out whether he is stepping into a water puddle or an illusion. Seeing all the opulence and mesmerizing spectacles around him, as he feels confused, angry, and envious of the wealth, power, and fame of his cousins, he loses his mind. When he sees Draupadi standing and watching him and hears her laugher reverberating through that hall, he feels insulted, becomes angrier, and vows to avenge the affront, ignoring that she did not mean to belittle him and the thought of annoying him was far from her mind. Indeed, it was in the hall of illusions that the seeds of the great Mahabharata war were actually sown, which germinated and ultimately consumed the whole Kuru clan, bringing them untold misery and great destruction in the end. The epic Mahabharata shows, through an epic narrative and complex relationships, how human beings can bring misery and destruction upon themselves and others through their actions caused by delusion, ignorance, egoism, desires, attachments, selfishness, pride, envy, and other weaknesses that are induced by the gunas.

The world in which we live is not much different from the hall of illusions in which Duryodhana lost his mind and way. It is a world of appearances, transient phenomena, and ever-changing vistas. The invisible world is much larger and more enigmatic than the world that we perceive through our senses. Therefore, we cannot be certain of what it is and cannot take it for granted. Although we live in it, we do not know whether it is an entity by itself or an illusion created by the association of numerous forces, things, and phenomena it contains. As mortal beings, we also find it difficult to know ourselves truly and be ourselves. Deluded by the gunas and clouded by desires and attachments, we fail to discriminate between truth and falsehood and engage in actions that draw us out and involve us deeply with the world and its attractions. Seeking things that seem to enhance us due to attraction and aversion induced by the modes, we develop an attachment to them and ignore the truths hidden within our consciousness. If someone reminds you that you are a divine soul, you may not believe them. Firmly fixed in your gross physical identity, you may find it hard to accept your spiritual nature and your imperceptible subtle bodies. Inherently, we want to live forever, free from aging, sickness, and death. Still, we find it difficult to accept the assurances given by our religious scriptures or self-realized masters about the possibilities that await us in the spiritual realm or the possibility of achieving immortality through spiritual effort. We need proof for the mystic experiences spiritual people claim to have experienced, which we cannot have unless we are willing to make sacrifices, let go of things we cherish and are attached to, and spend time and energy to purify and discipline our minds and bodies.

One of the unique features of Hinduism is the concept of maya, or the veiling power of Prakriti, which subjects us to ignorance and delusion. Maya literally means the wheel of the Mother or the dynamic force of the Mother. This world is her creation. She creates the world and veils the truth hidden in it with her deluding power. Hence, our scriptures declare that the world is veiled by Maya and filled with Maya, and until that veil is removed, we cannot see the resplendent Self hidden in all. Thus, at the personal level, maya is the delusion everyone experiences, even with all the knowledge and awareness. At the universal level, it refers to the power that prevents us from seeing the truth of things and things as they are. It is responsible for the delusion we experience about ourselves, the world, and the objective reality we perceive through our minds and senses. Because of it, we believe that what we see is real, become involved with the material world and pursue worldly pleasures, ignoring our divine nature and our bondage to samsara. The scriptures commonly use the metaphor of mistaking a rope for a snake to describe the nature of maya, or the delusion humans experience in this world.

Thus, the concept of maya is central to Hindu philosophy. It is one of its core concepts that carries great importance even in spiritual practice, as the reason to cultivate discernment through pure intelligence. Indeed, it is common to all the religions that originated in India, and its realization forms an important milestone in our spiritual progress. In Hinduism, it signifies how truth is concealed and distorted by the Play and Power of God in the world of transient phenomena, appearances, and deceptive formations to keep us distracted and occupied with our mundane existence. Maya is His concealing and deluding power only. He is the Magician who casts the net of maya to keep us bound to this world and ensure the orderly progression of creation. The concept helps us understand how we become entangled with the objects of our desires and weave in the process a web of deception around ourselves, forgetting who we are and what the true purpose of our existence is.

Maya is a state, as well as a condition, in which we believe and think genuinely that we are separate and distinct from the rest of creation and God Himself. This separation creates in us fear, insecurity, anxiety, desires, attachments, and the need to secure our lives and fill the great vacuum and perplexity we experience in the vastness of His creation. Our scriptures suggest that our world is a trap, and maya is the trapping mechanism. Nature employs it to entice individual souls into her Field to embody them and create the jivas, the mortal beings, subjecting them to the triple modes and various impurities that arise from them. Through attraction and aversion to dualities of life and through desires and attachments, she keeps them in her trap and under her control until they see the truth and strive for true freedom. When we are bound, we forget our essential nature and become involved with the material world and with the process of becoming and being. We become imprisoned by our thoughts, feelings, and desires, suffer from births and deaths, and bind ourselves to the consequences of our actions. Who unleashes this potent force? Our scriptures say that God Himself unleashes it. He is the grand master of illusion, the supreme Conjurer (Mayavi). He casts His net of illusion and ensnares the individual souls to remain deluded and bound to the world.

Maya thus becomes a very potent force in creation. Its purpose is to move the wheel of life and keep the world and creation moving forward as destined. It is the binding force that ensures a place for everything and everything in its place. The gunas aid in the process. They induce desire-ridden actions and subject the deluded jivas to the twin modes of attraction and aversion so that they do not think much beyond their physical reality, their daily routine, and the simple pleasures they experience and remain satisfied with them. According to our scriptures, God is not only a Conjurer but also a Concealer. He conceals the truth of Himself, His omniscience, and omnipresence. He conceals the divine Self that is hidden in each jiva from them so that they remain deluded until they overcome their delusion and realize their true nature. He hides Himself from them while remaining in it, and thereby perpetuates the belief that He is not present, is distinct, is elusive, is not what He is, or is different from what He seems to be. Maya is thus not only a deluding and distracting mechanism but also a concealing mechanism. The first ones lead to indiscretion and the latter to ignorance.

The Bhagavadgita explains how delusion arises and how we may overcome it. Lord Krishna states that deluded people bind themselves to the cycle of births and deaths through desire-ridden actions because they lack discrimination (buddhi). They assume ownership and doership and fail to discern the presence of God amidst them. They indulge in actions that bring them misery and suffering. However, there is a ray of hope for everyone. With effort and through the practice of yoga, everyone can overcome their delusion and work for their liberation. To achieve a correct understanding of the mechanism of maya is vital. We discuss below how maya is deeply embedded in our consciousness, entwined with our lives, and influences our thinking and actions.

1. The senses

The senses are ten in number: five organs of action and five organs of perception. The mind is the eleventh. Apart from these, we can also mention the five subtle sensory experiences (tanmatras), which connect the senses to their objects, and are responsible for our feelings of attraction and aversion to the things we perceive. The five tanmatras are hearing, touching, seeing, tasting, and smelling. The ten sense organs, together with the mind and these subtle senses, are the main instruments through which Nature connects the jivas to the objective world and deludes them, subjecting them to desires and attachments to worldly objects and keeping them distracted from knowing themselves and their concealed reality. According to the Bhagavadgita, out of desire comes attachment, and out of attachment, a person becomes deluded by seeking things in order to satisfy their craving.

Even from our daily experiences, we know that the senses are not reliable sources of knowledge and truth. Their perceptions and actions are distorted by many obstacles, which modern psychology calls cognitive distortions. The world is not what it appears to be. The truths hidden beneath the surface of apparent reality reveal to us a different picture of the world in which we live. There is an invisible world, very much a part of the physical world, which we cannot see with our senses. We also lack a holistic vision that encompasses all. Things appear differently when we view them from different perspectives and consider them as aggregates of things. The Bhagavadgita, therefore, urges people to look beyond the appearance of things into the essential reality that pervades them and envelops them as their source and support. The same power manifests differently in different things. We should not only understand 'That' (Tat), which has this power, but also experience it within ourselves to become free from the world of illusion and duality. That manifesting power is God, the Supreme Lord of the universe. His manifestation is what we perceive with our senses and mistakenly consider it as the sum of all reality. This is the delusion we must overcome to be free. When we shift our attention from His manifestations to Himself and from the projections and modifications of our own minds to our inherent, essential nature, we become aware of the transcendental reality that exists beyond our minds and senses.

2. Loss of buddhi (discrimination)

When our intelligence is clouded, we cannot discern truth from falsehood. It is like looking at the world through an impure prism. When we pursue sense objects with deluded intelligence, we are easily drawn into the world by our senses, become involved with the world, and engage in desire-ridden actions that bind us. We ignore the profound truths that are not immediately perceptible, thereby missing the central purpose of our lives, which is achieving liberation with righteous conduct. Deluded by the senses, the mind, and intelligence, we do not know the truth from falsehood. We accept the visible world as true, ignoring the concealed source that is responsible for it or the transcendental reality that exists beyond the visible reality. When we do not know who we really are, we accept our physical identities as the totality of our existence and make decisions from a very narrow perspective, ignoring the possibilities of our existence beyond life and death and the consequences of our actions upon our future lives. The senses, as we have discussed before, contribute to these deluded notions that we entertain in our minds about our existence and ourselves. Those who depend upon them solely for direction and guidance cannot go beyond the visible and perceptible world and experience the reality that exists in the stillness of their tranquil minds. Our delusion results in ignorance or the loss of knowledge and wisdom to discern reality from unreality, truth from untruth, the divine from the demonic, and right actions from wrong actions. Out of the ignorance thus born, embodied souls (jivas) indulge in wrong actions and become bound to the mortal world. When we do not have the right knowledge, we make wrong choices, perform wrong actions, and suffer from consequences. When we do not know how our suffering arises from our desire-ridden actions and their consequences because of the gunas and the impurities they induce, and do not practice restraint or withdrawal, we become bound to them. However, through yoga, we can cleanse our consciousness and open ourselves to the transcendental truths. By becoming aware of the need for self-transformation and cultivating purity, we can establish our minds in equanimity, stability, and sameness towards all. We realize the true meaning of renunciation and learn to perform actions without seeking their fruit. The study of the Bhagavadgita helps us greatly to overcome our delusions and know our identities. Its study will help us discern truths concerning God and ourselves. With our intellect refined by its knowledge, we will overcome our delusions and work for our liberation.

3. Desires and attachments

Under the influence of the gunas, which are the instruments of Maya, the deluded ones are always attached to the world and its objects. They are attracted to not only worldly things but also their egoistic personalities, memories, thoughts, opinions, and relationships. Those attachments arising from attraction and aversion can be positive or negative, and both bind them to the world. Memories pursue them, time haunts them, and thoughts possess them as they are driven by desires to seek things and fulfill themselves. Having become attached to the world and conditioned by memory and accumulated knowledge, they develop many negative qualities such as envy, selfishness, pride, fear, greed, anger, malice, caprice, cruelty, callousness, lust, and intense desire for success and personal advancement. They view life as a battleground in which they must always win and reach their goals at any cost. For them, failure and weakness are not options. Attracted to pleasures, repelled by pain and adversity, fearful of loss and hopeful of gain, unable to resist the lures and temptations of the world, although aware at times that all is vain in the end, they plod on, striving and struggling as if death would never touch them. The state of liberation is indeed the state of freedom from desires and attachment. The yogi who transcends desires, wants, and needs is a free person. He is liberated even if he does not attain oneness with the Self. He becomes pure, even if he does not practice yoga or devotion.

4. Sense of duality and multiplicity

Both the individual Self and the Supreme Self are eternally independent, whereas beings (jivas) are dependent entities. Even when the Self is in association with Nature, it remains independent. The beings exist in relationship with things and beings, whereas the Self exists by itself. The relationships they form result in the delusion of duality and the conflicting experiences of union and separation from things, which in turn lead to many emotional disturbances and mental afflictions. We are drawn to objects because we consider them separate and distinct. We seek them because we develop an attachment to them through our gunas and senses. This duality leads to desire-ridden actions and our bondage to earthly life. When we depend upon our senses, we perceive duality and diversity and experience attraction and aversion to the pairs of opposites. This leads to the delusion of ownership and doership and the compulsion to perform desire-ridden actions and perpetuate our individuality and beingness.

5. Transience, instability, and destructibility

The phenomenal world in which we live and which we call samsara is subject to modifications, impermanence, and destruction. It is driven by cause and effect, induced primarily by the gunas. Our physical personalities are part of this world and subject to the same qualities. We accept them as true because we cannot see the real Self that is hidden within us, which is eternal, immutable, and indestructible. Arjuna suffered from sorrow because he had the same delusion. He thought that he was a destructible being and that his actions would lead to the death and destruction of others. He did not consider death and destruction the modifications of Nature that are put in place to facilitate the soul's journey upon earth. In the phenomenal world, because of the gunas, our physical selves overshadow our true selves. When we are established in them, we accept ourselves as limited beings subject to death and destruction. When we purify our minds and bodies, we realize our immortality and experience peace and stability. Our existence is not impermanent. The modifications are. Our impermanence is an outer aspect, a mere phenomenon, like a dream, which will vanish when we realize our true nature and become absorbed in it.

6. Ego and false identification

Just as Nature manifests an alternate reality in the universe of God, it manifests an alternate reality in the microcosm of each individual in the form of ego consciousness, whereby each being identifies itself with its name and form rather than its inner Self. The ego is an illusion, but we perpetuate it because we spend our lives protecting it and promoting it. It is the false center of our consciousness. It acts as the Knower of the Field, whereas the Self is the true Knower (Kshetrajna). It acts as the enjoyer of the perceptions arising in the field of consciousness, whereas the true enjoyer is again the Self. It also assumes ownership and doership, whereas the Self is the true owner and doer. These misconceptions induced by the ego lead to the jiva's attachment, delusion, and karma.

The ego is responsible for our self-preservation instinct and our tendency to engage in actions to promote our interests or fulfill our desires, even if it means we have to compromise or ignore our spiritual progress and well-being. Left to itself, the ego will promote and perpetuate demonic qualities, whereby the jiva whom it represents does not know how to perform actions correctly with the right attitude, what constitutes righteous conduct, or how to practice it (16.7). As the Bhagavadgita states, a jiva, under its influence, develops a false sense of identity and thinks he is the lord, enjoyer, and the perfect one (16.14).

Thinking thus, he engages in desire-ridden actions. In some cases, he engages in destructive and terrible actions, which lead to his spiritual downfall. The ego is both the cause and effect of delusion. It is responsible for ownership, doership, duality, corporeality, materiality, and bondage. It keeps the mind in a state of flux and prevents it from experiencing stability, equanimity, and self-absorption. Under its influence, the deluded ones offer sacrifices for name, wealth, or pride. As a result, the Lord casts them into sinful and demonic hells.

7. Incorrect relationship with God

Because of ignorance and delusion, mortal beings cannot perceive God even though He is omnipresent and hidden in every aspect of creation. Therefore, their knowledge of God remains largely incomplete and incorrect. This ignorance interferes with their ability to form meaningful relationships with God and worship Him with the right attitude. In the Bhagavadgita, Lord Krishna mentions four types of devotees who worship Him, namely men in distress, seekers of knowledge, seekers of material wealth, and men of wisdom. Of these four, He declares the last one the best. Apart from these, He also mentions others whose wisdom is carried away by desires and who worship other gods through sacrifices for the fulfillment of their desires. He also mentions those who worship Him as the Unmanifested or who consider Him as the unmanifest having manifestations (avyaktam vyaktam). He further adds that people develop these wrong notions about Him because of His divine power (yogamaya) and fail to recognize Him as the unborn and imperishable Supreme Self (7.24-25).

The knowledge we gain from the study of scriptures does not help us to experience Brahman's absolute reality unless we develop corresponding inner purity that can bring us into direct contact with our inner Selves. Thus, most people, even after years of study and devotional services, remain largely ignorant of God and His manifestations. Even Arjuna, with his direct vision, saw but one aspect of God as Time (Kala). None can, therefore, comprehend God truthfully even after transcending their senses. They may understand Him, but in parts. They may enter His consciousness but cannot recollect the full extent of their experience since the distinction between the knower and the known is absent in transcendental states. As a result, our relationship with God remains largely personal. Ignorant people cannot truly realize the greatness of God. Even if they do, they cannot contain that experience in their limited consciousness. Only a few know Him, even at the time of their death, that He is the Lord of all gods (adhidaivam), Lord of the material universe (adhibhutam), and the Lord hidden in each living being (adhyatma).

8. Mortality and the cycle of births and deaths

Prakriti unleashes her deluding power of maya to veil their true nature and keep the beings ignorant and bound to the world. Through maya, she perpetuates ignorance by overshadowing their knowledge and discernment, whereby they pursue sense objects through selfish and desire-ridden actions and develop attachments to them. The dependence leads to karma and bondage. The Bhagavadgita states that all beings remain under Prakriti's deluding power during their existence in the mortal world, become subject to attraction and aversion, and engage in desire-ridden actions. She keeps the beings deluded as long as possible so that they do not easily escape. As a result, beings are born repeatedly until they evolve spiritually and achieve liberation. Those who fail to achieve liberation will remain bound and will be withdrawn by the Creator at the end of the world. The scripture also describes two paths that are available to the bound souls that determine their fate after death. Those who do not achieve liberation will travel by the southern path (dakshinayana) or the gray path to the world of ancestors and live amidst them. They will eventually return to the earth according to their karma and take birth again. However, those who attain liberation travel by the sunlit path of gods (devayana) and go to the immortal heaven of Brahman. They stay there permanently. Beings return to the earth because of unfulfilled desires and unfinished tasks arising from their latent attachments and unexhausted karmas. Depending upon their previous actions, they take birth in different wombs and live under different circumstances to repay their past debts and continue their mortal existence. This process goes on repeatedly until they overcome their ignorance and delusion, perform selfless actions with the right knowledge, and achieve liberation.

9. Deliverance from Maya

Mortal existence is temporary. Maya works so long as the beings choose to remain ignorant and perform desire-ridden actions under the influence of their egos. Their delusion manifests in several ways, most importantly as the duality between the subject and object and as desires and attachments due to attraction and aversion to things. Fortunately, this condition does not last forever. It persists as long as beings pursue their desires and worldly pleasures. This offers a ray of hope for the bound ones. It means they do not have to wait until the end of the world for their deliverance. They can escape from Nature's hold and samsara and return to their eternal state through self-purification, by subduing and transcending their gunas, by overcoming their ignorance with the right knowledge and the grace (prasada) of God, and by controlling their desires through detachment and self-control. Most importantly, they can resolve their karma by practicing karma sannyasa and offering their actions and their fruit to God. When one succeeds in these efforts, one attains sameness, stability, and freedom from karma. Remaining established in the Self and practicing exclusive devotion, they can overcome all the impurities, earn God's grace, and reach Him.

As a spiritual guide, the Bhagavadgita can lead the aspirants on this path. By following its teachings, they can qualify for liberation, cultivating purity and stabilizing their minds in the contemplation of God. Whoever practices yoga and experiences the advanced states of concentration, meditation, and self-absorption has a chance to reach Brahman quickly. The scripture also offers a shortcut. One can achieve liberation by remembering God at the time of death. It states that whatever humans remember at the time of their death, they attain that. Hence, those who can stabilize their minds in God and remember Him constantly at the time of final departure will also attain him. Even evil people have a chance to redeem themselves if they change their ways and worship God with devotion. They become righteous quickly and attain everlasting peace (9.31).

10. Overcoming Prakriti, the Field

We are conditioned to live and act according to our perceptions and experiences. Since we cannot look beyond the visible and apparent reality of the world, we come to believe that accepting our physical identities is the best way, as far as we know, to survive in this world and ensure our continuity. Veiled by maya, we seek peace and happiness by acting according to the laws of Nature and doing what is naturally possible and permissible to deal with the problems and challenges of life. We learn from experience that whenever we transgress Nature, we have to endure pain and suffering. Alternating between the contrasting realities of life, we try to stay within the circle of our cognitive experience and our comfort zones to maintain and ensure our sanity and security. Nature employs ignorance and delusion to keep us bound to the phenomenal world and its objects.

We live under the illusion that the knowledge we gain from our interactions with the world is true and reliable. It is indeed true, although in a limited sense. In fact, our empirical knowledge arises from our minds and senses, which are subject to the delusion of duality and diversity. It does not help us much in knowing the transcendental truths that are hidden from the faculties of Prakriti or with our liberation. Worldly knowledge (vijnana) may offer solutions and possibilities about reaching our goals or securing peace and happiness, but it cannot remove our delusion or ignorance. For that, we need a more reliable and substantive reality that is permanent, indestructible, absolute, and self-existing.

The truths we know through empirical experience are not absolute truths. They are standpoints or perspectives to which we become attached emotionally or egoistically and defend them as if we are defending ourselves. They are but relative truths that do not stand the test of time. We can justify them or refute them according to our convenience, worldviews, beliefs, prejudices, and preferences. The purity and divinity of our knowledge, memory, and intellect depend upon how free we are from our desires and how well we have adjusted to a life of renunciation and detachment. Therefore, as instruments of truth, they are unreliable unless we are pure and firmly established in sattva. A mind that is free of delusion assimilates truth without being oppressed or limited by it. It can harmonize and integrate conflicting facets or truths of life as diverse aspects of the same reality. It can hold the various experiences and perceptions we go through in our lives as complementary aspects of one holistic truth.

Truth is such. It is everything: eternal, multidimensional, indefinable, and all-encompassing. It reconciles everything into itself and resolves every duality into one harmonious whole, which our human minds are not habituated to do, accustomed as they are to relative thinking and limited perceptivity. This limitation of human intelligence arises from the divine play of maya. It is what happens to your intelligence and knowledge when you come under its influence and do not even know that what you experience is an illusion. The world that you see is an illusion, not because it does not exist, but because you see it from a limited perspective, through the narrow prism of your desires, fears, and egoistic considerations. The duality you experience is in itself a delusion that arises from your experience of attraction and aversion to things.

The world in which you live is an illusion because you perceive it and interact with it through the filters created by the faculties of your mind. It is an illusion because it exists in your mind and does not necessarily correspond to the outside reality. Besides, it is impermanent, and your mind cannot keep pace with the changes that happen in the world every moment. Therefore, much of the impression of the world that exists in your mind is a poor copy drawn from your memory. It helps you minimize the complexity of dealing with the world or managing your relationship with it. However, it does not help you know the truth about yourself. It is shaped by your desires and expectations. You relate to it according to your nature, intelligence, knowledge, and understanding. Since it is inside your mind, you project it outwardly upon the world to delude yourself that there is no contradiction between what you perceive and belief to be true. You do not see it as it is, but as filtered by your dominant desires and mental modifications.

Your mind mixes up your past impressions with your current perceptions to create the illusion that what you experience in the outside world is true or corresponds to its reality. Indeed, in reality, it is but a concoction of your mind and senses. It is not true knowledge, but a mental construction without true foundations, an edifice that can fall apart if you poke it enough with insightful awareness and inquiry. Our existence is such that we do not know when we are truly awake and when we are asleep, why we are here, or to what end all this leads.

An inner awakening is the first step to cut through that illusion and see the truth hidden beyond the lid that envelops the mind.

The True Meaning of Bhakti

The most popular meaning of bhakti is spiritual devotion, reverence, attachment, worship, etc. Rakti is a closely related word to bhakti with a similar meaning. However, it has more physical, emotional, and worldly connotations and is usually used in connection with worldly relationships and attachments. In the early Vedic tradition, bhakti was less important than knowledge, duty, and virtue. Bhakti became an important part of the Vedic belief system after the rise of Shaivism and Vaishnavism. These were essentially theistic movements centered around devotion and the worship of their central deities. Indeed, bhakti attained its highest glory in Vaishnavism. Shaivism is less emphatic on devotion and more on knowledge, asceticism, self-purification, and contemplative practices. In the Bhagavadgita, bhakti finds its greatest support. One may even look upon it as the foundational text of the bhakti movement, which became popular subsequently and added a new dimension to Hindu ritual and spiritual practices. Vaishnavism also found its greatest support in bhakti, which led to its phenomenal rise in the medieval period. The Bhagavad Gita stipulates two conditions to practice devotion. One, devotion must be to the highest, supreme Lord. Two, it must be undivided, unwavering, exclusive, and free from the impurities of egoism, desires, and attachments.

Although the Vedic tradition did not give much importance to the practice of bhakti, it may be surprising to know that the concept of bhakti came to us from Vedic sacrifices and is deeply associated with the ritual terminology of the Vedic religion, especially with the offering of sacrificial food. Bhakta means sacrificial food, any cooked or boiled rice or grains, or a portion of food served to the gods. Many compound words are also associated with it. For example, a bhaktakar or bhakti-upasadhak means a cook. A bhakta-abhilashak is someone fond of food. Bhakti-kamsa means a dish of food. Bhakti-chhdam means appetite. Bhakti-rochanam means stimulation for the appetite. Bhakti-shala means a dining hall. A bhakta also means a bound or enslaved servant who serves or works for a master for food or maintenance.

These words amply convey the hidden connection of bhakti with sacrificial food and suggest that bhakti was originally associated with rituals, ritual food, and food-related rituals or service. As time passed by, the idea became more refined and sublimated as the highest expression of love and sacrifice. With ritual offerings and sacrifices giving way to devotional worship, the word became increasingly associated with devotion as an act or expression of giving oneself to God or a deity as food or sacrifice. In the sacred relationship between God and His devotee, the devotee became a sacrifice or sacrificial offering (bhakta) who not only symbolically offered himself to the Deity as a mark of his unconditional surrender and commitment but also dedicated himself to his worship and service.

The bhakti movement gained traction in India in the post-Vedic period with the emergence of Upanishadic literature, internalization of Vedic rituals, the elevation of sacrifice as a yogic practice, and the emergence of new religious movements. Symbolically, it is deeply associated with Vedic rituals and maybe even animal and human sacrifices, and the ascetic practice of self-mortification as the means to escape from the bonds of Nature. Bhakta means food, or what has been sacrificed. Bhakti is an act of sacrifice or an offering of whatever is dearer to you to your dearest Deity. Bhokta refers to the deity who receives the ritual offering or sacrifice and enjoys it. In a ritual sense, a bhakta is the one who offers himself or ends up becoming a sacrifice in a sacrificial ritual. Mostly, animals used to be offered as a sacrifice with the belief that they would attain liberation through it. Bhakta (devotee) also means he who offers sacrificial food (bhakta) as an offering to God, the final recipient, the Enjoyer (bhokta) of all material things, and the devourer of all.

Bhakti (devotion) is thus a deeply spiritual and emotive gesture of becoming a sacrificial offering to God, really or symbolically. The result or the fruit of this sacrifice or offering is God's mercy or grace (prasadam). This is symbolically represented in Hindu rituals by the sacrificial food offered to the deity. The hosts of the rituals share the food with priests, family members, and guests. It is deemed beneficial, since it is believed to have been blessed and purified by God and is infused with His divine power. In Hindu ritual practices, devotees patiently wait until the ritual is completed and the remains of the sacrificial food are distributed as prasadam. They do not leave the place until they receive their share of it. Indeed, in recent times, this sacred tradition has devolved into a commercial practice, where many temples prepare prasadam in large quantities and offer it for a price while distributing a small portion of it during the rituals.

Thus, devotion originally meant a sacrificial act or offering in which devotees earn God's grace by offering Him their bodies or possessions, including food and other belongings, as a sacrifice. The most popular meaning of bhakti is having and expressing reverence, emotional attachment, and unconditional loyalty to God. The result of that offering is divine grace (prasadam). For the ignorant ones, it means the food they receive at the end of a ritual. Many people attend religious functions for that purpose only. However, knowledgeable ones know what it means and signifies. For them, the food offered in a religious ritual represents the collective devotion of all those who participate in the worship and share the fruit of karma that emerges from it as divine grace. It represents the ideal that one should perform sacrifices as an obligatory duty and make regular offerings to God, who is the source of all, rather than accumulating things for oneself and incurring sin. The sin you accumulate through selfish actions becomes your burden.

In the end, you must account for it because by engaging in desire-ridden actions for worldly possessions and enjoyments, you engage in the sinful conduct of steya, taking what does not truly belong to you. You cannot wash that sin away by visiting a few temples or giving charity. It can be washed away by karma sannyasa only, performing actions without desires and offering the fruit of your actions to God, the source of all. This is the true sacrifice, the mark of true devotion. God's exclusive devotees engage in this sacrifice persistently. They carry the sacrifice of devotion with them everywhere and into every action and aspect of their lives. They transform their lives into devotional sacrifices and, through that sacrifice, worship God reverently to a point where they can no longer bear any separation or distance from Him. The most pious ones exhaust their energies in His service and contemplation, like the candles or incense sticks that burn themselves into extinction.

Each offering, therefore, is an unmistakable expression of devotion (bhakti), a sacred action that brings you closer to the doors of immortal heaven, and the best spiritual solution with which you can resolve the problem of karma. As the Bhagavadgita states, God reciprocates your offerings with abundant love and grants you His grace (anugraha) with which you can enter His heaven. Hence, in the Bhagavadgita, Lord Krishna states that when you eat food for yourself without offering to Him, you will eat sin. It will bind you to samsara and limit your spiritual progress. When you offer to God the food you want to eat, it becomes prasadam, the fruit of your devotion, and no matter how impure it may be, by eating it, you will not incur any sin. God's exclusive devotees worship Him with single-minded devotion as if nothing else matters. Out of unconditional love, they offer to Him whatever they have or what happens to them as God's grace. Their devotional sacrifice lights their path to liberation as their actions cease to produce karma or impede their progress. Through that sacrifice, they also attain freedom from all karmas arising from their actions (naishkarmya siddhi).

Bhakti is a sattvic feeling whose location is in the heart region, the seat of the Self. True devotion of the exclusive kind, which leads to liberation, arises in those who have discerning wisdom (buddhi vikasam) and disinterest (virakti) in material things and who are free from attachments arising from the impurities induced by the triple modes. The gross body does not experience devotion as much as the subtle bodies since they are more illuminated by the Self. It arises in those whose minds and bodies are filled with the radiance of sattva. Therefore, the practice of devotion is considered an advanced practice of yoga that is not possible for everyone. Bhakti leads to freedom (vimukti) from attachments or liberation (mukti). If you are attached to Nature and passionate about material things or worldly enjoyments, you cannot attain liberation (mukti).

How does such devotion arise in people?

According to the Bhagavadgita, true devotion arises when one achieves perfection in the yoga of action (karmayoga), the yoga of knowledge (jnanayoga), and the yoga of renunciation. A true devotee exemplifies divine qualities, having purified himself through these methods. He surrenders to God and remains ever-absorbed in His thoughts and contemplation. Free from the impurities of egoism, vanity, desires, and expectations, and characterized by an attitude of reverence rather than craving, his devotion is pure and exclusive, without attachment and demonic passions, and is not sustained by fulfillment of desires but by sacrifice. Hence, it liberates rather than binds.

Devotion must be selfless. Only then will the devotion be one-pointed, with the mind focused on the object of devotion rather than oneself. When devotion is used to fulfill one's desires, it denotes that the devotion is to oneself and one's well-being. That is not true devotion, and it does not liberate. Selfless devotion can be expressed in different ways: by not seeking anything for oneself, by renouncing desires and attachments, by praying for others, or by serving others selflessly with kindness.

Deluded people may worship God for material gains, but it does not qualify as true devotion. Sacrifice is the basis of true devotion. It makes devotion an act of offering rather than receiving. Exclusive devotion of the selfless kind is the culmination of perfection in many yogas and is not easy to practice. Hence, although it seems easier, it is the most difficult to practice. When you worship God, you give Him whatever you have, surrender to Him unconditionally and selflessly, and make your life an offering, out of profound love, reverence, and gratitude as a true devotee. Instead of enjoying the fruit of your labor, you offer it to God as a sacrifice and live freely without the burden of sin. Devotion can be translated into a sacrifice or a loving act of giving and serving. The great saints and seers of Hinduism exemplified it in the past. Many exemplify it even today. With each act of giving, they exhaust their karma and unburden themselves of the sins of their past. For a devotee, it is one of the noble ways to express his bhakti and become a true bhakta.

Life's Lessons From the Bhagavadgita

Many timeless lessons are hidden in the sacred text of the Bhagavadgita. They reveal themselves to the extent you probe into them. To know them and practice them correctly and effectively, you require discipline, purity, faith, and devotion. The following are a few important ones.

1. Know that you are an immortal Self, a living god

One of the first revelations of the Bhagavadgita is that you are not your mind and body but an eternal and indestructible soul. This helps one overcome the deluded notion about oneself as a mortal being subject to birth and death. Your mind and body are impermanent and subject to change and impermanence. They wither and fall away while you remain forever. The bondage and suffering are temporary. They are gone as soon as you achieve liberation. Therefore, everyone should ideally resolve to work for their liberation. Unfortunately, it does not happen frequently in real life. People seek impermanent things and remain stuck in the impermanent and turbulent samsara. The pure Self that resides in all is immortal, ageless, and divine, untouched by the impurities of life or its limitations. It is blissful, since it is free from afflictions and modification and not subject to the dualities such as heat and cold or happiness and sorrow. Therefore, the Bhagavadgita suggests that we should realize this truth about ourselves and become established in that identity to remain indifferent to the chaotic conditions of the mind and body. The rest of the Bhagavadgita is about how to achieve liberation by remaining established in this identity. It states that when you cultivate divine qualities through self-purification and are centered within your divine nature, remembering that you are a pure and divine Self, you will accept the dualities and difficulties of your life with stoical wisdom. In short, the scripture teaches you how to live like a god on earth, without accumulating sinful karma and carrying the burden of suffering and bondage.

2. Overcome attraction and aversion

One of the main reasons why we experience desires and attachments, or the modifications of the mind, is that we are subject to attraction and aversion. Due to the constant interaction of the mind and senses with the objects of the world, we develop likes and dislikes, which result in the craving or the desire to have something or not have something, and to be with something or get rid of something. This is the main source of our bondage and suffering as we become selective and avoid the wholeness of life that is meant to teach us valuable lessons and set us free. The world is a beautiful place to live, but it is also a big trap set by Maya. Your freedom is an illusion. When you seek things, you are not free. When you depend upon things for your happiness, you are not free. When you suffer from fear and anxiety, know that your expectations bind you. Your free will also is not truly free. It is bound to your desires, expectations, and the consequences of your past actions. It is bound to the interplay of the gunas that are active in you and their influence. You are a prisoner of your desires and attachments. Through them, you remain in the grip of Nature. Through them, the world binds you to its things and holds you in control. Your relationship with it is your undoing. It is the source of your suffering. If you want to be truly free, you must overcome attraction and aversion and become indifferent to what life offers or does not offer and what fate is in store for you. By that stoical indifference, you can remain uninvolved with the world and set yourself free.

3. Life is unpredictable. You need divine help

Life does not always happen as we desire or expect. We may control some aspects of it, but not every aspect of it. While we face insurmountable problems often in life, we are endowed with limited knowledge, faculties, and energies to deal with them. While your abilities are limited, your knowledge of what guides you, helps you, harms you, obstructs you, or controls you in your thinking and actions is also limited. Some causes propel you into actions and reactions despite your best intentions. They are clearly outside your control. Although some causes arise from you or your essential nature, you cannot control them enough or their functioning. While you may be tempted to carry the burden of your life and karma all by yourself, it is better to seek divine help. You will lose nothing, except perhaps your pride, if you turn to God and seek His help in difficulties. God's devotees do not suffer in adversity as much as God's naysayers, critics, and skeptics. They live with the assurance that their prayers will be heard and their problem will be resolved. Therefore, accept your limitations, cultivate humility, surrender to God, and seek His help. In the Bhagavadgita, He gives us the assurance that if you turn to Him and truly love Him, He reciprocates your love and takes upon Himself the burden of your life.

4. Find the ultimate purpose, why you are here

The Bhagavadgita teaches us that Dharma, Artha, and Kama are not the most important aims of our lives. They are necessary and important to perform your obligatory duties and serve God. However, the most important purpose of your life is Moksha, the final liberation. It is because you are an eternal Self, presently bound to Nature and imprisoned in the body she creates and controls. You must escape from it to return to your pure and blissful state to complete your journey in the turbulent samsara. For now, you may be a mystery to yourself and others because you are still bound to Nature. Your existence may be a mystery, and you may not know why you are here and what purpose you serve. These are temporary problems. Have faith in God and keep working for your self-purification, living your life morally, dutifully, and righteously. Gradually, your mind will become clearer, and you will understand why freedom is important and how you can achieve it. There is a mysterious aspect about life that no one can fully comprehend, even with all the knowledge and intelligence in the world. However, if you keep observing it, some truths may emerge which may help you make the best use of your time while you are here. You can live consciously, conscientiously, mindfully, and virtuously, doing your duty, meeting your obligations, and helping others. With the right knowledge and wisdom, you can light up your consciousness, without unduly worrying about what may happen in the future and how your actions may turn out eventually. Once you settle with your ultimate purpose, your path becomes clearer, and your faith and resolve strengthen.

5. Honor your duties and responsibilities

Desires and attachments are the root cause of our suffering. If you perform actions with desires and expectations, you will suffer from their consequences. Because of the karma arising from your actions, wherever you live and whoever you are, you are bound to this world according to your desires and passions and not free. Our scriptures unequivocally validate this. If you struggle unwisely for your liberation, Nature will tighten its hold upon you and make your existence even more difficult to endure. If you give up in the middle, you will remain trapped and cannot escape. You must, therefore, find the right way and employ the right means, using discretion and moderation, giving up whatever is necessary, and strengthening whatever lightens you up and sets you free. You must know that desires and attachments increase your sinful karma, strengthening your involvement with the world, and along with it the suffering that arises from it. Therefore, for peace and equanimity, you must give them up and transform your actions into sacrifices or devotional offerings to God. By that, He will take responsibility for your actions and deliver you from karma and rebirth. Through sacrificial actions on the path of karma sannyasa, you can strengthen your devotion, purify yourself, cultivate nearness to God, and attain liberation.

6. Whatever Path you choose, cultivate purity and righteousness

The gunas are responsible for desires and desire-ridden actions. They are also responsible for the impurities of the mind and body and the modifications to which they are subject. A person lives and acts according to his essential nature, which is, in turn, shaped by his predominant modes. Although sattva is beneficial on the spiritual path, it is still a problem because it induces certain desires that can prevent liberation or exclusive devotion. Therefore, one should aim to transcend the gunas to cultivate utmost purity through righteous conduct. The Bhagavadgita lists many qualities by cultivating which one attains purity and sameness. The world is riddled with good and evil. A householder must live righteously, avoiding evil desires and performing his obligatory duties. On the other hand, a renunciant (sannyasi) who has given up worldly life must cultivate sameness towards both good and evil and remain indifferent to them. The wise ones know both are here to stay and inherent in us. The world is a battleground where the two sides engage in a constant battle. It goes within our minds and bodies, and in the outside world. In this battle, you must decide on which side you are and what qualities and tendencies you should strengthen in you. It is difficult to be a good person and practice virtues when the world seems to be falling increasingly under the sway of evil, but the choice is important because it will decide your fate. If you live righteously and grow the divine in you, you will progress towards truth (sat), light (jyoti), and immortality (amritam). Otherwise, you will enter the sunless worlds of utter darkness (asurya lokas) and perish.

7. Your faith is a reflection of your essential nature

As you are so your devotion and faith. Your faith arises from your essential nature. The gunas influence both. Since the gunas induce different behaviors and attitudes. It is challenging for humans to live by their faith without suffering from doubt and despair. In adversity, sustaining faith and devotion is even more difficult. Believing in God is not easy, especially when we are uncertain whether He heeds our prayers or not and whether He responds to our calls for help. However, faith and devotion are the only means by which you can connect to God and escape from this world. The Bhagavadgita makes it abundantly clear that everything happens because of God, and He alone can rescue us from samsara. Therefore, we must do our best to earn His grace through unwavering faith and devotion.

8. You are never separate or distant from God

In the Bhagavadgita. Lord Krishna devotes a whole chapter to His glories and manifestations to emphasize that He is hidden in all aspects of His creation. He describes how He radiates beauty, symmetry, perfection, harmony, radiance, and other qualities in the manifested world. Through these descriptions, He conveys that we are indeed never separate from Him and are connected to Him through all His creations. We see the world, His universal form, every day. He also exists in us as our very Self and higher nature. Yet, we question His existence and fail to acknowledge His presence or importance in our lives, as we are conditioned to see Him as a Being or a Deity. Everything around us is permeated with God's sacred presence. By purifying and training our minds and senses, we can discern the universal presence of God in all the things around us, in the silence of the night and radiance of the day. We can see Him in the space that permeates and envelops us. With our eyes, we can see all the beauty and splendor He created for us to enjoy and assure us that we are always connected to Him and are never separate from Him. We may not see Him directly or the infinity and vastness of His creation, but he has endowed us with supreme intelligence so we can estimate the dimensions of the material universe and its vastness. The descriptions found in the scripture also help us know that we are a part of the universe, live in it, and are made up of it. Our material knowledge (vijnanam) arises from knowing it. We are its dependent realities, united by our purpose in furthering its causes. We are made up of the same materials as the universe, share the same elements as found in stars, planets, and galaxies, and possess the same energy that pervades all creation. We live in the womb of existence, as its constituent forms, eyes, ears, and limbs. When you remember this universal God constantly and mindfully, devotion will gradually arise in you wherever you are and whatever you do.

9. The world is not what it appears to be

Another important lesson we learn from the Bhagavadgita is that we should not develop any attachment or relationship with the world because it is unreal and not what it appears to be. The world is a trap, a play by Maya. It attracts our minds and senses and keeps them engaged, distracted, and bound outwardly so that we will remain oblivious of our true purpose and our essential nature. Hence, Lord Krishna teaches that we should withdraw our minds and senses from the world into ourselves and establish them in the contemplation of the Lord who resides in us as our very Self. Through that, we will not only escape from bondage and suffering but also attain oneness with Him. Our minds and senses are limited in their ability to comprehend the reality of the world and its secrets. We may rely upon them, but we must question our assumptions and unverified beliefs when we make decisions or act upon them. Your senses are the windows to the world, but they also present to us a world of contradictions and duality. Much of the reality about this world and ourselves is hidden from us because of them. Hence, we must keep our minds open, cultivate wisdom, and learn to discern things clearly so that we will not be trapped in the illusions of our own making. Most importantly, we must control our senses rather than letting them run wildly in all directions in the pursuit of our desires.

10. You become what you think

This is one of the inferences we can draw from the Bhagavadgita. Our gunas tend to strengthen themselves through repetitive thoughts and desire-ridden actions. They produce sinful karma, which, in turn, determines your fate and future, including your future births. As you continue to indulge in repetitive behavior and habitual actions and thought patterns, you reinforce your essential nature and remain stuck in the cycle of births and deaths. Therefore, if you want to transform your life and destiny, you must resolve your gunas, changing your thoughts, purifying your mind and body, and replacing your lower nature with the divine one. In other words, as long as your essential nature, thoughts, and actions keep reinforcing each other, it will be difficult for you to accomplish any transformation within yourself. It is as if you have drawn yourself into a self-induced vortex in which you become the cause as well as the effect or the subject and object of your suffering from which escape becomes elusive. This is karma at the most basic level, which makes your suffering increasingly difficult to resolve. You are the sum of your thoughts, actions, and accumulated karma. They sow the seeds of your suffering. Through your thoughts and actions, arising from your desires and expectations, you create your suffering and victimize yourself in the process. Your suffering continues as long as you remain ignorant of their underlying causes and do not find the means to escape from them. Hence, you must know that any reform, improvement, or purification must begin in the mind. Your mind is the source. It creates your life and future from your thoughts and actions, which also arise from it. To break free from this endless loop and create a new beginning or future for yourself, you must focus on controlling, purifying, and stabilizing your mind. By controlling your mind, purifying your thoughts, and stabilizing it in the contemplation of God, you can control your desires and achieve liberation.

11. Practice exclusive devotion to attain liberation

For the Bhagavadgita, God is the Supreme Lord and the center of all existence. He is the sacrifice, the host of the sacrifice, the material poured into the sacrifice, and the result of the sacrifice. Nothing happens without His command. Therefore, to escape from the world, it recommends the highest form of devotion: exclusive devotion (ananya bhakti) or single-minded devotion (ekanta bhakti) to the highest God, stating that yajnas and other rituals are important, but they are incomparable to the practice of devotion to the Supreme Lord. They may help you in achieving material goals: Dharma, Artha, and Kama, but do not lead to liberation. Through exclusive devotion, devotees can earn God's grace, which is necessary to escape from samsara. Similarly, devotion to the highest God is important since those who worship gods, demigods, and other beings go to them, whereas those who worship the Supreme Lord go to Him without doubt. Lord Krishna also says that none is dearer to Him than those who worship Him exclusively, with their minds absorbed in Him, contemplating Him always, and spending their lives in His service.

12. Practice karma sannyasa, offering your actions to God

Many people do not realize that God plays an important but imperceptible role in their lives. They attribute their successes and failures to themselves, taking pride when they succeed and falling into despair when they fail. The Bhagavadgita suggests that this attitude puts them on the rollercoaster of life, subjecting them to mental instability and suffering. Therefore, it is necessary to acknowledge God's role in the unfolding of your life. By attributing your failures and successes to Him and renouncing the ownership and doership of your actions to Him, you can pass on to Him the burdens of your life and live in peace. Worldly people take credit for their actions and shift the blame elsewhere for their failures. Even if they do not acknowledge

God, they should realize that many extraneous factors and fortuitous circumstances play an important role in their lives and destinies. Much of what happens to you happens because of various factors, most of which are not under your control, including your birth and death. Apart from your actions, numerous factors contribute to your life and achievements. Indeed, you and your life are the result of the actions and contributions of countless people, both living and dead. For example, without parents or ancestors, you would not even have taken birth. All the modern amenities, luxuries, devices, programs, applications, inventions, and discoveries that you currently use and enjoy are due to the contributions made by numerous others. We should, therefore, live in gratitude, without taking credit for our actions. Still better, we should offer all actions to God, who is the source of all and who manifests in this universe in diverse forms and helps us in numerous ways.

Endearing Qualities of a Pure Devotee

Who is a true devotee? What are his endearing qualities? Who earns the grace (prasada) of God? Does the practice of devotion require prior preparation? What qualities lead to devotion of the highest kind that ensures our union with Him? How should we worship Him to secure our liberation? In the Bhagavadgita, we find answers to these and other questions about devotion and its importance in our liberation. It declares that ritualistic devotion and halfhearted measures, without purity and perfection in one's thinking and attitude, do not lead to salvation. It may lead to better karma and better rebirth, but not to liberation. Devotion is an act of offering, not receiving. It is a sacrifice in which you surrender to God and put your life at His disposal. True devotion can be expressed in many ways. Serving others by seeing God in them is also an expression of true devotion, which many seers and sages exemplified through self-example. That value still holds good. The concept of Bhagavata, the servant of God, is also rooted in the three eternal principles: sacrifice, service, and devotion. True devotees exemplify them. They win over the Lord through exclusive devotion.

Devotion and renunciation go together. You cannot practice true devotion without renouncing desires and attachments to worldly life. One may earn meritorious karma (punyam) from devotional services and obligatory duties performed out of a desire to go to heaven or attain a good birth in a family of pious people in the next life. However, they do not lead to salvation. In the heart and mind of a true devotee, there is no place for desires or desire-ridden devotional service. In the early stages of practice, one may entertain positive desires to be good or do good. However, in the later stages, one must renounce all desires to attain purity and perfection since desires in any form can bind the soul to samsara.

Therefore, God's true devotees give up everything and worship Him with wisdom, knowledge, detachment, and dispassion. They do not seek Him to reach their other aims. They worship Him without desires and expectations and offer Him unconditionally whatever they have.

A pure devotee, who practices exclusive devotion with no other goal or aim, remains firmly established in purity (sattva samavistah) and thoughts of God. He does not detest disagreeable actions, nor does he favor agreeable ones (18.10). He gives up attachment to his actions and even to their fruit. He sees God in all and considers them His numerous manifestations. If you see a devotee craving for money and worldly pleasures in front of God, know that he has a long way to go on the path of devotion.

A true devotee does not engage in vain rituals and sacrifices to prove his devotion or show off his power or wealth. He is devoted to God through unconditional love and humility, not desire or vanity. Demonic people engage in conditional and agenda-driven worship and devotion. They perform sacrifices out of desire, vanity (dambha), or egoism. A true devotee worships God because he loves Him truly and cannot bear separation from Him. His mind remains absorbed in Him as he remembers Him in every action he performs. He is not a seeker but a giver. He is not motivated by suffering, curiosity, or worldly desires to practice devotion or worship God. His life revolves around Him. He remembers nothing but the name and form of God. In his heart, nothing exists but the light of God. If you look into his mind, you will hear nothing but the silent reverberation of his reverential prayers and the chanting of His names and forms. His surrender is so pure and complete that he does not act upon the prompting of his ego or desires. His devotion expresses itself in his sacrificial actions and renunciation of desires, ownership, and doership. He identifies himself with God so completely that he does everything for the sake of God and nothing for himself.

The lives of Hanuman, the Alvars and Nayanars of southern India, and great saints like Kannappa, Chaitanya, Vallabhacharya, Mirabai, Kabir, Tulsidas, Tukaram, and Sri Ramakrishna are a few examples of how humans can express exclusive devotion and attain the highest perfection. Their lives prove that with effort, faith, and discipline, human beings can reach out to God through single-minded devotion, overcoming mental and emotional barriers induced by their egos and self-preservation instinct. The Bhagavadgita assures that a true devotee of God never perishes. God becomes His support and guardian, taking care of his wants, needs, and welfare personally. However, those who trouble them may earn God's wrath.

Outwardly, a pure devotee may not be impressive enough to attract others' attention. He may even appear withdrawn, delusional, and depressed, but his devotion distinguishes him from others. He is dearer to God because he remains connected to Him through his heart and consciousness. His devotion draws him closer to God and earns him His grace and love. An inseparable bond arises between them that cannot be erased by external forces because God reciprocates their devotion and nurtures their relationship out of compassion. The Bhagavadgita portrays God as the merciful and generous Being who readily responds to His devotees' calls and attends to their daily needs as if they were His own. At the same time, He readily punishes the wicked and evil ones by casting them into the wombs of lower life forms and darkest hells.

Pure devotion arises from the predominance of sattva. It means that you cannot experience the devotion of the highest kind until you reach perfection in the practice of karma, jnana, and sannyasa yogas. It arises when the mind is empty, the heart is free from passions and emotions, and the ego is silent and subdued in the silence of the senses. Devotion of the exclusive kind and distraction do not exist in the same space. They cancel each other. If you are distracted, you will have devotion mixed with passions and emotions, but not pure devotion. A distracted mind may be devoted to the things of the world, but it cannot experience pure devotion. To experience true devotion, a devotee must surrender to God unconditionally. He must lay down his life at His feet without fear or anxiety and offer to Him everything he has, becoming an oblation or sacrificial food in the sacrifice of his life. His actions must be burned in the fire of detachment and dispassion so that they will not raise their hoods to strike him. When he achieves perfection in karmayoga and jnanayoga and when he practices renunciation and detachment with complete sincerity, his heart is ready for the flutter of devotion and the dawn of wisdom.

Devotion arises with the predominance of sattva and with the resolve and faith of the sattvic kind. When rajas and tamas are suppressed, and sattva predominates, certain rare qualities manifest themselves in a devotee. The Bhagavadgita identifies them as divine qualities, which strengthen divine nature and devotion and bring the devotee closer to the Lord. The following are a few important aspects of God's true devotees that arise from their divine nature and exemplify their conduct. They facilitate their spiritual growth and lead them on the path of liberation.

- They are pure, intelligent, and stable
- They are skillful, impartial, and undisturbed
- They renounce ownership and doership
- They are solely devoted to God and meditate upon Him always
- They worship only the Highest Supreme Lord with unwavering faith
- They are steadfast in their faith and resolve
- They seek truth and knowledge and renounce ignorance and falsehood
- They always focused on the thoughts, names, and forms of God
- They practice compassion and humility as they see Him everywhere and in everyone
- They know that Isvara is the eternal Seed of all things and beings
- They identify themselves with God completely
- They are born after many births and intense practice
- They practice devotion with a sattvic resolve
- They work for his liberation
- Always singing His glories, prostrating before Him with firm vows, they worship God with exclusive devotion out of love but without desires and expectations
- They practice detachment and renunciation and remain indifferent to the world
- They are free from desires, envy, hatred, or ill will
- They are friendly, compassionate, and forgiving
- They are free from egoism as they surrender to God and attribute all their actions and their outcomes to Him
- Whatever they do, whatever they eat, and whatever oblation they pour into the sacred fire, they offer that to God
- They practice virtues such as non-violence, non-stealing, non-covetousness, truthfulness, and cleanliness

- They are free from evil passions, cruelty, delusion, and egoism
- They practice self-restraint, silence, and solitude when they are not engaged in devotional or spiritual practices
- They practice sameness and remain equal to friend and foe, honor and dishonor, heat and cold, pleasure and pain, and such other dualities
- They are equal to praise and criticism, and attribute them to their fate or God's play
- They remain stoical and silent in both honor and dishonor and do not attempt to defend themselves
- They are content with whatever they have or whatever happens
- They are usually without a fixed abode, except in special circumstances
- They willingly promote Dharma and serve God's creation
- They are balanced and stable as they are free from joy, envy, fear, anger, and excitement
- They do not disturb others, nor are they disturbed by the actions of others
- They neutralize karma as they renounce desires, seeking, striving, and doership in both auspicious and inauspicious works and offer their fruit to God
- They are pure, impartial, and nonjudgmental in their thinking and attitude

Devotees who possess these qualities are indeed extremely rare. Most of them reflect a few qualities fully or partially. A true devotee strives to follow the immortal Dharma faithfully as ordained, holding God as the supreme example. His faith and devotion remain strong as he accepts life as the fruit of God's will. Teaching the Bhagavadgita or spreading Lord Krishna's message from it is also a form of devotional service alone. Lord Krishna declares firmly in the scripture (Ch. 18) that among His devotees, those who teach the knowledge of the Bhagavadgita, those who study it, and those who hear it from others are dearer to him in the same order than the rest. A true devotee, therefore, not only practices devotion to the Lord but also enlightens others about His greatness by speaking about Him and sharing his knowledge with them.

Stages in devotional worship

In the 12th Chapter of the Bhagavadgita, Lord Krishna explains the alternative ways in which He can be worshipped. He states categorically that one should not worship the Unmanifested (avyakta) Brahman because it is difficult and painful. Then, He proceeds to explain how one can worship the Manifested Brahman. He says that the best way to do it is through surrender, meditation, and single-minded devotion. Worshipping Him with devotion and concentration is the highest form of devotion one can practice in an embodied state. He promises to rescue those who are capable of practicing from the ocean of mortal existence. He lives in the hearts of those whose minds are fixed upon Him and whose intellect dwells in Him. However, everyone cannot think of God constantly or worship Him exclusively. Hence, he gives other options. If devotees cannot fix their minds upon Him, they can still practice meditation (abhyasa yogam). If they cannot do it either, they can perform actions for His sake and attain perfection. If they cannot do even that, they should take refuge in Him and renounce the fruit of their actions to Him with self-control. Thus, Karma Sannyasa, which sets the stage for the journey of purification and liberation, can also be the starting ground for the cultivation of exclusive devotion.

The gunas, which are responsible for every action and intention, play an important role in shaping our devotion. Sattvic devotion is the purest. It is free from evil desires, egoism, vanity, and selfishness. A sattvic devotee indulges in constructive desires that are beneficial, produce peace and happiness for the self and others, or lead to the welfare of all. He prefers the company of God to the company of people and worships Him without desires, attachments, and doership. He practices equanimity and self-control, withdrawing his mind and senses and remaining equal to the dualities such as pain and pleasure and success and failure. Rajasic devotees are driven by passions, desires, and emotions. They worship different gods and demigods to satisfy their passions and worldly desires or promote their self-interests. Due to ignorance and delusion, they see themselves as distinct and separate from them or God and approach them with duality. Since their devotion is conditional and they lack self-control and equanimity, they are easily disappointed and distracted if their devotion does not result in the fulfillment of their wishes. In short, rajasic devotees worship God with expectations and strive hard to please Him through their worship and service. They also have a poor understanding of what constitutes Dharma and Adharma and what should be done or not done (18.31). Tamasic people, who are delusional, negligent, inattentive, rebellious, and destructive by nature, worship God conditionally with evil intentions, even to hurt and harm others. Their devotion vacillates between the extremes of positive and negative emotions and mood swings. They are ignorant and delusional about their methods and practices, and often invent their own methods and practices, even if they are unconventional, harmful, disapproved, or prohibited by the scriptures. They worship out of vanity, egoism, pride, and envy with ulterior motives. Sometimes, they resort to extreme measures to please the deities they worship and obtain their favors. Tamasic devotees are unskilled, imperfect, crude, stubborn, deceitful, malicious, depressed, and procrastinating. They hold perverted opinions and usually end up hating God or opposing Him. Some choose lower gods and evil spirits as the objects of their worship and do not mind invoking them for destructive purposes. Thus, comparatively, of the three types, the Sattvic devotees are the best. However, Lord Krishna says that in the end, devotees must transcend the gunas and remain the same in all conditions and situations. The best devotee is the one who conquers the gunas and remains firmly established in the thoughts of God with exclusive devotion.

Atma Samyama Yoga, Realizing the Self by the Self

The yoga that comes closest to the Classical Yoga of Patanjali is the Atma Samyama Yoga described in the sixth chapter of the Bhagavadgita. It is the yoga of knowing the Self by controlling the Self through concentration, meditation, and self-absorption. In this yoga, also called Atma Yoga, you practice intense self-purification and self-control to align and balance your mind and body (atma samyama) according to your spiritual goals and the demands of your spiritual practice. By practicing it, a skillful yogi manifests within himself divine qualities, virtues, and the highest ethical standards and conduct that are enumerated in the scripture and necessary to achieve liberation. From the Bhagavadgita, we may deduce that by itself, this yoga may be difficult to practice, but in conjunction with other yogas, it will yield excellent results. The yoga will help you remain absorbed in contemplation by withdrawing from the outside world. By restraining your egoistic thoughts and your natural inclination to seek worldly objects and enjoyment for fulfillment, you transcend the limitations of your mind and body and experience the deeper states of self-absorption. By suppressing desires and attachments and transcending the gunas through self-control, you develop the resolve and strength to restrain your mind and senses, and you attain peace, stability, and sameness that are essential for stabilizing your mind in the contemplation of God or the Self.

Atma Samyama Yoga is meant to remove the impurities of the lower nature, which is driven by primitive desires and instincts and animal tendencies, and silence its craving and striving so that one may perceive the Self that is hidden deep beneath layers of accumulated memories and habitual thought patterns. This is accomplished by practicing the various methods of yoga, such as following rules and restraints, regulating breath (pranayama), withdrawing the mind and senses (pratyahara), concentrating (dharana) on the object of devotion, meditating or observing the mind (dhyana), and entering into a deeper state of self-absorption or mental absorption (samadhi). When you achieve perfection in these disciplines and practice the last three methods simultaneously and effortlessly, you excel in this yoga.

The mind is turbulent by nature. However, as Lord Krishna says, it can be controlled through regular practice (abhyasa) and dispassion or detachment (vairagya). We do not find peace and stability in the outside world. We must find them within ourselves by locating the point or the state where it is possible to be at peace and in harmony with ourselves. It requires effort, determination, discipline, and self-control. We do not experience peace if we are in conflict with ourselves. We do not achieve perfection in yoga if we engage in halfhearted measures. We cannot attain peace and harmony if we are preoccupied with our egoistic and selfish desires and pursuits. God does not enter our consciousness if we do not let Him in through surrender, renunciation, and devotion. We may seek God's mercy (Isvara prasadam), but it comes only when we empty our minds of all selfish and egoistic thoughts and fill them with exclusive devotion.

The Bhagavadgita states that we must practice renunciation by giving up desires and attachments and the fruit of our actions. It is true renunciation, not taking vows and wearing orange robes, while the mind is still impure and the ego is still plotting its survival and continuity in another mode. No one becomes a skillful yogi (yukta) without renouncing the thoughts of the world or the desires induced by the gunas. Indeed, it is a tall order, possible only for a few extremely dedicated, disciplined, and devoted yogis who can practice self-control without torturing their minds and bodies and with strong faith and devotion to continue tenaciously amidst dualities, difficulties, and disturbances.

As the scripture states (6.3), for a sage (muni) on the path of self-realization, selfless work is the means to unite with the Self. Once he accomplishes perfection in his actions by means of renunciation, serenity becomes the means for him to progress further toward the highest perfection, which is oneness with the Self. Therefore, Lord Krishna says that one should uplift the Self by the Self but not by degrading the Self and not performing actions that are in conflict with the goal of self-realization. This advice is relevant to the practice of Atma Samyama Yoga because, as the Gita says, the Self is the only friend of the Self, and the Self is the only enemy of the Self. For him who has conquered the lower self by the higher Self, the Self is the friend, and for him who has not done it, it is his enemy.

Therefore, self-discipline is at the crux of Atma Samyama Yoga. A self-disciplined and serene person (jitatma) becomes established in the contemplation of God and remains equal to the pairs of opposites (6.7). Indeed, discipline is vital to any practice. Through discipline, one must become a conqueror of the senses (jitendriya) and the mind. It is hard to imagine whether progress is possible at all in any field without discipline and self-control. While indiscipline may not pose problems in some aspects of worldly life, there is no place for compromise or complacency in spiritual life. Discipline is important in spiritual practice because one can realize the Self only when the mind and body are completely pure and filled with sattva. For mental stability and inner peace, which are imperative for the practice of samyama, one must be free from the impurities of rajas and tamas and desires or attachments.

How one can practice Atma Samyama Yoga is also described by Lord Krishna (6:10-19). He states that a yogi should select a clean place and arrange his firm seat (sthira asanam) there, which should be neither too high nor too low. He must cover it with kusa grass, deerskin, and a cloth one over the other. Sitting on that seat, he must keep his mind and senses under control and practice meditation and concentration for self-purification (atma visuddhi). Holding his body, neck, and head in one straight line, sitting stable and still, concentrating on the tip of his nose, undistracted, with a peaceful mind, without fear, he must practice celibacy (brahmacharya) and subdue his passions. With his mind in control and firmly in God alone, as he continues the practice, he will attain peace and the Supreme Goal of liberation (6:10-15).

This yoga does not give scope for practicing extremities (6.16-18). One must follow the middle path of moderation and restraint both in practicing it and following the discipline to achieve balance and equanimity. As the scripture affirms, Atma Samyama Yoga is neither for those who eat excessively nor for those who do not eat at all. It is neither for those who sleep for long nor for those who remain awake. Skillful yogis (yuktas) who practice it must control their eating, enjoyment, sleeping, and waking times to destroy their sorrow. Resting their controlled minds (vinaya cittam) in the Self, without desires and craving for sense objects, they must practice until they subdue all passions and become equal to the dualities. Their minds become like a lamp in a windless place, as their minds remain stable, without flickering, in that state of equanimity. Thus, with their minds withdrawn from the external world, with their egos absorbed in their higher nature, the conquerors of their minds and bodies become the conquerors of themselves (jitatma) and remain satisfied within themselves (6:20). Resting in that august state of peace and freedom, they arrive at the ultimate goal of yoga, which is disassociation from the union with pain and suffering (6.23). They enjoy the extreme bliss of union with Brahman and develop the unified vision of the Universal Self, seeing the Self in all and all in the Self.

The yoga of self-control is indeed difficult for those who cannot restrain their minds and senses or develop indifference. Perfection in self-absorption and samyama is best possible when the mind and body are still, and the modifications are subdued. Self-discipline is, therefore, important. A yogi must keep his mind and senses firmly under his control and establish them in divine contemplation. What happens if he fails to control his wandering mind? Would he fall into darker worlds? When Arjuna asks this question, Lord Krishna replies that any effort in the yoga of self-control does not go to waste. He sees neither downfall nor destruction for those who are engaged in such auspicious deeds, here or hereafter. (6.40). If they fall from yoga, they may not attain liberation but would go to heaven or the world of righteous people and live there for a long time, enjoying the merit of their actions. Once their karma is exhausted, they would return to the earth and take birth in the families of pious or prosperous people (6.41 & 42). There, they regain the knowledge and intelligence of their previous lives and strive again with greater vigor and determination to achieve liberation (6.43).

In terms of principles and practice, as well as goals, Atma Samyama Yoga, as described in the Bhagavadgita, bears a close resemblance to the classical yoga of Patanjali. It has all the ingredients of Patanjali yoga, but unlike the other, it is theistic. The purpose of Atma Samyama Yoga is to attain Brahman or union with God, while that of Patanjali Yoga is to attain union with Isvara, the Lord of the body, or absorption in Him. Lord Krishna declares that the yoga of self-control is higher than the yoga of knowledge and the yoga of action. He advises Arjuna to practice it and become skillful. He also says that among the yogis, those who practice this yoga are considered the most skillful. They are superior to ascetics, men of knowledge, and men of action (6.46). Even among them, those who are full of faith and whose thoughts are absorbed in Him are considered the best. The practice of this yoga also requires the cultivation of divine qualities, which would lead to the predominance of sattva. This is the same as the practice of yamas and niyamas in classical yoga for self-transformation. The divine qualities, which are vital for the practice of this yoga, are listed in the 16th and 17th Chapters.

Transforming the Physical Self

The Bhagavadgita is essentially a scripture on transformational wisdom, probably one of the earliest expositions on self-development through self-control and self-purification. It suggests the ways and means to transform your mind and body, achieve the chief aims of human life (Dharma, Artha, and Kama), and achieve liberation (Moksha), making oneself and one's actions continuous offerings in the sacrifice of life to the Supreme Brahman. It prescribes several yogas or paths to achieve it. Of them, at least four yogas are the most important: the yoga of action (karma yoga), the yoga of knowledge (jnana yoga), the yoga of renunciation (sannyasa yoga), and the yoga of devotion (bhaktiyoga). Indeed, it offers an integrated approach combining the essential aspects of these four into a holistic approach. Its emphasis is on purifying and divinizing the physical, mental, and spiritual aspects of our personalities and making them fit for attaining and containing higher and purer states of consciousness and divine nature. It describes other yogas also, which are equally important. We may regard them as ancillary yogas that form part of a comprehensive transformative program that leads one from the impure states of ignorance and delusion to the state of knowledge, discernment, and self-awareness.

In the context of the Bhagavadgita as well as Patanjali Yoga, purification or self-transformation involves suppressing the impurities of rajas and tamas and cultivating purity or sattva. Of the three modes, sattva is the purest and conducive to the flowering of divine nature. All the divinities and luminous objects in the universe are said to have sattva in predominance. If we increase sattva in our bodies, we become increasingly divine-like and reflect divine qualities. Rajas and tamas make us passionate, egoistic, delusional, ignorant, materialistic, or worldly, whereas sattva refines and purifies our gross and subtle bodies, improves our perceptions and discernment, and brings us closer to our divine potential. Intuition and other paranormal powers (siddhis) arise from its predominance only. It is also responsible for rationality, wisdom, and intelligence in us. Sattva elevates our thinking, whereas rajas and tamas degrade it. Rajasic nature makes people increasingly worldly and selfish, while the mode of tamas brings out the worst in humans and leads them to demonic and destructive behavior.

The Bhagavadgita emphasizes the importance of self-transformation and inner purity to qualify for liberation. It prescribes the yoga of action (karmayoga) with renunciation of desires (karma sannyasa) to overcome attraction and aversion for sense objects and attain freedom from karma. It does not say that you must renounce the world or its riches, but only the desire for them. It recommends the yoga of knowledge to cultivate the right knowledge about our true nature to overcome egoism, ignorance, and delusion about ourselves. It prescribes the yoga of renunciation to overcome desires and attachments and cultivate detachment, discernment, and sameness. When one excels in these yogas, sattvic devotion manifests in the hearts of the yogis, which helps them subdue their egoism and traces of any other impurities that persist in them.

Thus, the various yogas suggested in the scripture help the yogis purify and transform the five layers of their bodies, namely the gross food body, the breath body, the mental body, the intelligence body, and the bliss body. Persistent practice of these yogas not only leads to purification but also excellence in each of these yogas, which will collectively set the stage for the practitioner's final liberation. By that purification, the yogis harmonize their lower and higher natures and become stable-minded and firm in wisdom (sthithaprajna). In the human personality, the physical body is the animal component, the mind is the human component, and the heart is the spiritual component. The body is a playground of Prakriti and Her various forces. The human mind, with its reasoning power, is the receptacle of accumulated knowledge, impurities, and modifications. In the heart alone, one experiences the stirrings of the Self and subtle feelings and emotions that are peculiarly human and arise in moments of spiritual exultation. The yogas proposed in the Bhagavadgita aid in the purification and integration of these three components into a harmonious whole and lay the groundwork for reaching the highest goal. The process is not easy as she tenaciously holds the jivas in her net of Maya and does everything in her capacity to bind them to samsara and make their escape difficult. Building many walls of impurities around them, she keeps them ignorant and deluded for as long as possible.

The Bhagavadgita identifies the body as the playground of Nature and as the Field (kshetra) of the Self. It describes the body as the city of nine gates, in which the Self, the Knower of the body (kshetrajna), is held in bondage. For liberation and the practice of yoga, one needs to know the distinction between the two clearly. The body is made up of various tattvas: intelligence, the ego, mind, senses, the five gross elements, and the triple modes. It is subject to desires, passions, attachments, dynamism, consciousness, and modifications. It is perishable and unstable. It needs to be transformed so that it will become a vehicle of divine virtues such as humility (absence of pride), honesty, non-violence, tolerance or forgiveness, purity, sincerity, stability, self-control, detachment, dispassion, absence of ego, equanimity, even-mindedness, unwavering devotion to God and preference for loneliness. When they are firmly established through inner purification, one attains immortality.

The body is also a battlefield in which both the good and evil tendencies battle for supremacy while the Knower of the Field remains in the background as the Witness and Enjoyer. The conflict between these opposing forces is essentially a conflict between the gunas, which try to suppress each other and induce conflicting states of desires and attachments. Yogis should aim to cultivate purity by practicing virtues and transcending the gunas by regulating the food they eat, the actions they perform, and the virtues they practice. They should also transcend the triple gunas, described in the scriptures as the triple gates of hell, namely lust, anger, and greed, by suppressing them and remaining indifferent to the desire they induce. As the Bhagavadgita states, whoever is free from the gunas and the triple gates of hell acts for the welfare of his Self and reaches the highest goal (16.22).

In the journey of self-purification, transcending the gunas is of utmost importance. Until then, one must focus on removing the impurities of the mind and body and cultivating purity (sattva). As the scripture says, purity is the fruit of pious and selfless actions (14.16). Therefore, a householder must practice karma yoga and engage in sacrificial actions with the spirit of renunciation to overcome selfishness. He must perform pious and virtuous actions and uphold Dharma. He should follow the righteous path in matters of faith, worship, sacrifices, austerities, penances, charity, and mundane actions such as eating, speaking, listening, thinking, etc., as described in the 17th Chapter. From sattva arises the knowledge and wisdom necessary to practice jnana yoga, the yoga of knowledge. With increasing sattva and increasing knowledge, he qualifies to attain good births. If he persists and purifies himself further through self-control (atma samyama), he becomes skillful in the yoga of renunciation and devotion and goes beyond the gunas (gunatita). Knowing that the gunas alone act, he remains indifferent and undisturbed by their actions. Remaining the same in sorrow and happiness, self-reliant, equal to all, steady, balanced in censure and praise, equal in honor and dishonor, equal to friends and foes, renouncing doership, he establishes his mind in God with exclusive devotion and an unwavering mind.

Purifying the tattvas in the body

The Bhagavadgita prescribes various methods to transform the mind and the body and cultivate even-mindedness, detachment, and divine qualities. They facilitate samyama and advanced states of self-absorption and equanimity. The following account is based on the methods suggested in the scripture to purify the various tattvas and attain perfection.

The organs of action

The organs of action are five: speech, hands, feet, excretory organ, and reproductive organ. For self-control, to overcome desires and attachments, or to excel in any yoga, one must restrain them and engage in sacrificial actions without desires, offering their fruit to the Lord. The organs of action cannot be silenced forever since it is natural for the body to engage in actions and movements, either voluntarily or involuntarily. Indeed, as the Bhagavadgita states, no one can remain inactive even for a moment because of the gunas. Even when the body is asleep, certain organs in the body keep functioning to keep it alive. Their presiding deities are always awake and keep a watch on the body as guardians. For effective self-control, one should restrain not only the organs of action but also the senses and the mind. Hence, the scripture (3.7) says that a yogi should excel in the yoga of action by restraining his organs with his mind, unattached.

The organs of perception

There are also five organs of perception: eyes, ears, nose, tongue, and skin. They, too, must be controlled to stabilize the mind in the contemplation of the Lord or to excel in any yoga. Since they are responsible for attraction and aversion, desires, attachments, and passions such as anger and envy, they are still more difficult to control than the organs of action. Because of their outgoing nature, they are responsible for the turbulence of the mind, attachment, desires, delusion, confusion of memory (smriti bhrama), and loss of discrimination, and disturb the minds of even those wise people who practice self-control. The withdrawal of the senses (pratyahara) is one of the effective ways to restrain them and stabilize the mind in peace and equanimity. As the Bhagavadgita states (2.58), when one withdraws one's senses from sense objects as a tortoise withdraws its limbs, one becomes stable in thinking and intelligence (sthithaprajna). The sense objects cease to trouble those who do not enjoy them through their senses. The taste for them may last for a while in memory, but even that will fade when one sees the Self seated in the heart.

The mind

The mind (manas) is the lord of the senses. It is considered the eleventh sense since it can often perceive things intuitively without the aid of the senses. However, since it constantly extends itself into the world through the senses, it cannot remain free from their influence or the turbulence they cause. The scripture states that the mind is a major obstacle on the path of yoga since it is fickle (chanchalam) by nature, turbulent, and difficult to control, and without controlling it, one cannot attain equanimity, sameness (samsiddhi), and freedom from karma (naishkarmya siddhi). The Bhagavadgita describes the ideal state of mind, which is stable, balanced, even-minded, equal, and indifferent to the dualities, and free from the modifications arising from impurities, such as delusion and ignorance. It likens the subdued mind of a yogi to a lamp in a windless place and to attain lasting peace by achieving it, it suggests the withdrawal of the senses, concentration, meditation, self-absorption, living in solitude, self-control, celibacy, moderation in eating and sleeping, and freedom from desires (6.1-10). Therefore, a yogi should rest his disciplined mind in himself alone.

Seeing himself abiding in his divine nature and the silence of his mind and senses, he remains satisfied within himself, ever contented, and seeking nothing other than the desire to worship the Lord and remain absorbed in his contemplation.

Intelligence

In the body, intelligence (buddhi) is the highest tattva of Nature, which is modeled on Brahman's pure intelligence (prajna). The Bhagavadgita states that discerning wisdom arises from intelligence (buddhi) that is stable, one-pointed, and free from attachments and the impurities induced by the gunas. It is also Nature's highest aspect present in us, but the Self is still higher than the intelligence (3.42). When it is pure, it radiates the brilliance of the Self. Delusion and ignorance arise when the mind is restless and subject to craving and attachments. Due to the lack of discernment and right knowledge about themselves, deluded people worship neither God nor other divinities. They pursue wrong aims and identify with their physical nature (mind and body). The Bhagavadgita states that discerning intelligence does not arise in those whose minds are unsteady (2.66). Their wisdom is carried away by their disturbed minds as a boat is carried away by turbulent waters (2.67). Therefore, one should aim to keep the mind steady and concentrated. When the mind is stabilized through the withdrawal of the senses, selfless actions, detachment, and sameness, intelligence becomes stable and one-pointed, whereby we distinguish right from wrong and knowledge from ignorance. With increased wisdom and knowledge, we become aware of the eternal nature of our existence and work for our liberation.

The ego

The ego (aham) is the false self. It represents our individuality and identification with our names and forms and induces attachment to our minds and bodies, whereby we become deluded about our true identity and eternal nature. The ego in each jiva is both a friend and an enemy of the Self. It is a friend when it is pure and facilitates virtuous conduct and self-realization, and an enemy when it is impure and engages in desire-ridden actions to bind us to worldly enjoyments and samsara. For liberation, the ego must be restrained and offered to the divine will as a sacrifice. Detachment, self-restraint, the yoga of action and knowledge, surrender, and devotion are the best means to purify it and transform it into a divine instrument. When the ego is subdued and desires are controlled, one develops even-mindedness, which is necessary to transcend the gunas. The ego must always be kept under control by practicing detachment and renunciation, restraining the senses, doing selfless service (12.4), and practicing devotion. Surrendering all actions to God, worshipping Him, and meditating upon Him with single-minded devotion, a yogi should gradually replace his egoistic thoughts with divine thoughts and his ego-identity with his spiritual identity. These methods increase sattva, suppress rajas and tamas, and bring a fundamental transformation in one's thinking and attitude. Purity is essential to cultivate divine nature. When the divine nature is fully established, the ego remains subdued. The practice of jnana, karma, and sannyasa yogas helps a devotee to achieve purity and perfection and stabilize his mind and body in exclusive devotion, which will ultimately lead to liberation.

How to distinguish a person who attains purity and transcends the modes? The three gunas are problematic since they induce desires and attachments through attraction and aversion, and keep the mind and senses outgoing. Although sattva strengthens purity and divine qualities, it still binds the pious ones through noble intentions and attachment to righteousness. One should therefore strive to cross them and become free from their influence. The fourteenth chapter of the Bhagavadgita describes the distinguishing marks of a person who has transcended the gunas. It says that a person who achieves that rare distinction remains indifferent and free from aversion when he is awake and engaged with the world, when his senses are active, or when his mind is deluded. He does not let gunas disturb him or induce desires in him, knowing that all actions arise from the gunas, and he is not responsible for them and does not cause them. He remains balanced, indifferent, and equal to pain or pleasure, the pleasant or the unpleasant, praise or criticism. With a steady and unwavering mind, he looks upon equally a lump of earth, stone, or gold. Equal in honor and dishonor, equal to friend and foe, not taking sides, giving up initiating desire-ridden actions, says Lord Krishna, whoever attains this state by transcending the modes is fit for entering the state of Brahman.

Liberating the Self with the self

As the Upanishads suggest, there are two selves within each jiva. One is the physical, temporary, and impermanent self, and the other is the eternal, indestructible, and pure Self. The physical self must act in harmony with the goal of liberation and strive for purity and equanimity through the practice of yoga to help the pure self escape from samsara. In that transformative process, the physical self must cease to be a problem and an obstacle by undoing itself and falling into silence. We learn from our enlightened masters that liberation is not a learning process, but an unlearning, unwinding, and unburdening process. If you want to attain liberation, you must practice yoga, withdraw from the world, and let your mind and senses become still so that you can look within yourself and know who you truly are. Logically, it is an inverse process, in which the Self returns to the point from where it begins the journey as an embodied Self, ending an accumulative process in which Nature weaves herself around Him as His body, the Field of Play. You may attain that state in innumerable ways, due to the play of Maya, bondage, births and rebirths, but eventually you must discard your materiality and accumulated impurities to return to your pure state. For the Self, its embodiment as a jiva is but an interlude in its eternal existence, in which it undergoes no transformation and suffers from no modifications despite its existence in the impure samsara. All the commotion and chaos it witnesses in the jivas arise in the Field of Nature only, the lower self or the not-self, while the pure Self remains a Witness.

When you look at the colorful diversity of the world, in a state of duality, you, as the embodied Self, are drawn into an alternate illusory reality that binds you and does not let you see things as they are, discern the truth of yourself, or discriminate between the real and the unreal. However, when you withdraw from the Field in which you are engaged through your mind and body, and look within yourself, you will subdue your desires and passions and realize in a state of unity that you have been an eternal Self all along. Hence, liberation is indeed a process of realization rather than transformation since the Self is eternally the same and unchangeable. Transformation and purification are for the physical self or the mind, and the body only. In this transformation process, you do not destroy anything. You bring the various tattvas of Nature that make up your physical self to their perfect best so that they can be closest to your true Self or your divine nature in terms of purity and divinity. Even God is associated with Nature in His manifested aspects. All His manifestations are made up of the two selves or components, Purusha and Prakriti, or the spiritual and material Selves. Isvara, the Lord of the Universe, is a pure Being (Isvara tattva), with Prakriti acting as His playground for His enjoyment. The purpose of yoga is to attain the highest level of purity so that a yogi can reflect His qualities in himself and qualify to attain oneness with Him.

The individual Self is always pure, eternal, and immutable. When you become a jiva, you do not know who you are or what you represent. When you remember it, you become Shiva, the eternal. As a jiva, you enter a state of ignorance and delusion and forget who you truly are. When you overcome them and realize that you are verily the pure Self, you automatically regain your pure and eternal state and become free from the hold of Nature even if you continue to exist in the body as a liberated soul (jivanmukta). The Bhagavadgita teaches you how to return to that pure and resplendent state, not by avoiding actions and the battles of life, or escaping from their consequences, but by staying right in the middle of the battlefield of life and doing your duty with peace and equanimity. It suggests how you may lead a divine-centered life and work for your salvation with knowledge and awareness in a state of surrender and devotion. The scripture is not a dogma or a hypothesis. It is a practical philosophy that can be practiced and tested by anyone. It has been a source of inspiration since ancient times and continues to do so even now. Countless devotees followed it to transcend their ignorance and achieve liberation. It still enjoys a special place in the hearts of millions of devout Hindus even today.

Stable Mind and Self-Realization

In this chapter, we will discuss the nature of Sthithaprajna, the one whose mind is stable and whose intelligence shines like the resplendent sun, and how that state is attained.

The human mind is the most amazing, powerful, and complex creation of Nature. It enables us to know our individuality and the world in which we live, and use that knowledge intelligently and rationally to regulate our lives and actions according to our needs and desires. Our self-awareness, knowledge, and intelligence arise from the various faculties of our minds, which are collectively mentioned in our scriptures as the internal organ (antahkarana). With our minds, we can fathom the depths of our being, consciousness, and the universe and understand their structure, mechanism, and relationships. We may not always be right in our knowledge and actions, and we may not always have complete knowledge of everything. However, through effort, training, testing, and learning, we can discern the right way from the wrong way and the right knowledge from the wrong knowledge to perform any action or reach any goal. We can improve our methods, decisions, choices, and solutions, and succeed in any effort. In this discussion, we will use the mind in the popular sense as the seat of consciousness, intelligence, and all mental activity rather than in the traditional Hindu sense of manas as the receptacle of memories and other mental objects.

From an evolutionary perspective, we may consider the human mind the most developed instrument of Nature. However, our scriptures indicate that it is still an incomplete and imperfect organ or creation of Nature, having both light and darkness or shades of gray, and subject to instability, impermanence, and disintegration. It is vulnerable to modifications (vrittis), afflictions (kleshas), ignorance, and delusion. Unless you train your mind vigorously and control it, you cannot keep it stable or peaceful. You cannot stabilize or concentrate your mind on anything unless you restrain your senses and withdraw them. You cannot hold peace or light in it if you cannot free yourself from afflictions, modifications, doubt, delusion, and despair. Your existence upon earth is defined greatly by the state of your mind and your perceptions. Your mind helps you experience and make sense of life and the world and its reality in all their hues and colors. It may help you soar to the heights of heaven in your thinking and imagination in a positive state, or plunge you into sorrow and depression when you are in difficulties.

One of the chief weaknesses of the human mind is its restlessness and instability caused by desires, duality, and the twin problem of attraction and aversion. In seeking what gives us pleasure and happiness and in avoiding what is unpleasant and painful, we become caught in the dualities of life and experience diverse mental and emotional states. They keep our minds turbulent and carry away our poise, wisdom, and discernment. Caught between attraction and aversion and the desires and attachments they induce, we experience modifications and mental turbulence. The happiness and pleasure that arise occasionally in the interlude between those chaotic moments are fleeting because although we can control some aspects of our lives through our actions (karmas), we are still subject to acts of God (adhidaivam) and Nature (adhibhutam). When we do not obtain what we like or when circumstances force us to accept what we do not want, we feel disturbed, anxious, and emotionally upset. In those disturbed moments, we fail to recognize the causes hidden in our problems, discern the right solutions, or make the right decisions.

The Bhagavadgita recognizes human intelligence (buddhi) as the higher mind, different and distinct from the ordinary mind (manas), which is considered a mere receptacle of thought forms and accumulated memories. Intelligence (buddhi) is the highest evolute of Nature. In the universe, it manifests as the Great Intelligence or the Cosmic Mind (Mahat), distinct from the Pure Mind or the Pure Consciousness (sat chit) of Brahman. Buddhi in a being is the microscopic aspect of the Cosmic Mahat. As an aspect of Nature, it is a part of Nature's Field (kshetra), whereas Pure Mind or Pure Consciousness is the eternal and immutable state of Brahman, the Knower of the Field (kshetrajna), who is above all.

According to the Bhagavadgita, our consciousness (citta) is prone to disturbances when our minds and intelligence (buddhi) are clouded by the impurities of the triple gunas. Driven by desires and subject to duality, delusion, and ignorance, we fail to discern truth. Due to the repeated contact of the mind and senses with the objects of the world, we develop attraction and aversion, which in turn produce desires and attachments. As we act on these desires, we experience varied passions and emotions such as anger, fear, envy, and the like. Under their influence, we become deluded, believing we are only mortal beings, forgetting our divine nature and connection to God, and indulging in indiscriminate actions that result in karma, rebirth, and bondage to samsara. Thus, mental modifications and instability arising from desires and attachments are real problems, which a yogi must resolve by practicing self-control, selfless actions, renunciation, contemplation, and exclusive devotion.

Mental instability and disturbances are part of our daily experiences. We are seldom free from the restlessness of our minds and senses. They are constantly in a state of flux and turmoil, swinging between conflicting emotions, feelings, and mental states. Unless we train them, we cannot calm them down. Most of the time, we are not even aware that we are restless because we become used to our mental and emotional states and accept them as natural. We cannot effectively resolve this problem with half-hearted measures or with our mental or intellectual knowledge and faculties alone. They might help us experience peace and stability to some extent, but they do not provide permanent solutions. Our knowledge of the world and material things, including our bodies (vijnanam), arises from our perceptions and memories stored in our minds. It does not solve our material or spiritual problems permanently, free us from bondage and suffering, or find solutions to the problems whose causes we cannot easily ascertain.

In fact, instead of solving them, this knowledge often worsens them by playing on our fears and fueling our doubts and confusion. Further, it does not help us recollect the memories that are deeply buried in our consciousness and contribute to our mental afflictions or help us understand their causes. Therefore, whatever solutions we may find with our mental faculties and knowledge are inadequate. If this were not so, people in today's world would not face so many problems. Hence, what we need are comprehensive and lasting solutions to achieve lasting peace. For that, we must reduce our involvement with the world and withdraw into ourselves to know the hidden truths about ourselves and find peace and happiness. We must look for that center of stability in us, which is impervious to the noise and turbulence caused by our senses, and serve as our sanctuary where we can remain calm and equal amidst the storms and tempests of life.

The Bhagavadgita portrays the mind's restlessness as a natural condition and an intentional design of Nature (Prakriti) to keep us deluded, distracted, and controlled by our inherent nature. In that deluded and disturbed state, we do not realize the need to practice spirituality, know ourselves, or change our worldly ways. Perpetuating these attitudes and propensities, Nature keeps us under control and achieves her objectives. The scripture goes to the root of the problem and suggests that all these problems arise from the triple gunas. They are pervasive in our bodies and influence our thinking, actions, and intentions. Since they are invisible, we can only know them by their influence and the nature and actions they induce or by the results or effects they produce. As the scripture affirms, the gunas are responsible for our desires, attachments, and desire-ridden actions. Since desire-ridden actions lead to karma and desires arise from the gunas, logically it follows that they are also responsible for our mortal existence and continuation in samsara. One may assume ownership and doership of actions, thinking that actions arise from free will. However, according to the Bhagavadgita, there is no free will. All actions arise from the triple gunas. Because of them, beings are helplessly driven into actions. As long as they are active, no one is truly free. True freedom arises from liberation when one transcends the gunas and conquers desires. A wise person knows it and practices yoga to control and suppress his gunas and desires. When he succeeds in that through persistent practice and detachment, he remains undisturbed by his conditions, experiences, circumstances, actions, and their results. He renounces doership and ownership, knowing that his actions arise from the gunas and he is not their cause.

The gunas tend to compete and suppress one another for predominance. Under their influence, the jivas are attracted to things in which their corresponding gunas are predominant and repelled by those in which they are absent. Thus, sattvic beings seek sattvic objects, rajasic ones are attracted to things that are predominantly rajasic, and tamasic ones are drawn to tamasic objects that promote delusion and inertia. In this competition that goes on indefinitely at every level in the constitution of a jiva, the jivas indulge in desire-ridden actions, without knowing that they are naturally induced to act under the influence of their predominant gunas. Engaging in desire-ridden actions and forming attachments to the objects of like nature, they become bound to the cycle of births and deaths.

The three gunas bind jivas in their respective ways. Sattva binds them through pleasures, rajas through passions, and tamas through ignorance and delusion. Ideally, humans must transcend all three to achieve liberation from births and deaths. However, if it is not possible, one must at least try to cultivate sattva and achieve mental stability, peace, and equanimity, which will set the stage for further transformation and progress. When sattva predominates, we become spiritual and strengthen our divine nature. We turn to God and work for our liberation. As we advance on the path of self-transformation, we experience unity and self-control (atma samyama) and self-absorption, which will gradually burn away latent impressions and prevent the seeds of karma from fructifying.

It is not an exaggeration to say that the Bhagavadgita primarily aims to teach us how to live spiritually and experience peace and stability, without renouncing the world or our basic human duties and responsibilities towards our families and society. Its teachings are meant to calm the nerves and address the problem of ignorance, delusion, and human suffering as exemplified by Arjuna. Indeed, the objective of the Patanjali yoga is also the same: to achieve peace and stability through self-transformation, which is a major challenge in any age or society. Yoga is one of the simplest and most direct means to address this problem. The Yogasutras begin with the assertion that the purpose of yoga is ending the mind's modifications (*yoga chittavritti nirodhah*). By declaring that, it brings to the forefront the central purpose of human life, which is knowing and becoming one's pure Self.

The Bhagavadgita consistently emphasizes the importance of equanimity, stability, and sameness in the pursuit of liberation, which is considered paramartha, the ultimate aim of human life. The purpose of buddhiyoga is to sharpen the intelligence and develop discernment, both of which lead to the same goal. If your mind is unstable, you cannot free yourself from the modifications of your mind and body, nor can you think clearly and rationally.. A disturbed mind cannot focus on anything for long. In such a state, we cannot withdraw from the world or remain focused on the ultimate goal of liberation. One might superficially renounce the world, but without proper training, one cannot truly escape desires and attachments. Even if you go to the Himalayas, without discipline and self-control, you will not find peace within yourself, except perhaps in sleep, if you manage to sleep at all. If you have attachments and desires, you remain preoccupied with worldly thoughts, and the world follows you even into the deepest caves or the recesses of your mind. There is no sanctuary, externally or internally, for those who cannot control their minds and senses or their desires. To excel in yoga and tame your restless mind, you must practice self-control with faith and resolve, overcoming all desires and attachments.

According to the Bhagavadgita, when we are disturbed, we cannot think clearly or make the right decisions due to the loss of discrimination. When we take refuge in our egos, we fall into false notions of ourselves, believing we are mortal beings subject to impermanence, death, and destruction. This is the state of delusion, which produces fear, anger, envy, pride, lust, and other negative passions. It happened to Arjuna on the battlefield of Kurukshetra when he was overcome with the fear of sin and retribution. He used his learned knowledge to speak about family, duty, virtue, heaven, and similar topics. When he experienced fear, he thought of leaving the battlefield and living on alms as a beggar. Then, he rationalized his fear and weakness to create a credible argument about his predicament to justify his decision to escape from the harsh realities of war and his duty as a warrior.

Our scriptures say that the mind is a conjurer. It creates its make-believe reality of self-induced delusions, to distract us from the real problems we face in our lives, or temporarily protect us from them, or from the pain and suffering they cause. This tendency of our minds (prvritti), which is so natural that we may not even notice it, is a major obstacle to achieving peace and liberation. If we let the mind indulge in cognitive distortions and resort to its defensive mechanisms, we cannot think or resolve problems effectively. For that, we need a stable mind so we can focus uninterruptedly, think intelligently, respond adequately, and keep ourselves free from mental afflictions and self-induced delusions.

Most of our problems are self-created. We create them largely because of our ignorance and inability to think clearly and correctly. Our wisdom becomes evident in our decisions and actions. Disturbed people make disturbing decisions. We aggravate our problems and suffering when we are not peaceful and when we are not in harmony with ourselves. Wise men, skillful in yoga, choose to be part of the world, but do not get involved with it and do not lose their balance with indiscriminate actions. They restrain their minds and senses, practice detachment, and remain indifferent to external events. Things in themselves have no power over you. You give them the power by giving in to your desires and passions. You seek them in the hope and illusion of securing them to fulfill yourself or fill the emptiness or inadequacy you feel within yourself. Caught between attraction and aversion and unable to restrain your seeking and striving, you barter away your freedom, peace, and happiness. You do not realize how deeply you have become involved with the world and how much freedom you have lost until you become introspective and observe your cravings and longings with the intelligence and awareness you acquire through yoga.

A silent mind is ideal for liberation. When we are calm, we allow our intelligence to shine. When we are free from disturbances, we think clearly and focus firmly. The Bhagavadgita shows us the way to attain this ideal. It states that mental stability (sthithaprajna) arises from one-pointed intelligence. If you want to control your mind, you should sharpen your intelligence with knowledge and wisdom and purify it, so that you know intuitively how best to practice it and reach the goal. A person of stable intelligence is not fooled by the appearance of things. He knows what is happening around him and inside him. Established in yoga, performing actions such as seeing, hearing, touching, smelling, tasting, walking, dreaming, and breathing, he thinks he is doing nothing (5.9). While engaged in actions and dealing with the world, he remains untainted like a lotus leaf in the water. (5.10). He looks upon things equally, and with his intelligence firmly fixed in his inner Self, he attains the state of non-return (apunahvritti).

The Bhagavadgita rightly identifies desire as the root cause of our suffering. Out of desire, we become bound to the world. We seek objects or avoid them, hoping to find peace and fulfillment by possessing or accumulating the things we desire most. When we do not achieve expected results, we feel disappointed, angry, or frustrated and blame ourselves, others, God, or circumstances. On this perilous path, we experience pain and pleasure intermittently, but cannot secure permanent peace or stability since we cannot control much of what exists or happens in the outside world. The world cannot control us unless we yield to it and succumb to its temptations. The happiness or suffering that arises from our interaction with it is also limited since it is impermanent and never the same. However, the happiness or the contentment that arises from within you, independent of the external world or circumstances, rests on the firmer foundation of your essential nature, character, and integrity. It is longer-lasting, easier to control, and more reliable since you are better equipped by Nature to control the world that exists in you than the world in which you live. By controlling it and stabilizing it, you can experience peace and stability even when the world is disturbingly chaotic.

Thus, mental stability is best achieved through self-effort, self-control, and self-transformation by controlling your desires and attachments and removing the impurities that keep you involved with the world and its attractions instead of focusing on your true purpose of attaining freedom from Nature, the world, and their influence. Controlling the world or exerting influence over it is not as important as withdrawing from it or remaining detached from it through renunciation and self-control to attain freedom and lasting peace. You conquer the world not by rushing into it but by withdrawing from it. You cannot control what you desire unless you silence your thoughts and remain stable and equal to all circumstances. You cannot be free from the influence of the world and its temptations unless you redefine your relationship with it from a spiritual perspective, knowing that to control anything on which you depend or without which you cannot be happy, you must overcome the dependence and the attachment associated with it.

Peace and happiness arise when we exercise self-control by restraining our minds and senses, becoming indifferent to attraction and aversion, and letting go of attachment to the world. Those who seek fulfillment through worldly possessions and relationships remain trapped by their desires, like prisoners, whereas those who master themselves can live freely without depending on the world for happiness or security. This freedom does not come from sattvic desires, rajasic passions, or tamasic delusion, but from detachment, tolerance, and enduring patience and resolve. In short, we attain peace and happiness, not by having or accumulating material things or using them, but by practicing moderation and contentment and giving up our ego-induced desire to possess them or depend upon them for validation. True freedom arises when we are detached and do not let the world or its objects influence our thoughts and actions. Whoever is free and content within is free from the world.

Liberation may be difficult, but not impossible if you have a sattvic resolve or firmness (dhriti), which, according to the Bhagavadgita, (18.33), arises when a yogi stabilizes his mind, vital breath, senses, and actions by practicing yoga. Practicing obligatory duties with detachment (vairagyam) and controlling his desires with sattvic resolve (18.26), he cultivates pure intelligence (18.30), which enables him to know the difference between indulgence and abstinence, action and inaction, and bondage and liberation. They will eventually lead him to stability, sameness, and freedom from karma and bondage. With mental stability arises undisturbed and unending calm. All sorrows cease for the yogi whose mind is stable and cravings have ended. Free from desires and craving, he remains equal to all and satisfied within himself, neither grieving for what he does not have nor rejoicing for what he has. Whatever happens to him or whatever life brings to him, he accepts it stoically as divine providence (*yaddruchch labha samtushta*) and deals with it with sameness and indifference. By conquering his inner world, overcoming his limitations, and becoming disinterested in the world, he transcends duality (dvandatitha), delusion, and egoism and remains undisturbed and indifferent always. Free from ignorance and delusion, he sees clearly the beauty and splendor of God in every aspect of creation and within himself. Having become united with Him through his consciousness, he sees himself in all and all in himself.

Living in a complex world, we know how important peace and equanimity are for our mental and spiritual well-being. In this regard, the Bhagavadgita is very clear. It suggests that you must look for solutions to the problem of your suffering within yourself, and even God helps you internally by illuminating your mind and intelligence and removing impurities. If you surrender to Him and seek His guidance, He gives you the knowledge and wisdom to achieve this goal. To experience peace, you do not have to renounce your duties and obligations or the world, but your desires and attachments and desire-ridden actions. If you do not live for yourself or pursue selfish desires, you will not be tainted by the impurities of samsara. The shaktis of Maya do not trouble you. Instead, they transform into higher Shaktis and help you in your transformation and progress. If you offer your actions to God, He will assume responsibility for their consequences and help you in your practice. If you bring Him into your life, He will guide you safely beyond the reach of Death into the world of eternal freedom.

Purusha and Prakriti

In creation, all things come in pairs. Like the positive and negative charges of electricity, they act like twins and together complete the circle of life. We call them dualities (dvandva) or pairs of opposites. They exist even at the highest level of God's manifested realities. Although Brahman is one, He manifests in creation as two: the Self and the not-self. He creates His twin aspect, an opposite, which is responsible for the materiality, dynamism, and diversity we find in our world. We recognize them as Purusha and Prakriti or as the Self and Nature, respectively. They also go by different names as the Universal Male and Universal Female, Father God and Mother Goddess, Pure Consciousness and Pure Energy, God (deva) and Goddess (devi), Shiva and Jiva, and others. Universally, they represent the twin realities of Brahman. In Him, they remain indeterminate and indistinguishable, while they manifest as distinct realities in Isvara, His highest manifestation, who acts as the Lord of the Universe and the Creator of all. One of the distinguishing features of Hinduism is that it is gender fluid. There is no universal male or female human or jiva in Hinduism. All humans, as well as the rest of the jivas, are a combination of male and female aspects. The invisible Self is male, and the visible Prakriti is female. In the jivas, they are represented by pure consciousness and the body.

In the physical dimension of the universe, these fundamental polarities of existence appear as space and matter or consciousness and materiality. Both are said to be eternal and indestructible. However, Purusha is said to be independent and self-existent, and Prakriti is said to be dependent upon Purusha as His dynamic principle or executress. In other words, She needs the support of God. However, not all schools of Hinduism agree with this. Some believe that both are eternal, separate, and independent, but come together in creation as equals to manifest the worlds, objects, and beings for the duration of each cycle of creation. According to some schools, Purusha is both the efficient and the material cause of the creation, and Prakriti is inseparable from Him. Some believe that He is the efficient cause, and Prakriti is the material cause. The Bhagavadgita upholds the former view that God is the source and controller of all, while Prakriti executes His will as His dependent and eternal aspect. Some even believe that Prakriti acts as both, while God remains passive and does nothing except as the enjoyer and witness. Whatever the truth may be, they participate together in their manifested states to initiate, execute, control, and regulate the creative process, which is responsible for whatever exists and whatever we perceive and experience as existence.

Etymologically, Prakriti (pra + akriti) means the power or the energy (pra) that creates and supports all manifested forms (akriti) that appear in creation in their natural and unmodified state. It also means the power that creates and sustains all living and breathing (pra) forms (akriti). Its popular meaning is a natural condition, state, disposition, or form of anything found in its natural and pristine state, which has not undergone any change, distortion, or alteration from its original condition. In philosophy, it generally refers to Nature, materiality, or objective reality found in creation. When it undergoes change or modification in creation, it becomes vikriti, meaning artificial, ugly, altered, or recreated from its natural state, quality, or condition.

Purusha (puru + usha) means "the eastern dawn," or the morning light that appears in the east, which symbolizes the rising Sun, Isvara, the Self, or the Manifested Brahman, who heralds the dawn of creation by appearing in the endless space (akasa) as the Cosmic Being and sets in motion His dynamic energy and creative consciousness to bring forth all the beings and worlds. In the ninth chapter of the Bhagavadgita (9.7), Lord Krishna declares that at the end of each cycle of creation, all things and beings enter His Nature, and at the beginning of each cycle of creation, he brings them forth. He further states in another verse (9.10) that under His watchful observation, Nature brings forth both the moving and nonmoving things. The deluded ones do not know this and disrespect Him, while the wise ones know it and worship Him as the inexhaustible source of all. Purusha and Prakriti constitute the two distinct realities of creation and our very existence. In each of us, Purusha is the Self or pure consciousness, and Prakriti is the body. The organs in the body represent her tattvas. The self-effulgent Purusha, the Lord in the body, illuminates them since they lack illumination of their own.

According to the Bhagavadgita, Prakriti operates at two levels. Her lower nature is eightfold: earth, water, fire, air, ether, mind, and reason, and also the ego (7.4), while her higher nature consists of that (life force) by which all the living entities are upheld (5.5). All the beings in the universe originate from this twofold Nature (5.6). The Adhibhuta, which is responsible for all physical events, represents her elemental aspects (8.4). At the end of each cycle of creation, all manifested things and beings dissolve in Brahman. The gunas regain equilibrium as Nature becomes inactive and withdraws into her primal condition as Adi Shakti, the Primal Goddess. When the next cycle of creation begins, Brahman manifests them again (9.7). He becomes Purusha, and seated in Prakriti, He creates all classes of living beings (9.6), and the rest of the entities, both moving and non-moving (9.10). The relationship between Purusha and Prakriti is symbolized creatively in the Shivalinga, which represents Creation or the whole existence as the union of Purusha and Prakriti and their union as the source of all. All living beings are living examples of this great union. Nothing happens until they come together and work together. Life arises from the Non-Being (Shiva) when he joins with Prakriti and transmutes into numerous beings (jivas). In those forms, He subjects himself to her deluding power and experiences duality and delusion.

In a being, the body represents Prakriti, while the Self represents Purusha. The body, consisting of different organs or aspects (tattvas), is known as the Field (kshetra), and the Self is known as the Knower of the field (kshetrajna). The Field or Prakriti has parts and diversity. It is subject to modifications, whereas Purusha is indivisible and free from modifications. Prakriti is subject to duality and change, while Purusha is indestructible, immutable, and inexhaustible. Purusha exists in all as the pure, egoless consciousness, beyond the reach of the body and its parts, such as the senses and the mind. Even though He is bound to materiality and enveloped in delusion, He is not subject to any modifications. Purusha is the Adhidaiva, the Great God (8.8), the Ancient, the Omniscient, the Universal Enforcer of Law, and the Supporter of All (8.9). In the body, as the indwelling Spirit and inner Witness, He becomes Adhiyajna, the Lord of the Sacrifice (8.4). He is the Witness, the Guide, the Bearer, the Enjoyer, the Great Lord, and the Supreme Self (13.22).

Purusha is the universal Cosmic Male, the supreme Brahman, who emerges out of nothing to manifest the worlds and beings for unfathomable reasons. He is the subject as well as the object of sacrificial ceremonies. According to the Vedas, His self-sacrifice in remote antiquity resulted in the manifestation of the worlds and beings. Since He is the source of all, and is considered the Sacrificed as well as the Sacrificer, by making sacrifices to Him, one qualifies to attain immortality and enter the worlds of gods or immortal beings. The concept of Purusha as the Creator and Nourisher is well documented in the Vedic hymns, especially in the Purushasukta of the Rigveda, which describes how Purusha manifested the worlds out of Himself and established social order.

The Bhagavadgita describes two types of Purushas, the perishable and the imperishable. Creation is perishable. Brahman is imperishable. The jivas are perishable, the Self or the souls in them are imperishable. The body is perishable, while the pure consciousness in it is Imperishable (15.16). In other words, it acknowledges life as a combination of the movable and immovable or permanent and impermanent parts or aspects of existence. In their ultimate essence, they represent the same absolute and indivisible reality, Brahman. In creation, they represent the fundamental duality or polarity. Although Prakriti appears as distinct, she is an essential aspect of the eternal Brahman. In a living being, Prakriti is the physical self or the perishable Purusha, while the individual Self (atman) is the imperishable Purusha. The Supreme Purusha, God (Isvara) Himself, is, however, said to be neither of these, because He is beyond the perishable (Prakriti) and higher than the Imperishable inner Self, and sustains the three worlds by entering into them (15.17). Since He is beyond the perishable and higher than the Imperishable (Self), He is called the Supreme Purusha (Purushottama) (15.18). It means, although the individual Self has the same essence as the Universal Self, just like Prakriti, it is considered an aspect (amsa) of the Universal Self only. The Universal Self pervades the whole creation. There is no end to His manifestations (vibhutis) (10.40), which He holds by a single fragment (ekamsam) of Himself (10.42), including the individual Selves.

Prakriti is responsible for the illusion and the duality we experience in our interactions with the objective world. All modifications (vikarams) and modes (gunas) arise and exist because of Prakriti only (13.19). With the help of the gunas, which induce desires and passions, she binds the jivas to samsara and causes their birth in both good and evil wombs (13.21). The Bhagavadgita declares that in the performance of actions, Prakriti is the cause, while in the case of pleasures and pain, Purusha is the cause (13.21). Our ignorance and attachment arise largely due to the impurities of our minds and bodies. When they are present, we cannot discern the truth of anything clearly. Our senses are imperfect instruments of knowledge. With their help, we may perceive things, but only superficially. We cannot look into the nature of things and see them as they truly are without delusion. In the perception of things, truth is lost due to the distinction that exists in our perception between the knower and the known or the subject and the object. As long as the object and the objectivity associated with it remain in our perception, our experience of knowing and our perception of its reality remain incomplete. The same is the case with knowing the Self. To know it really, we must overcome the duality between the knower and the known and become absorbed in it.

The Self in the body is known as the indwelling witness and lord of the sacrifice (Adhiyajna). According to the Bhagavadgita (8.4), when Purusha, who is also known as the Controlling Deity (Adhidaiva), resides in the body as the inner witness, He becomes the Lord of the Sacrifice (Adhiyajna). He is the lord of the sacrifice because in the sacrifice of life, He (the Self) is the ultimate recipient of all offerings. Perceptions, the vital breath, and food are enjoyed by Him only. It means that Purusha and Prakriti manifest in the macrocosm as well as the microcosm as inseparable twins and as the two sides of One Absolute Reality. We may conceptually distinguish them through our intelligence, but we do not know much beyond what we can perceive or understand, since the hidden creation is much vaster and more complex than the visible one.

The indwelling Self is also known as the embodied Self (jivatma). In its essential nature, it is the same as the liberated soul (muktatma). However, it is bound to the body (Prakriti) and caught in the field of illusion from which it cannot easily escape without persistent spiritual effort. To perceive the Self in the body, knowledge and discernment alone are insufficient. You must overcome your attachment to your name and form and establish your identity fully in your spiritual identity or higher nature. As the Bhagavadgita states, a striving yogi perceives Him as the Lord seated in the body enjoying the sense objects, while the ignorant ones, whose hearts are impure, cannot perceive Him even after much striving (15.11).

For the Self, the Purusha, the body or Prakriti is like an outer garment. Until liberation is attained, He remains bound to samsara and keeps returning to the earth to attain new bodies and continue His association with Nature. When the jivas die with their unfinished karmas, their elemental bodies (bhutatma) return to Nature. The Self in each body leaves it and goes to the ancestral world. While departing, He takes away with Him the deities presiding over the organs like the wind carrying away the fragrances so that He may continue to enjoy the objects in his afterlife (15.8). The final moments of a dying person are crucial. The scripture says that whatever a person thinks, at the time of his death, he attains that (8.6). Whoever departs from the body thinking of God attains Him without doubt (8.5 & 8.13). From this, it is evident that the mind should be purified and trained to remember Him always so that no effort would be required to think of Him at the time of death (8.8).

The time of death is also important since it has a bearing on the fate of humans after death and where they may go. A yogi who dies during the period of the northern solstice goes to the deathless world of Brahman by the sunlit path of immortals and lives there forever. He never returns to the world or suffers from karma and bondage. Those who depart from here during the southern solstice go to the ancestral world by the path lit by the moon. They do return to the earth after exhausting their karmas partially and take birth variously according to their past merit. However, those who are demonic by nature perish, which means they have fewer chances of attaining human birth. They either fall into the lowest hells (16.16) and suffer there for a long time or are reborn in lower life forms.

According to the Bhagavadgita, the eternal Supreme Purusha is said to be neither a Being (sat) nor a Non-Being (asat). He is omnipresent with hands and feet, eyes, heads, faces, and ears everywhere. He envelops everything without moving. He is the source of the sense organs, but does not have them or use them. Although detached and indifferent to all, He is the sustainer of all. He is without qualities, but all qualities arise from Him only. He is within and without all beings, moving and unmoving, very subtle and incomprehensible, far away but also very nearer. Though Undivided, He is also situated in all beings as divided. Bearer of the beings, He is also known as the devourer and the illuminator. Among the illuminated, He is the illumination and the illuminator, and is also said to exist beyond darkness. He is the knowledge that is known and the knowledge that is yet to be known. He is also the goal of all the knowledge that can be known. He resides in the hearts of all, and yet is not a part of them. The scripture declares that Prakriti is for performing actions, and Purusha is for enjoying the life that happens because of them. Indeed, He is said to be the Overseer, Regulator, Bearer, Enjoyer, the Great Lord, and the Supreme Soul. He is Purusha, the transcendental Soul (13. 12-22), the Universal Witness.

The knowledge of Purusha and Prakriti helps us understand the perishable and imperishable aspects of our personalities and the world in which we live. By knowing these distinctions, we can understand how to integrate them into our spiritual practice and work for our liberation. We will know where to focus our efforts and what methods we should use to facilitate that process. When we know that the body is a temporary dwelling place for the embodied Self, we develop dispassion and detachment towards it and turn to our spiritual nature to become absorbed in it. The Bhagavadgita affirms that those who know Purusha and Prakriti along with the gunas will not take birth again in this mortal world even if they are engaged in actions (13.22). They go to the Supreme Lord (13.34).

Conquering the Ego, the False Self

In this world, it is very difficult to live without identity and individuality. These two aspects of our personalities define us and introduce us to the world. Without them, we cannot manage our lives or relate to others meaningfully. Imagine what happens if you wake up one day and forget who you are. Your life will be in chaos. It happens to some unfortunate individuals when they wake up from a long coma or suffer from damage to their brain tissue. Your identity is like your address in God's creation. It grows with you, and so does your individuality. They keep changing as you accumulate knowledge and experience and learn to manipulate your way through the world and relationships. Your individuality is what you build and live with. You may consider it an asset or a burden. For spiritual people, it is a problem as well as a burden, but for the worldly, it is an asset and the means to draw their respective territories and establish their zones of influence. People spend their whole lives defending it, upholding it, promoting it, and protecting it. You do not know how your life will be if you silence your individuality, do not know who you are, or become a different person by chance.

The ego is the sum of the experiences, perceptions, memories, knowledge, and relationships gathered by each being in the course of its existence upon earth. It is an illusion created by their aggregation. It does not actually exist except as a notion in the consciousness of each being. You will not find the ego in its parts, but only in the things and experiences with which it becomes associated or for which it engages in actions. It survives by actions, attachments, possessions, and relationships. You remove its parts from the equation, and the ego disappears instantly. Hence, your individuality is a self-created myth that perpetuates for a lifetime and controls the jiva as its false master. You defend it, uphold it, and promote it as if it is all that matters. In the end, you will pay the price for all the excesses you committed to satisfy its demands and desires and ensure its survival. When the diverse components of your individuality disperse or return to their sources, your ego vanishes. What is left after that is a mystery, which we have been trying to understand since the dawn of our civilization. Is there anything knowable beyond your known identity and individuality? "Yes," say the Hindus; and "No," say the Buddhists. You do not have to agree with either of them. You have a choice. You can wait until Nature disintegrates and disperses your ego and all that you build in the vain hope of surviving death, or you can do it yourself through yoga and self-transformation and see what happens. The yogis do it. Painstakingly, they remove or weaken the forces that keep their egos intact and active. When they do it, they fall into silence. They become the silent ones (munis) with subdued egos, desires, and attachments. Unfortunately, most of them do not feel the need to let others know what goes on in them or what happens when their egos fall into silence. They live as if they do not exist. Perhaps, they want to convey this important lesson by setting an example through their conduct. When the ego falls silent, all the seeking and striving come to an end as one becomes almost nonexistent and immaterial to the material world.

In worldly life, the ego is the facilitator, but in spiritual life, it is an obstacle. It is also often described as the false self or the lower self, which is even compared symbolically in some traditions to the enemy within or the demon. It is responsible for our individuality, duality, and beingness. It creates and perpetuates in us the idea that, individually, we are distinct and different from the rest of the world, and we need to work for our survival and well-being. Because of egoism, we assume ownership and doership and perform actions to satisfy our desires and secure our attachments.

The ego touches every aspect of our worldly existence. It is our spokesperson, our message, and our front. The life that we lead here upon earth is essentially its creation. The Bhagavadgita is very much a conversation between the human ego and the eternal Self. Arjuna stands symbolically for the ego-self, while Lord Krishna represents the individual Self or the Supreme Self. Arjuna's suffering is the suffering of an ego bred on ignorance, delusion, egoism, passions, desires, and attachments. It arose from his limited knowledge, his sense of separateness, his identification with his name and form, his attachment to his body, his belief that he was the doer of his actions, and his anxiety about the outcome of his actions for which he thought he was responsible. He suffered from doubt and despair when he assumed responsibility for his actions, for waging a terrible war against people with whom he developed attachment, and thought of the consequences arising from them as directly influencing his life and future. In that state of anxiety and confusion and taking upon himself the burdens of his life, he did not remember God as the all-pervading Supreme Lord or His role in his life or the lives of all others, even though Lord Krishna, God-incarnate, was right in front of Him, acting as his charioteer.

Clearly, Arjuna was acting under the influence of his ego, which suffers from fear, anxiety, and confusion in stressful situations because of its limited knowledge and inability to comprehend the bigger picture or the role of God in our lives and destinies. The ego is bound to the knowledge it accumulates. It is created by that knowledge only. Hence, it cannot see anything beyond duality and distinction or beyond its limited perspective. For the same reasons, conflict and confusion are rooted in its consciousness, actions, and reactions. These tendencies were well reflected in Arjuna's suffering and the doubts and moral problems he expressed about fighting the war against his relations and acquaintances. He had delusions about his own identity as he identified himself with his name and form, and thought of others in the same way.

Identification with one's own name and form is considered egoism. However, identification with the inner Self or the Supreme Self is not considered so, although the Self is also an ego (aham) of the transcendental kind. When you identify yourself with your pure Self completely in a state of withdrawal and self-absorption, it leads to your transformation and the realization that you are none other than Brahman only (*aham brahmasmi*).

According to the Bhagavadgita, the earth, water, fire, air, mind, intelligence, and ego constitute the eightfold division of the material Nature of Brahman (7.4). Lord Krishna describes it as His inferior Nature. In the beings, it represents the physical Self or the ego-self. At the highest level in creation, it represents the whole creation which arises from Him as His projection: Isvara, Purusha, Brahma, or all Manifested Materiality (sambhuta), all His creative energies, manifestations (vibhutis), worlds (lokas), gods, goddesses, celestial beings, demons, and living beings (jiva-bhutam). The dualistic schools refer to it as His universal form (visvarupam) or cosmic body. The pure

Self and the physical self both exist in the same body, but as distinct entities with no relationship or correlation whatsoever between them. However, in the journey of liberation, their relationship assumes greater significance. The ego must be purified, subdued, and transformed into a friend of the Self, so that it ceases to be an obstacle to liberation and the source of delusion and desires. As the scripture declares, in the ignorant and deluded ones, the ego is the enemy of the Self, whereas in those who conquer the lower nature by their higher nature, it becomes a friend (6.5). They become the conquerors of their minds and bodies (jitatma), remaining the same in cold and heat, pain and pleasure, and honor and dishonor (6.7). Therefore, Lord Krishna says that His devotees who aspire for liberation should take refuge in the inner Self and surrender to God, performing actions without desires and renouncing the fruit of such actions as a sacrifice. In other words, they must surrender their ego, recognize God as the doer of all their actions, engage in karma-sannyasa, and desist from acting as their spiritual enemies.

In the Bhagavadgita, we find many references to ego (aham) and the importance of transforming it for perfection and success in yoga. It identifies it as one of the tattvas of Prakriti and the body as the Field (kshetra) (13.6), which is subject to modifications, such as aging, sickness, birth, death, rebirth, sorrow, anger, and the duality of attraction and aversion. The ego is subject to the influence of the gunas. It is responsible for the modifications (vrittis) of the mind, aiding and abetting desire-ridden actions and keeping the mind and senses in the outward mode. Hence, the Bhagavadgita says that a person who is without ego (anahamvadi) is dearer to God. Egolessness (nirahamkaram) is a divine quality (13.12), which arises from the predominance of sattva (18.26), and leads to peace (2.71) and equanimity. He who is without ego, he alone is fit for self-realization (18.54). Actions do not taint him because he acts without egoism (ahamkritva bhava). Since he does not let his ego participate in his actions, he does not act even if he acts (18.18). Therefore, he is not bound. In contrast, demonic people act egoistically. They perform actions selfishly for themselves or to satisfy their egos. Selfishness is a demonic quality. Since it arises from the ego, egoism is also a demonic quality (17.6), which leads to ignorance and downfall. Men of demonic resolve perform severe penances and torture their minds and bodies without discrimination, out of vanity, pride, delusion, and egoism (17.6). Their actions lead to bondage and suffering rather than liberation.

Because of egoism, we believe that we are the doers of our actions and are responsible for them and their outcome. Because of it, we crave things and perform actions out of desires and attachments. In the process, we become bound to the mortal world. The Bhagavadgita says that it is delusional to think that you are the source of your actions. You perform actions because of the gunas that are inherent in you. They induce desires and desire-ridden actions. They perform all actions as they tend to compete and suppress each other for predominance and control. An egoistic and ignorant person wrongly believes that he is the doer (3.27) while performing actions, whereas he performs them under their influence. The wise ones know it. Therefore, when they perform actions, they think that the gunas in them are active, and their bodies perform actions because of them. The first step to overcoming the problem of karma is to recognize this fundamental truth and offer all actions and their fruit to God, not taking any credit or discredit for their outcome. A karmayogi, who is pure in his heart and restrains his mind and senses, overcomes his egoistic thinking and limited vision, and practices karma sannyasa. He sees himself in all living beings and remains free even though he is engaged in actions (5.7).

Depending upon how we approach it, the ego-self can become either an ally or an impediment in our spiritual liberation. If we purify it and align it with our spiritual values, it becomes our friend and facilitates our liberation. Conquering the ego, therefore, is vital to achieve perfection and skillfulness in yoga. He who subdues and silences his ego and all the traces of individuality and separation from his consciousness earns the right to enter the Abode of the Supreme Self. He remains stable and serene in all circumstances. When he reaches that state, he becomes free from anger, pride, greed, envy, fear, and delusion. Freed from all desires, passions, and attachments, he believes that he does nothing while seeing, hearing, touching, smelling, tasting, walking, sleeping, and breathing (5.8). With his ego subdued, he attains union with the Universal Self and develops a unified vision through which he sees the Self in all and all in the Self (6.29). He finds

God everywhere and worships Him as the Inhabitant of all beings (6.31). He reaches the profound conclusion that he is indeed none other than Brahman Himself.

Achieving egolessness

How can we overcome egoism and achieve egolessness? Egoism manifests in many ways and perpetuates itself in many ways. The ego fights for its survival until the end. The problem we have in subduing our egos is that we have to do it within ourselves using the very faculties that tend to support it and are influenced by it. In other words, you must subdue yourself by yourself. This, indeed, is very difficult. You can fight against external enemies. However, fighting against yourself within yourself and by yourself, living as if you do not exist and do not matter, is a huge challenge. Many advanced yogis, who spend years transforming their minds and bodies to subdue their egos, also find it very difficult to achieve complete success. Their egoism shows itself in weak moments when they are careless, disturbed, opposed, or challenged.

Egoism does not mean having pride or attachment to your identity and individuality only. In spirituality, it has wider implications. It is not only having the notion that you are a distinct person or entity separate from God and the rest of creation, but also entertaining any thought, desire, or feeling to which you may be particularly drawn and with which you may identify. In other words, if you have any opinion, any selfish thought, any desire to protect and defend yourself, any notion of ownership or doership, know that your ego is still active and exerting its influence upon you. If you feel the need to defend yourself or your views and opinions, know that you have an ego. If you react to any situation or event in any manner due to anger, fear, pride, or envy, know that you have an ego. If you are preoccupied with yourself or with your interests, that is also a sign of egoism. Any sign of restlessness and disturbance also denotes that your ego is still active. In short, if you defend yourself, promote yourself, speak for yourself, take credit for something, seek recognition, have expectations, claim ownership, or experience fear, anger, greed, envy, or pride, know that you are not yet free from your ego. We know from observation that even after spending years in practice, yogis may still experience egoism in their thinking and behavior. The Puranas show how even seers and sages often succumb to their egos and act irrationally under their influence, creating problems for themselves and others.

The Bhagavadgita touches upon some very important truths about the problem of ego and how it influences our thinking and actions. By meditating on them, we can develop deep insight into the nature of the ego and how it can be purified and subdued through spiritual practice.

1. Ignorant people identify with their minds and bodies, but in truth, each jiva in their pure essence is an eternal and indestructible Self. One should identify with it rather than with the physical self or the ego-self.
2. The body is like a garment. In each life, the Self wears a new body at birth and discards it at death. Similarly, in each life, it assumes a new person, individuality, or ego. Therefore, devotees should not develop any attachment to their minds and bodies or their egos. Cultivating detachment and remaining satisfied within themselves, they must overcome their desires and delusions.
3. All actions arise from the gunas. The gunas arise from Prakriti, and Prakriti is an integral part of God, the Lord of the Universe, who is the real doer and the source of all. Therefore, one should renounce egoism, delusion, ownership, and doership and engage in actions as an offering to God and without desiring their fruit.
4. The gunas and the impurities they induce strengthen the ego. To overcome this, one may cultivate sattva in the initial stages, but eventually, a yogi must transcend all the gunas since the ego remains active as long as the gunas are active.
5. The ego is difficult to overcome. However, it can be subdued through detachment and persistent practice of karma sannyasa, offering all actions to God and practicing sameness, self-control, and exclusive devotion.
6. Attachment to your name and form is a lifeline and major source of nourishment for your ego. Any weakness on your part keeps your ego alive. When you are devoted to your ego, you will remain under its influence and serve its aims.

Therefore, you must become a God's devotee rather than your ego's devotee and cut it from all sides by not letting it control your thoughts and actions and not nourishing it by any egoistic effort or undertaking. When you saturate your mind with devotion to God, your ego gradually loses its influence and falls silent.

7. Knowledge and wisdom are essential to discern things clearly and overcome egoism, ignorance, and delusion. When you cultivate discernment and right knowledge through self-purification and the practice of yoga, you become centered in your pure Self rather than your ego, overcome the duality and delusion arising from your ego, and experience oneness.

Divine Qualities of Pure Souls

Good and evil constitute one of the fundamental dualities. Human beings must choose their side and which qualities they want to reflect. The Bhagavadgita puts significant emphasis on inner purity and unwavering sincerity in the practice of yoga for liberation. The inner Self is the witnessing Self. It is ever awake and attentive to our actions and mental formations, but completely untouched by them and the phenomenal world. It is forever pure, even when it exists in the body of the lowest organisms. It watches our actions, interactions, and modifications and enjoys the perceptions brought in by our senses without becoming involved and without participating in them. In contrast, the mind and the body are vulnerable to various forces: our actions and impurities (adhyatma), the actions and impurities of others and the world (adhibhautika), and the actions of God or Fate (adhidaivika). Even a simple and vague subconscious thought, memory, or suggestion can hurt you and delay your progress. A spiritually active person must, therefore, be careful about his thoughts and actions and remain on guard always, examining his motives and paying attention to his hidden desires and unresolved passions.

In the practice of yoga, purity, sincerity, and honesty are important. You must be true and honest with yourself, acknowledging your faults and mistakes, and without deluding yourself. You must also make the necessary effort to correct yourself, going the extra mile if necessary, to remove any traces of evil. Self-realization is a mirage for those who indulge in outward religiosity, without discipline and without making the corresponding effort to purify themselves. To experience peace and equanimity, you must fill your mind and body with sattva and suppress rajas and tamas. Without purity, you may practice yoga for years, but you will remain vulnerable to your passions and desires. A yogi who is balanced and skillful (yukta) in his methods and practice is always on guard. He would not allow his ego to take control or defend him. A spiritualized ego is an even bigger problem in overcoming selfishness and attachments than an ordinary and simple ego that is content with its habitual actions and does not indulge in delusions of grandeur. Unless we are careful, the very religion that intends to deliver us from sinful actions may become a tool in the hands of our manipulative egos and a major source of delusion and distraction.

When we bring our worldliness into our religious practice and develop attachment to a particular religion, God, scripture, or guru, we fall into the trap of our egos, set by Maya, and lead ourselves astray. In such cases, people may also develop negativity and aversion towards other faiths and become involved in harmful actions, negating the very principles they are supposed to follow. It is equally detrimental to our spiritual progress if we become attached to our gods and religions and forget the purpose of overcoming dualities and cultivating sameness, which the Bhagavadgita equates with yoga or the highest state of yoga. God's true devotees should stay away from these negative and destructive tendencies, which arise from the gunas. As the Bhagavadgita declares clearly, one should neither be the cause of disturbance to others nor be disturbed by them. They are considered the stable-minded yogis (sthithaprajna). They attain the highest state of yoga by transcending both attraction (raga) and aversion (dvesha), not only in worldly matters but also in spiritual practice. In the final stages, they even become detached from their objects of worship and their methods of practice, renouncing all striving and seeking, and surrendering themselves to God and His will.

On the path of liberation, our success depends very much on our transformation and purification and on developing certain auspicious qualities that strengthen our divine nature and bring us closer to God. Self-purification is of the utmost importance in the practice of yoga and is the foremost purpose of any spiritual practice in the early stages. We may read scriptures or perform rituals and sacrifices out of genuine interest, but they are of no value unless we remove the impurities of our minds and bodies and practice virtues unconditionally. Without purity, no one can achieve self-realization. No one can cross the ocean of samsara with an impure nature. No one can realize the Self if the mind is filled with passions and emotions. On the path of yoga, inner cleanliness (antar-suddhi) is more important than even physical purity. A yogi may live in an unclean place or ignore his bodily care out of pure indifference, as followers of some ascetic traditions do. However, spiritual practitioners must keep their minds clean and pure and under firm control. If the mind is enveloped in ignorance and delusion, it remains this worldly, bound to Nature and its modifications. Impure souls cannot join the pure souls of the immortal world even during the final dissolution. This is an undeniable spiritual truth affirmed in the Vedas. Unless one practices self-discipline and cultivates divine qualities that are enumerated in the Bhagavadgita, it is not possible to experience self-absorption (atma samyama) and oneness with the Self. Unless the higher mind (buddhi) is made pure like a clear diamond, with rules and restraints (yamas and niyamas), withdrawal of the mind and senses, concentration, meditation, and balance (samyama), it can neither reflect the radiance of the Self nor reveal the truths that are hidden beyond the objective realm.

The human personality is a mixture of both divine and demonic qualities. We are part animal, part human, and part divine. Our consciousness is permeated with them and the qualities and nature they represent. We have the potential to manifest them, strengthen them, or weaken them according to our nature, actions, aims, and aspirations. We can either rise to the heights of virtue or fall into the depths of sin. We can fill our lives with God and light or plunge ourselves into utter darkness. We channel divine or demonic energies, depending upon whom we nourish through our actions and sacrifices. The Bhagavadgita, therefore, offers us a choice: whether we want to act constructively or destructively and whether we want to be our own friends or enemies. It wants us to decide whether we prefer to achieve liberation and escape from this world through yoga by cultivating divine nature and surrendering to God, or cultivate demonic qualities and remain bound to samsara. The paths to Brahman are many, and we may reach Him by any path and from any direction. What matters is achieving liberation. Lord Krishna affirms clearly in the scripture that in whatever direction people worship Him, He strengthens their faith in that direction. A devotee may practice sattvic, rajasic, and tamasic devotion according to his nature. Each of them leads to different ends. Sattvic people worship God, restraining their minds and senses. Rajasic people worship God's creation and worldly things to satisfy their passions and desires. Tamasic people worship whatever appeals to them with delusion and ignorance. The first approach leads to salvation, the second one to bondage and rebirth, and the third one to delusion and spiritual downfall.

To achieve liberation, spiritual people must cultivate purity, subdue their egos, overcome delusion and desires, and nurture or strengthen their divine nature, so that they remain in harmony with their noblest and highest ideals in a state of peace and equanimity. They must divinize their lower nature so that it becomes a friend to their higher nature rather than its enemy and is illuminated. In simple and practical terms, this means that a yogi must lead a virtuous life and practice virtuous conduct. At every crucial moment in his life, he must turn to God for solutions and follow the guidance found in the scriptures or the examples set by others who have traveled a similar journey in the past. A true devotee does not compromise his ideals; he will not forsake virtue. He will remain loyal to God by practicing the divine qualities He embodies. This process gradually removes all notions of separation and distinction from Him and allows His radiance to shine through. When your mind becomes pure and divine, it opens up to higher intelligence and remains stable in the contemplation of Brahman. True knowledge arises from sattva, and devotion becomes possible only when your mind and heart are filled with it. We will be able to perform desireless actions without seeking their fruits only in a sattvic state.

Divine qualities

The Bhagavadgita provides ample information on the role of the triple gunas: how they manifest different qualities, traits, tendencies, likes, and dislikes, and influence our nature, character, and conduct. It describes the divine qualities that result in divine nature, virtuous conduct, and liberation, and the demonic qualities that lead to evil conduct. By explaining what leads to liberation and what leads to suffering and spiritual condemnation, it encourages us to live righteously, perform our obligatory duties, cultivate divine qualities instead of the demonic ones, and work for our final liberation. The scripture lists several divine qualities (daiva sampada), such as the following, that are helpful to cultivate nearness to God and attain oneness with him.

- Fearlessness (abhayam)
- Predominance of sattva (sattva samsuddhi)

- Knowledge (jnanam)
- Charity (danam)
- Self-restraint (damah)
- Study of scriptures (svadhyaya)
- Austerity (tapah)
- Simplicity (arjavam)
- Non-violence (ahimsa)
- Truthfulness (satyam)
- Freedom from anger (akrodha)
- Self-giving (tyaga)
- Peacefulness (santih)
- Non-slandering (apaisunam)
- Compassion (daya)
- Absence of greediness (aloluptam)
- Gentleness (mardavam)
- Modesty (hrih)
- Unwavering (achapalam)
- Radiance (tejah)
- Forgiveness (ksama)
- Resoluteness (dhritih)
- Cleanliness (saucam)
- Without malice and treachery (adroham)
- Without self-importance

In addition to these qualities, Lord Krishna also describes qualities of those devotees who are suitable for liberation or have achieved excellence and perfection in yoga. They are stated below.

- The perfected ones are non-deluded. They know Brahman as the unborn (ajam), without a beginning (anadim), and Lord of the world (loka mahesvaram) (10.03).
- They know Him, His manifestations (vibhutis) and divine powers (yogas), and worship Him with the utmost devotion (10.07), as the source and origin of all (10.08).
- Meditating on Him, with their minds forever absorbed in Him, surrendering to Him, speaking of Him, and enlightening one

another about Him, they live their lives devoted to Him exclusively (10.09).
- Restraining their senses with sameness, they take delight in the welfare of beings (bhuta hitam).
- They are firmly balanced and settled in contemplation (yuktatamah), endowed with supreme faith (sraddhah), and ever worshipful (12.2).
- They have intelligence, knowledge, compassion, truthfulness, sameness, and mastery over their minds and bodies (10.04).
- They meditate upon Him as the omniscient, most ancient, universal lord, smaller than the smallest, upholder of all, of inconceivable form, golden-hued and beyond darkness (8.9).
- They are free from malice and hatred, compassionate, egoless, devoid of ownership, detached, forgiving, even-minded, skillful, pure-minded, impartial, and free from sorrow, joy, impatience, fear, and distress (2.13, 14 & 16).
- Their minds are placid and absorbed in Brahman. With their rajasic nature subdued, they are without impurities (6.27).
- They are impartial, detached, and desireless. Hence, they regard all equally, whether one is a Brahmana, a learned person, a person of virtue, a cow, an elephant, a dog, or even a lowly and unclean person (5.18). They are disinterested in gain and loss, treating all conditions and circumstances with equal sameness (5.20).
- They live as if they do not exist and do not matter, do not disturb anyone, and are undisturbed by anyone. They are free from joy, impatience (amarsa), fear, and distress (12.15).
- They neither rejoice nor hate, nor lament, and renounce both auspicious and inauspicious moments and situations (12.17).
- They worship God with exclusive faith, regarding Him as their Supreme Goal (12.20) and the inexhaustible source of all beings (9.13). Always speaking highly of Him, striving with firm vows, and offering their salutations to Him, they engage in yoga to attain Him with undivided minds and steadfast devotion, forever absorbed in Him (9.13 & 14).

Demonic Qualities of the Wicked

We have learned about divine qualities in the previous chapter. Let us now focus on the demonic qualities (asura sampada) or the evil tendencies (prvrittis) that manifest in God's creation. Both divine and demonic qualities are a part of the illusion of the dualities He creates with His manifesting and deluding power (yogamaya) to control His creation. They are opposed to each other and try to suppress each other wherever they have an opportunity. As long as they are in balance, creation remains stable. When that balance is lost, the worlds fall into chaos, necessitating divine intervention.

Demonic qualities are negative traits meant to create chaos and disorder, provide a stark contrast, and offer humans a choice or an alternate way of life. They interfere with our spiritual practice, cause mental afflictions (kleshas) and disturbances (vrittis), and lead us in the wrong direction (durgati) away from our divine nature. The demons represent the evil forces of the universe. They are forever in conflict with the gods, the forces of light. God is the balancing power. He makes sure that the demons stay in their ordained spheres and do not disrupt the universal order or spread chaos and terror, which they love to do whenever they get an opportunity. The demons not only live in the sunless worlds (asurya lokas) where the light of Brahman does not reach due to the thick cloud of impurities that envelope them, but are also found in various aspects of creation, including our minds and bodies, as tendencies, potentials, and impulses. When they invade humans or prevail in them, they personify demonic nature, lose their virtue, knowledge, and intelligence, and indulge in senseless acts of violence, anger, cruelty, delusion, greed, pride, and lust.

According to our tradition, the earth and human life have a special significance in God's creation. Liberation is not possible unless souls take birth in a human body in the mortal world and work for it. Similarly, the risk of committing sin and falling into the lowest hell also arises when souls are born in the mortal world and engage in desire-ridden actions. Even gods cannot attain liberation unless they are born in our world. Hence, whoever from the higher worlds wants to attain liberation must take birth in our world and engage in spiritual practice to qualify for it. The same is true for demons. They must take human birth to enhance their powers or acquire spiritual powers.

This world is a battleground for gods and demons where they have a chance to increase their numbers and strength. The gods need humans for sacrificial food, and demons need humans to gather strength or spread their evil influence by feeding on our evil thoughts, passions, and impulses. Both sides are always looking for opportunities to prevail over each other by establishing their control over mortals. They do it mostly by influencing our thoughts and actions so that they can derive their nourishment from us. If humans practice virtues, cultivate divine qualities, and nourish the gods, the gods will gain strength. The opposite will happen if they cultivate demonic qualities and nourish the demons through their thoughts and actions. Thus, our lives and the fate of our world are shaped mostly by how we interact with gods and demons, which qualities we cultivate, and whom we support and nourish through our thoughts and actions.

Those who seek liberation must know how demonic nature arises and manifests in humans, how it can interfere with our lives and actions, and how we can protect ourselves from it. The knowledge will help us remain on the bright or right side of things. By avoiding demonic qualities and staying away from those who possess them, we can minimize our chances of falling into degradation. If you know how demonic people live and act, you can shun their company and save yourself from a great calamity, for it is a calamity, indeed, to fall into the company of demonic people or become like them. We need to know the distinction between divine and demonic qualities, so that we can develop discernment and make right choices in guiding our lives towards light and liberation, and for those who depend upon us or look to us for inspiration and guidance. By knowing the distinction between the two and cultivating proper discernment, we can lead righteous lives, perform our obligatory duties in obedience to the will of God, and qualify for His grace. At the same time, we can also avoid becoming vehicles of demonic forces and falling into depravity and degradation.

Being deluded and ignorant by nature, human beings have the potential to be good or evil depending upon the choices they make and the attitude with which they seek things and perform their actions. Since we are modeled after the Cosmic Being (Purusha), we contain within ourselves all the essential aspects of creation in the form of organs, components (tattvas), and energies. Depending upon our purity and propensity, we may nurture either the gods or the demons that reside in us. If we nourish the divinities with sattvic food and good thoughts and actions, we allow the divinities in us to grow in strength and help us in our self-transformation and liberation. In contrast, if we nurture the demons in us, they grow in strength and transform our minds and bodies into virtual hells. What we do and what we strengthen in our consciousness, therefore, is of utmost importance in our lives and our wellbeing. So is the case with the food we eat. If we eat sattvic food, we grow into gods. If we eat tamasic food, we let darkness prevail in us.

The Bhagavadgita describes demonic beings as destructive, cruel, and deluded entities who do not acknowledge God or His role as the Creator, Preserver, and Destroyer of the worlds. Because of their ignorance, they neither worship Him nor offer their respect. Instead, they detest Him or envy Him. Even if they do worship Him, they do so out of egoism and vanity, to satisfy their selfish desires and show off their power and status. For them, the physical Self is the real Self, and the material world is the only reality. They worship God when it suits them, but if it does not benefit them, they will oppose Him and fight against Him.

Impurity is for the mind and the body. The Self is always pure and resplendent, even in its embodied state. It is impervious to evil. However, if one engages in evil actions, it remains bound to the mortal world, enveloped in ignorance. The physical Self and the inner Self are the two fundamental aspects of a living being. By its actions and attachments, the physical self binds the immortal Self to the cycle of births and deaths. Therefore, for the deluded and ignorant, their minds and bodies become their chief obstacles to peace and equanimity. Unless they purify their minds and bodies and surrender themselves to God, they will remain deluded and distracted from the goal of liberation. We find a reference to these two selves in the Upanishads as the two birds perched on the tree of life; one eats and enjoys the sweet and bitter fruit of the tree, while the other bird, the Self, calmly watches.

The tree symbolically represents the body; the enjoying bird represents the ego or the physical self, and the witnessing bird represents the immortal Self. When the two are in harmony, peace prevails. When they are not, chaos and disorder will reign.

Due to the presence of impurities in our consciousness, we tend to indulge in actions that lead to our suffering and bondage. We live with the belief and the illusion that somehow the laws of life do not apply to us, and somehow we remain untouched by the consequences of our actions and the impermanence of life. With that assumption, we live as if Nature is going to make an exception out of us and keep us alive for long, free from the process of aging and dying. Alternatively, we do not believe in any of these and live as if God does not exist, and nothing remains after death. If it were not so, a majority of people on earth would live their lives responsibly and work for their salvation. Since this is not happening, it means most of us lack faith (sraddha) and remain wedded to our egoistic thinking and selfish actions. Some would even go to the extreme and become demonic. They completely give themselves over to demonic nature and create for themselves great misery.

The practice of virtue is necessary for our liberation. The rules and restraints prescribed on the path of yoga are vital to bring about a transformation in ourselves. Studying scriptures like the Bhagavadgita and assimilating their teachings helps us greatly to cultivate right conduct and lead god-centric lives on the path of righteousness. Knowledge comes in two ways, and both are essential to overcome our ignorance and suppress the latent demonic tendencies inherent in our nature. One is the intellectual knowledge, which arises from study (svadhyaya), and the other is the experiential knowledge, which arises from transcendental experiences arising from regular and persistent practice (abhyasa). Both lead to the refinement of character and discerning wisdom whereby we know what leads to liberation and what contributes to bondage.

In the 16th chapter of the Bhagavadgita, we find a very detailed description of the demonic qualities of the wicked people and the consequences arising from them. Lord Krishna explains that there are two types of beings in the world, the divine and the demonic. Divine tendencies lead to liberation and the demonic ones to bondage and suffering. The scripture declares that those who fall deeply into evil ways belong to the lowest of humanity. Because of their demonic nature, they are cast forever into unclean and demonic wombs. Born thus in evil wombs, birth after birth, they sink into the lowest hells (16.19 & 20). What leads to such a vile nature? Lord Krishna says that lust (kama), anger (krodha), and greed (lobha) are the triple gates of hell. They lead to one's downfall. Those who are liberated from them will work for their spiritual welfare. However, those who disobey the scriptural injunctions and act under the influence of their lustful passions attain neither perfection, nor happiness, nor the Highest Goal.

The Bhagavadgita's (16.06) assertion about divine and demonic beings is also attested by other scriptures. We also get a fair view of their respective qualities by studying them. According to the Upanishads, in the early stages of creation, Brahma created demons, gods, and humans in the same order. Human beings are vital to the other two classes. They not only share both types of qualities but also assist both groups by nourishing them according to their nature. Demons prefer darkness because of their tamasic quality, whereas gods prefer light because of their sattvic nature. Demons perform actions selfishly out of vanity and egoism. Gods perform them selflessly as an offering to God. By nature, demons are cruel and inflict pain to pleasure upon their targets. Gods are pleasure-oriented. After enjoying sacrificial food from the worshippers, they bestow peace and happiness on them. Demons are opposed to God. Gods obey Him and follow His laws and instructions. They uphold Dharma and assist God in upholding it. Demons love to spread chaos, confusion, and disorder. Gods spread peace, happiness, and orderliness. Demons regard the mind and the body as the true Self. Gods view the mortal bodies as temporary subjects to death, disease, and destruction. Demons live as if there is no life beyond death, although they are subject to death and destruction. They always look for opportunities to attain immortality but do not succeed, while gods are immortals and last until the end of creation.

The following list of demonic qualities is based on the teachings of the Bhagavadgita. They suggest why it is important to stay on the side of the gods rather than that of the demons.

- **Lack of discrimination**: Demonic people lack discrimination because their intelligence is deluded by ignorance and impurities.

They do not know what actions to perform and what to avoid (16.7). They consider the enjoyment of desires the highest goal instead of liberation (16.11).

- **Lack of balance**: Demonic people lack balance. They go to extremes in their actions and opinions, giving little thought to their strengths and weaknesses, and acting in disproportion to their wealth or power.
- **Lack of virtue**: Demonic people do not believe in virtuous conduct. They do not care about cleanliness or follow the traditions and customs (acharam) that are necessary to ensure order and regularity or avoid sinful conduct. They lack truthfulness. Filled with lust, vanity, pride, and arrogance, and because of delusion and ignorance, they pursue illusory things and engage in unclean actions. They are self-centered, selfish, egoistic, and narrow-minded, and indulge immediate gratification without worrying about the consequences (16.14).
- **Lack of knowledge**: They hold distorted views about the nature of the world and creation, thinking that the world is unreal, without foundation, and exists solely because of sexual activity (16.08). Deluded by ignorance, not knowing the true nature of their essential nature, they take pride in their birth, family lineage, wealth, and religiosity (16.15).
- **Lack of compassion**: Since they cannot discern the truth of their existence, they engage in hostile and cruel actions seeking the destruction of the world (16.09).
- **Lack stability**: Demonic people suffer from countless worries until their death, as they give themselves completely to the enjoyment of worldly pleasures (16.11)
- **Lack of respect for truth and justice**: Driven by expectations and given over to thoughts of lust and anger, they try to amass wealth by unjust and unlawful means for the fulfillment of desires.
- **Lack of respect for tradition**: Conceited, arrogant, proud, and intoxicated by wealth, they perform sacrifices insincerely or superficially due to vanity, often disregarding the norms and established traditions (16.17).
- **Lack of devotion to God**: Given over to egoism, vanity, strength,

lust, and anger, they hate God and envy Him, even though He abides in them and others (16.18). Carried away by delusion, they do not recognize Him as the supreme and Imperishable (7.13). Therefore, they do not worship Him (7.15).

- **Lack of respect for the inner Self**: Lacking knowledge and discernment, and not knowing His Supreme State as the Supreme Lord, they disrespect the Self that lives within their bodies (9.11). Instead of taking refuge in Him, they take refuge in their demonic nature (9.12)

Demonic people of the Age of Kali

In this age of Kali, the world will increasingly become vulnerable to demonic nature, whereby people lose their sense of right and wrong and become materialistic and excessively evil. As a spiritual guru once remarked, in the beginning, the demons used to live in distant lands of total darkness. Later, they began living in nearby places, where light could not enter. Now they are living within ourselves and amidst us, as the world is becoming increasingly evil and chaotic, and more people are falling under the influence of the impure gunas. As a result, now they are not only controlling us from outside but also from inside. The demons are on the verge of conquering the world, at least temporarily, until, hopefully, another incarnation manifests. Even religions and spirituality are not free from their sway. As Aurobindo once said, wealth, money, and their circulation are already under the control of demonic forces. Hence, we have so much inequality and suffering in the world, and more money is spent on wars and destruction by many nations rather than on the welfare of all. In the Mahanirvana Tantra, Goddess Parvati speaks about how evil nature manifests in the Age of Kali. Her revelations are summarized below [1].

- It will be an age of sin, full of evil customs and deceit, as Dharma will be destroyed, and people pursue evil ways.
- The Vedas will lose their power. The Shrutis (Vedas) will be forgotten. Many of the Puranas, which contain the glories of the past and describe the ways of liberation, will be destroyed.
- Men will grow averse to religious rites, lose their morality and virtue, and succumb to evil actions. They will lose restraint, maddened by pride, lustful, gluttonous, cruel… addicted to baser

habits..., becoming thievish, calumnious, malicious, quarrelsome..., losing all sense of shame, sin, and fear as they seduce the wives of others.

- The priests will live like the working class. Neglecting their daily sacrifices, they will officiate at the sacrifices of the low. They will become greedy, given over to wicked and sinful acts... Eating unclean food and following evil customs, they will...lust after women, be wicked, and readily barter for money, even their wives, to the low. In short, the only sign that they are Brahmanas will be the thread they wear. Observing no rules in eating, drinking, or in other matters, scoffing at the Dharma Shastras, with no thought of pious speech ever so much entering their minds, they will be bent on injuring the good and the pious.
- Since people of this age are full of greed, lust, and gluttony, because of those evil passions, they will neglect their spiritual practice and will fall into sin. Having drunk a lot of wine for the sake of sensuous pleasures, they will become mad with intoxication, and be bereft of all notion of right and wrong
- Some will violate the wives of others, some will become rogues, and some, in the indiscriminating rage of lust, will go with any woman, whoever she may be.
- Overeating and drinking will make many sick, depriving them of strength and common sense. Disordered by madness, they will meet their death by falling into lakes, pits, or impenetrable forests, or from hills and rooftops.
- While some will be as mute as corpses, others will be chatting endlessly, and yet others will quarrel with their relatives and elders. They will become evil-doers, cruel, and destroyers of Dharma

References

1. The Mahanirvana Tantra, Tantra of the Great Liberation, Translated by Arthur Avalon (Sir John Woodroffe), 1913.

The Body as a Vehicle of the Self

According to our tradition, that which is perishable with a beginning and an end and which is subject to modifications and impermanence is not real. The real must always be self-existent, not occasionally or conditionally but permanently. In other words, only that which is eternally and permanently independent, indestructible, and stable counts as real and standard truth. Everything else is unreal and temporary, a mere appearance that appears and disappears in the phenomenal ocean of life like a wave in an ocean. The ocean of absolute and pure consciousness is real, but the waves that rise and fall in it are not. Pure consciousness is real, whereas the formations or the colorations in that ocean are unreal. Brahman alone satisfies the criteria of absolute reality, while His creation does not qualify.

In Brahman's creation, we are like temporary waves, mere formations that rise and fall while the essence (water) in each of us is the same eternal consciousness. Based on this interpretation, we may consider that the physical self, of which the body is the most important aspect, is not the real self. So are the mind, the senses, and all that exists within their domain. They constitute the visible or the perceptible self or the outer sheath, inside which dwells the true Self (Atman) or the divine being. Identifying oneself with the physical self and accepting it as the true self - this is considered delusion. We all suffer from this delusion so long as we are subject to duality and rely upon our senses alone to discern things. This false identification, which arises from ignorance and the impurities present in our consciousness, is responsible for our bondage and continuation upon earth. We accept the false self as true because we cannot comprehend the truth that exists beyond the domain of the physical self and its instruments.

Arjuna was inundated with sorrow because he was steeped in duality. When he entered the battlefield and saw both the armies arrayed on each side, ready to fight, he saw them as separate and individual entities having distinct names and forms of their own. Therefore, he thought of the fate that was awaiting them and the extent of destruction the war was going to cause. On both sides were his friends and family, people whom he had known for a long time and whom he loved and respected. Fate brought them together. Fate put them in opposing camps. Fate had drawn the lines between good and evil. It had drawn a diverse range of people to the battlefield. Some came out of anger and vengeance to settle past scores. Some came out of social and family obligations. Some came in response to the command of their rulers and generals. Some came as part of their obligatory duties (dharma) to protect the lineage of the Kurus to whom they declared their allegiance. Some came out of pure love and friendship for the people whose victory mattered to them. Whatever the reason might be, they were conditioned to fight and stand for their principles and beliefs, which they believed even if they were wrong. A number of causes precipitated the war. They could have been avoided if good sense had prevailed. However, it was not meant to happen because a war of such magnitude was needed in the divine scheme of things to wipe out evil from the face of the earth and restore Dharma so that the world could once again move forward and progress as ordained.

Those people were not very different from us in terms of their justification for going to war. They resorted to the same approaches, reasons, arguments, and excuses we use in our lives to perform actions or resolve our problems and difficulties. At times, we are propelled by greed, desires, selfishness, anger, lust, or fear. At times, we are inspired by noble intentions and higher ideals to help others or work for their welfare. Sometimes we become overly preoccupied with our interests and ourselves, while sometimes we go out of our way to think of others and help them, even at the cost of our comfort and happiness. In all these situations, we act and react according to our worldviews, knowledge, intelligence, and judgment. We act both rationally and irrationally. In resolving our problems, we do suffer from certain limitations that we cannot easily overcome because of our ignorance, attachments, and our dependence upon our minds and senses. We may excel in the perception of things, but may feel limited in comprehending the ultimate truths of our existence. We cannot see reality through the prism of our minds because we cannot free them from attachments, the gunas, and the dualities of life.

These problems exist as long as we remain attached to our limited thinking and awareness, and as long as we build our dreams and aspirations with egoism and selfishness to protect and promote our names and identities. If we spend our entire lives in the pursuit of things that are impermanent in themselves, at the end of the journey, we feel exhausted and wasted. It is like devoting your life completely to digging a deep well only to know in the end that it does not have a water source. Most of us live our lives this way, striving and struggling for the sake of personal gains, taking pride in our power and position, or our family lineages. Our achievements do not last forever. They do not accompany us to the next world except as undercurrents or unfulfilled desires. When we leave this world, we take but the residue of our actions and aspirations.

Arjuna suffered from sorrow on the battlefield because he falsely identified himself with his physical self, unaware that he was an eternal, inexhaustible, and indestructible soul. He was concerned that the war would cause the death of many people, including great souls like Bhishma and Drona, and lead to the decline of his family. He thought so because he considered others and himself as physical beings and betrayed his attachment to his family and family members by expressing his concern about the impact of war upon them and the possible decline of his family. Like most of us, he lacked the conviction and the belief that he was an eternal soul who was immutable and indestructible. Most importantly, he ignored the role of God in creation. Until Lord Krishna explained to him clearly the difference between the destructible physical self and the indestructible inner Self, he did not look upon himself as an eternal self and consider his life upon earth as a mere interlude in the eternity of God and his existence. Until his mind opened to a new vision of him as an embodied self that lives in the city of nine gates as a temporary guest under the control of Nature, he did not consider his relationships and his attachment to his family an obstacle, and his duty as a warrior could be a source of liberation and self-transformation rather than sin and suffering. We all suffer from this problem, right now at this very moment. It is hard for us to focus on the belief that we are eternal souls. The idea may linger for a while in our minds when we read the scriptures or listen to a discourse, but as soon as we get down to our daily routines, we return to our physical mentality and act like mere mortals.

For liberation and principle-centered spiritual life, one must draw a clear distinction between the body and the Self is important. This knowledge alone has the potential to transform you and take you nearer to God or your pure Self. However, for that, you must live with the conviction that you are an eternal soul and the body is just an outer covering, a vehicle, or an instrument, which you will discard in the end at the time of your departure from this world. The Bhagavadgita draws this distinction clearly. It declares that the body is the Field (kshetra) while the Self is the Knower of the Field. As an instrument of Nature, the body acts as the vehicle of the Self. Your pure Self is not what you think you are. It is different from, and other than, who you think you are. In the deluded state of the jivas, the Self remains hidden. It is known only by those who suppress their desires and attachments and transcend their minds and senses.

An impure body is like a prison house for the Self, while a pure body is like a temple, where the Self radiates its brilliance and sanctifies everything that comes into its vicinity. The physical body is perishable, destructible, and subject to the process of aging, sickness, and disease. It is like the dress we wear. Just as people discard their worn-out clothes and wear new ones, the soul discards worn-out bodies and takes on new ones (2.22). Just as it passes within the same body from childhood to youth and old age in one life, it moves on from one body to another (2.11) from one birth to another. Therefore, the Gita declares that wise men are not deluded (2.13) and do not grieve over the dead or the living (2.11).

The body is an obstacle because it is made up of the gunas and aspects (tattvas) of Nature. It is also a facilitator in our liberation because with discipline and self-control, we can purify it and experience oneness with the Self. For the disciplined and self-restrained, the body is a friend, and for the irresolute and ignorant, it is an enemy. Liberation is possible only when the soul resides in the body as an embodied Self (jivatma). If it leaves the body without settling its past dues, it has to take birth again in another body. The body is thus a prison, but in that prison alone, you have an opportunity to practice yoga and work for your liberation. For a man of discernment, the body is a vehicle of liberation and a temple of God. By entering into that temple and closing all the doors, one can experience peace and unending joy. Therefore, one should treat the body with respect and reverence, without forming attachment to it and without subjecting it to cruelty or extreme austerities.

The body is an instrument of Nature. It is the source and support for the mind and the senses. It is a playground of the gunas and, therefore, subject to modifications. It is made up of five great elements (earth, fire, water, air and ether), the ego, intelligence, the senses (the ears, the eyes, the skin, the tongue, the nose, the hands, the feet, the mouth, the anus and the sexual organ), the mind and the sense objects (the sound, the taste, the touch, the smell, and the shape). Apart from these, the body is also the seat of desire, repulsion, sorrow, bodily parts (sanghatah), dynamism (chaitanyam), determination (dhriti), or will power (13.07).

In the phenomenal world, the body is a formation or secretion of Nature around the Self. Just as an oyster builds a pearl around the particles of dust in its womb, Nature shapes beings around the shining particles of the Supreme Self that are caught in its womb. Enveloping them in layers of ignorance and delusion, it continues its play, subjecting their minds and bodies to innumerable modifications. At the same time, the Self within them remains the Witness and the Enjoyer. The sources of these modifications are the gunas (modes), namely, sattva, rajas, and tamas. Their interplay and inherent tendency to dominate one another induce desires and desire-ridden actions in beings. Thus, the triple gunas are responsible for our delusion and existence upon earth as mortal beings. Under their influence, we suffer from attraction and aversion towards the pairs of opposites and indulge in desire-ridden actions. By assuming ownership and doership for our actions and seeking their fruit, we become bound to the gunas and the results arising from the actions they induce (3.29).

In our practice of yoga, we must cultivate the right attitude towards our bodies. Moderation is the ideal. The Bhagavadgita affirms that a karmayogi who engages his organs in desireless actions, keeping his body and mind under control, remaining mentally detached, offering the fruit of his actions to God, living only to perform bodily functions, becomes liberated from the bondage of birth and death and never returns to the mortal world (3.21-23). For a yogi who has mastered his senses and controlled his mind, even death can be a source of liberation. This is possible because whatever a person thinks and remembers at the time of his death, he attains that only (8.5).

Thus, if a person manages to remember God at the time of his death with complete devotion, practicing yoga and holding his breath between his two eyebrows, he will easily reach Him (8.10). Discipline and sincerity are important. Whoever tries to restrain his organs of action outwardly without inner control and detachment from the sense objects is a man of deluded intellect and a hypocrite (3.06). One should aim for inner control and balance. By closing all the openings of the body, establishing the mind in the heart, fixing the life energy in the head, and uttering the syllable "AUM," a yogi can easily attain the Supreme Self (8.12 & 13). Therefore, a seeker of liberation should restrain his senses and train his mind, practicing buddhi yoga and continuously thinking of God only.

The body has certain natural limitations. One should respect them. Those who ignore this instruction are considered men of demonical resolve. They practice rigorous and extreme penances that are either prohibited or disapproved by the scriptures. Under the influence of lust, delusion, etc., they torture their bodies and the Lord who dwells in them (17.05 & 06). Therefore, moderation is very important. The scripture makes this point clear. The yoga of self-control and liberation is not for one who is a voracious eater or a non-eater. It is also not for him who sleeps too much or who does not sleep at all (6.16). Moderation, regulated diet and relaxation, restrained actions, discipline in sleeping and waking, these practices lead to freedom from sorrow (6.17).

Thus, according to the Bhagavadgita, a yogi should primarily focus on purifying and transforming his body so that it can withstand the rigors of his practice. No one can achieve liberation without a body, so he must ensure that he does not unduly hurt or harm it in his eagerness to make progress. Since it is perishable, he must protect and guard it from harm. Since it is necessary to achieve liberation, he must purify and divinize it so it can become a true vehicle for the pure Self and be fully illuminated by it. The body is a means rather than an end in itself. It is not the sum of our existence but only a part of it. While it may not last forever, it plays an important role in our liberation. Therefore, a yogi must also overcome any attachments he may develop with his name and form. The Bhagavadgita suggests that by detaching oneself from the body, controlling one's mind, becoming aware of the influence of the gunas and the senses, constantly fixing the mind on the Higher Self, and performing daily duties with detachment, one should aim to overcome limitations and achieve liberation.

During spiritual practice, one must learn to live with the pain and the hardship experienced in the body as it goes through various stages of transformation and purification set in motion by austerities and spiritual practices. Sometimes, one may even fall sick as the body fails to absorb the stress caused by the rigorous practice. A yogi should therefore pay close attention to his body. He should take care of it, keep it clean and healthy, respect its limitations and vulnerabilities, and protect it from harm, injury, and the disturbances caused by the impurities and evil forces. He should treat it as a sacred gift from God, a true vehicle of internal and external sacrifices, and engage in bodily actions, such as eating and sleeping, as sacrifices with detachment, offering Him all his actions with surrender and devotion. Establishing his mind in the contemplation of God, seeing the body as his not-self, he should gradually detach himself from his mind and body, suppress all modifications, and attain oneness.

Hindu scriptures, such as the Puranas, suggest that all beings in all the worlds possess bodies. Some are subtle, and some are gross. Mortal bodies contain both gross and subtle aspects. Isvara, the Lord of the Universe, also has a body. The universe itself is considered His body. What Arjuna saw on the battlefield during the discourse was indeed His universal form. The Vedas also described Purusha, the Cosmic Being with innumerable hands, eyes, ears, etc. Indeed, the whole creation is God's universal body. It is so vast that it constitutes but a small aspect of His infinite and absolute existence. All the beings who appear in creation are part of it. As Arjuna saw, it is the sum of everything, past, present, and future. Ignorant people cannot comprehend His universal dimensions and mistake Him for a human if he appears among them in a human form.

Making Sense of the Senses

The sense organs are our windows to the world and our only link to it. Without them, it is impossible to know the world, make sense of it, or relate to the objects in our environment. With their help, we overcome the limitations of space and extend ourselves beyond our bodies into the physical world. Because of them, we have perceptions, dualities, relationships, desires, attachments, delusions, ignorance of transcendental truths, bondage, and suffering. While in the physical world, they are the means by which we gain knowledge, in the spiritual context, they are considered sources of duality, ignorance, and delusion and obstacles to cultivating discernment, sameness, and equanimity. They are also the main sources of cravings, attachments, attraction and aversion, passions, and mental modifications (chittavrittis). Hence, our scriptures emphasize the importance of withdrawing the senses and restraining them to achieve self-control and progress spiritually.

The senses are called Indriyas, which denotes their association with Indra, the lord of the heavens. Symbolically, they are considered the agents of Indra, the cosmic mind. In the Cosmic realm of Purusha, they represent the divine forces of Indra. In a human being, who is considered a replica of God (Purusha), the senses belong to the realm of the mind, which is comparable to Indra and consciousness to sky, heaven or the realm of gods (bhuva), while the body represents the mortal world or earth (bhuh) and the Self represents Purusha and the immortal heaven (suvah). At the individual level, the ego-sense represents the demonic force that is always intent upon overpowering Indra (the mind) and controlling the senses (gods). Philosophically, the senses represent the pleasure principle, peace, and happiness. They are compared to gods, and like gods, they are driven by pleasure and enjoyment, taking delight in pursuing what is pleasant and joyful. They show a strong aversion to the painful and unpleasant experiences, just as the gods are.

Hindu scriptures recognize ten or eleven senses: five organs of action (karmendriyas), five organs of perception (jnanendriyas), and, if we include the mind, which is considered the eleventh, the number comes to eleven. The eyes, ears, nose, skin, tongue, and mouth constitute the organs of perception. They are responsible for our knowledge of the world and the material things. The mouth (as an organ of speech), hands, feet, excretory organs, and reproductive organs constitute the five organs of action. They are responsible for the actions the body performs for the jiva's survival and continuity. They perform mostly body-related actions. There is a fundamental difference between these two types of senses. The organs of perception are outgoing. The organs of action remain attached to the body, while the organs of perception extend far beyond the body into the world and interact with it. The organs of action act according to the information the organs of perception bring and the desires and attachments they create. Both are essential for the survival of the jivas. Together, they constitute the ten senses (13.05). Then there is the mind (manas), which is likened to a sense organ in the Bhagavadgita (15.7). It is the Lord, or the controller of the senses. All the senses act under its control and influence.

In addition to the ten senses we discussed before, there are five other senses known as the subtle senses (tanmatras). They are the functions or purposes of the organs of perception, by which they connect to their objects, namely smelling, tasting, seeing, touching, and hearing. The organs of perception are also aligned with the great elements (mahabhutas): the earth, water, fire, air, and space. In fact, the five subtle senses are considered their source because we know their existence through them and their corresponding organs of perception. Thus, the earth element is associated with the nose and perceived through smelling. The water element is associated with the tongue and experienced through tasting. The fire (light) element is associated with the eyes and experienced through seeing. The air element is associated with the skin and experienced through touching. Finally, the space or ether element is associated with the ear and is perceived through hearing.

The senses are responsible for our awareness and knowledge of the objective world with which we interact. However, they are not perfect instruments of truth. Hence, they are not reliable sources of knowledge or useful in discerning truths from falsehood or reality from unreality. They are also not very useful in knowing transcendental truths beyond the physical domain. In fact, while they are considered vital for our survival upon earth, they are also considered obstacles to self-realization or liberation since they are enveloped by impurities and are chiefly responsible for ignorance, duality, delusion, desires, and attachments. They also limit our knowledge, vision, and wisdom as they induce desires and attachment to names and forms and remain involved with the external world, making the mind restless, distracted, divided, and afflicted. As the Bhagavadgita declares, due to repeated contact with material objects, beings experience desires. From desires, they experience attraction and aversion towards the objects and the dualities of the world. From that, they develop attachment to worldly things. From attachment, they experience conflicting emotions such as anger, fear, anxiety, greed, envy, and pride, which in turn lead to restlessness, instability, and mental afflictions.

Based on our daily experience, we know that we cannot completely depend on our senses to manage our lives or resolve our problems. We are not completely rational since we are subject to emotions and feelings, which interfere with our rationality. Our minds are also subject to several mental distortions that interfere with our perceptions, knowledge, and understanding. The senses provide a limited view of whatever we perceive, since their reach and field of perception are limited. This led people to believe in the past that the Earth was flat or that the sun and moon revolved around it. They believed that several oceans and continents surrounded the Earth, and the stars were shining objects that adorned the heavens. Now, we know that these were misconceptions created by their ignorance and limited knowledge. They also teach us an important lesson: we cannot totally rely upon our senses to know the truths of the world or ourselves. Even in the case of ordinary perceptions, we have to be careful because our perceptions can be colored by our thoughts, attitudes, emotions, beliefs, desires, and prejudices. We create our illusions and fanciful thoughts. We see what we want to see or in what we are most interested. Our opinions and conclusions may not always be right since they are influenced by our egos, desires, interests, and focus. What this means is that we must not assume infallibility but keep an open mind. At the same time, we must look for additional means to validate what we perceive to be the truth.

The Bhagavadgita highlights the negative role played by the senses and how they delude us into bondage and ignorance. It warns people not to rely upon them ignorantly, but to cultivate discerning wisdom so that they can see things as they are and act accordingly. It explains how duality, desires, and attachments arise because of them and how we may escape from their influence and transcend them to realize the transcendental truths. Cravings and the transitory feelings of heat and cold, pain, or the dualities of pleasure and pain arise from the activity of our senses. We cultivate sameness when we learn to tolerate such conditions and states of mind (2.14), and suffer from duality when we indulge in them (5.22). When we keep extending ourselves into the material world through our senses and constantly deal with worldly things, we experience attraction and aversion and engage in desire-ridden action. A yogi and a seeker of liberation should not come under their influence at all (3.34). In the second chapter of the Bhagavadgita, Lord Krishna explains how suffering arises from their actions. Repeated interactions between the senses and their objects lead to attachment, from which anger ensues. Anger leads to delusion, and from delusion arises confusion of memory. From confusion of memory arises loss of intelligence, and when intelligence is lost, the breath is lost (2.60-63). In other words, the senses are responsible for our involvement with the world. They strengthen egoism (ahamkara) and our involvement with the impermanent objects and pleasures of the world.

The scripture suggests withdrawal of the senses with detachment as a solution to stabilize the mind and cultivate equanimity and sameness towards the pairs of opposites. Since the senses are responsible for the instability of the mind and its delusions, they need to be silenced. They can be silenced only by withdrawing them from the external world into oneself and keeping them restrained. Logically, it makes sense because the mind becomes restless mainly because of the outgoing nature of the senses. When they are withdrawn, the mind enjoys temporary relief from the usual noise of the world and experiences peace and stability. The Gita says, by withdrawing his senses completely from the sense objects, the way a tortoise withdraws its limbs, a yogi gains mastery over his senses (2.58). Freeing himself from passion and dispassion, keeping his senses that are acting on the sense objects under his firm control, and by establishing his mind in the Self, he gains God's grace (2.64). Just as wind blows away a floating boat, the senses drive away intelligence when the mind is constantly engaged with worldly objects (2.67). Therefore, a yogi should firmly stabilize his intelligence with resolve by controlling his senses from all directions (2.68). Pratyahara, the withdrawal of the senses (pratyahara) from the objects into oneself, is one of the eight limbs of Classical Yoga. It is the foundational practice for perfection in other limbs, namely, concentration, meditation, and self-absorption.

Withdrawing the senses from the sense-objects with a correct understanding of the role of the senses in our lives is the first important step in stabilizing the mind. It is also the first step towards self-transformation and liberation. However, by itself, it does not guarantee perfection. We must also withdraw our minds from the external world and absorb them in the contemplation of God or the Self. As Lord Krishna says, he whose mind is constantly engaged in the contemplation of God becomes stable and attains liberation. He becomes an ardent devotee of God, whose welfare He personally takes care of. Attachments arise due to the activity of the senses. It, in turn, strengthens egoism and extends its sphere of influence in the objective realm as far as the mind and senses can travel. They take refuge in the ego and follow its commands. By performing desire-ridden actions under its influence, jivas incur sin and remain bound to the world. However, those who take refuge in the Self, practicing detachment and renouncing the fruit of their actions, attain the Highest Abode and never return. By controlling his senses dutifully, he becomes detached from the sense objects and regains his freedom from the compulsion to act according to his desires. With the elimination of desires, he achieves equanimity, peace, freedom from fear, lust, egoism, anger, and such other ungodly qualities. Firmly established on the path of liberation (6.24-29), he becomes stable like an ocean that remains undisturbed although waters from numerous rivers enter it from all directions (2.70).

Although the senses are responsible for our ignorance, delusion, and suffering, they are also helpful. They help us overcome our ignorance, worldly desires, and attachment to our physical selves as we engage them in studying the scriptures, performing selfless and virtuous actions, worshiping God, practicing yoga, participating in devotional services, or cultivating divine qualities. They also help us practice concentration, meditation, and self-absorption and achieve self-control, equanimity, and sameness. By withdrawing them into themselves and subduing their egos, yogis must become witnesses to the actions of their minds and bodies. By cultivating witness consciousness, thus, they must observe the world dispassionately without judgment and attachment to overcome their delusion and cultivate knowledge and discernment. In that state of withdrawal and mindful awareness, they can learn a great deal about themselves and their thinking and behavior. Thus, the senses that are obstacles to achieving peace and equanimity in worldly life can become agents of change and transformation on the path of liberation. When they are withdrawn and restrained, they help the yogis become established in sameness, attain perfection in karma sannyasa, the yoga of knowledge, self-control, renunciation, and devotion, and qualify for God's grace.

Descriptions of the Pure Self

One of the notable differences between Hinduism and Buddhism is about the Self or the soul. Hinduism believes in the existence of the eternal and indestructible Self, known as Atman, whereas Buddhism does not believe in a permanent self. Instead, it believes in the existence of an impermanent self, also called the not-self (anatma). This impermanent self, according to the Buddhist belief, is an aggregation or formation of diverse components, both physical and subtle, which create the illusion of a distinctive personality or individuality and egoism or the feeling of being distinct and separate from others. This not-self, the artificial formation of a being, continues from birth to birth, like a flickering flame, accumulating karma, memories, desires, attachments, and latent impressions, until it attains the indescribable state of nirvana and is fully extinguished. For the Hindus, the Self is immaterial and beyond the mind and the senses. For the Buddhists, it is material and can be discerned through the mind and senses. Since in Hinduism, the Self is unknowable, ungraspable, and indescribable, many speculative theories exist about its essential nature.

In Western traditions, the concept of the Self does not exist. They believe in souls and the world as real. For them, a soul or a spirit is a subtle entity that possesses an ethereal body with a distinctive form it acquires from the physical body during its existence on earth. When a person dies, this distinctive spiritual or ethereal body survives death and continues to exist in the astral realms or in heaven or hell according to its deeds. Hinduism also believes in a subtle body called the karmic body (karana sariram), consisting of karmic memories and latent impressions. However, it is distinct from the Self and works more as an appendage that accompanies the Self to the next world at the time of death. On the other hand, the individual Self is untouched by the being or its actions. It is eternally pure intelligence or consciousness without any materiality, identity, or individuality. Whether it is in the same class of jivas or different classes of jivas, it is always the same: infinite, all-knowing, indistinguishable, and indestructible. In fact, in Hinduism, puritans do not like to refer to the Self (Atman) as a soul because it has no characteristics that distinguish one from another. It is an aspect of God or God Himself, unlike the souls of Western religions that are human, inferior, and distinct from God or the Holy Spirit.

The mind cannot perceive the Self under any circumstances. One may imagine it or speculate about it, but it cannot be seen, heard, or touched. For humans, it is a mystery hidden in the deeper layers of our consciousness. We cannot discern it with our intelligence, nor can we experience it in the state of duality. It is incommunicable. Therefore, we cannot relate to it, except, perhaps, in the transcendental state of oneness where otherness and all notions of subject and object disappear. Since it is indescribable and beyond the mind and the senses, we cannot comprehend its essential nature in human terms. We do not have definitive answers to many questions concerning the Self. How does it exist in the body? How can it be absolute and at the same time have individuality? Where does it exist after its liberation? What happens to it when a being dies? How does it escape from the body, and where does it go after death? In a state of self-realization, do we become the Self or just become aware of its presence in the body? What is the state of a self-realized yogi, and how is it different from ordinary consciousness? These and many other questions are difficult to answer to everyone's satisfaction.

Speculative philosophies and ascetic traditions arose in ancient India to address such questions even before the birth of Mahavira, the last of the Jain Tirthankaras, and the Buddha, the founder of Buddhism. They tried to probe into the depths of the human personality and understand the different states of our existence and consciousness, starting from the wakeful to the deep sleep state. They relied upon various ascetic, meditative, and yogic practices to enter different states of being and experience duality and transcendence in varying degrees. The Vedas, especially the Upanishads, attempt to answer these questions by explaining what the Self is and is not. They conclude that the Self is certainly not the mind and body. They also suggest a special technique called neti-neti ("not this, not this") to distinguish it from all the known aspects of our existence. The sum of that process is that the Self is not a person with a mind and body or a name and form. It is also not the body, the mind, the senses, intelligence, ego, male, female, the world, Nature, and so on. Further, it is not the one who is subject to the duality of the knower and the known or anything that is impermanent, perceptible, definable, destructible, relatable, dependent, interdependent, etc. Even by excluding everything that we know or can imagine, it is still difficult to comprehend the Self. Surely, it is not of this world and does not belong to our realm or exist in any aspect of it.

The individual Self and the Supreme Self

Hinduism also describes two types of Selves: the individual Self and the Supreme Self. Various schools of Hinduism speculate on the question of whether they are the same or different and, if different, in what respects. The six schools of Hinduism, called the Darshanas (views or observations), deal with the cryptic nature of the Self and its relationship with the world and God from their respective perspectives and essential doctrines. Since they have many fundamental differences about the nature and existence of God and Selves, there is no unanimous opinion among them as to how the individual Selves exist in creation in relation to each other and God, if He exists at all. According to some schools, the individual Selves are eternally different from God, or the Supreme Self. According to some, they are notionally different, and according to others, they are always the same without any distinction. Some schools, the purely materialistic ones, which are not a part of these six schools, even go to the extent of denying both the individual Self and the Supreme Self. They believe that all existence arises from natural processes, independent of any God or efficient cause.

Among those who believe in the existence of the individual Self and the Supreme Self, there are different views. Some believe that the individual Selves are uncreated and exist eternally. Some believe that God creates them, releases them at the beginning of creation, so Nature can embody them, and withdraws them into Himself at the end. Some believe that the individual Self is an illusion. When a jiva attains liberation, the individuality of the Self disappears and dissolves into oneness like a drop of rainwater dissolving into an ocean. Some believe that although they are similar in their essential nature, they have subtle differences, which make them distinct but not so distinct (bheda-abheda).

None of these different theories can be proved conclusively or objectively. Whatever views we have about them are based on speculation or the spiritual experiences of yogis and adepts. Since they are based on their subjective experiences, one has to take them at their word.

Since many views and opinions exist on such eternal truths or realities, a great sage like Ashtavakra concluded that one should not rely upon the opinions of anyone or any scripture but upon one's experience. Since the human mind cannot discern transcendental truths definitively, there is no way any of these theories and conclusions can be proved. When you try to establish absolute truths with perceptual knowledge, there are bound to be problems since the mind cannot comprehend them or validate them.

Undoubtedly, the individual Self is beyond the reach of objective human experience and cannot be perceived or cognized directly. The only way to attain that knowledge is through subjective states of transcendental experiences, which arise only in the absence of any activity of the mind and senses and the duality of subject and object. Unfortunately, so far our studies concerning the Self have remained inconsistent and inconclusive, making it almost impossible to conduct any scientific enquiry into its essential nature and draw definitive conclusions that can be verified or validated universally. The Self cannot be discerned in duality. This is clearly accepted as an undeniable universal truth by those who have discerned the Self. The Vedas also validate it. Unfortunately, when we transcend the duality of the subject and object by withdrawing and silencing our minds, we do not remember what happens or what we witnessed or experienced, just as we do not remember anything in the deep sleep state. Thus, although the Self is theoretically within the reach of each person through transformative practices such as yoga, practically it is not within anyone's reach. One cannot even rule out the possibility of self-induced delusions masquerading as real spiritual experiences, especially in situations where impurities existing in the consciousness can interfere with the whole process.

There is also no unanimous opinion among various Indian religions about whether souls exist in all living beings or only in humans. Hinduism holds that all living beings, including plants and animals, possess souls. Jainism goes a step further and suggests that not only plants, animals, tiny insects, and bacteria but also all inanimate objects, such as water, stones, pieces of dead wood, and other substances possess souls. It also believes that souls may exist individually or in clusters or groups. The aggregates of souls make the practice of nonviolence even more difficult to practice, as souls may exist in the water one drinks, the air one breaths, or the food one eats.

The school of Vishistadvaita or qualified nondualism classifies souls into three categories based on their purity and degree of freedom, namely bound souls (baddhas), freed souls (muktas), and forever-free souls (nitya-muktas). Bound souls are those who are bound to samsara, or the cycle of births and deaths. Freed souls are once-bound souls, but are now liberated and exist in Brahman's immortal heaven. The forever-free souls are those who were never bound and who would never be bound. These last ones are again divided into bhaktas (devotees) and bhagavatas (servants of God). The bhaktas are devotees of God. They serve Him directly. The bhagavatas are also devotees who, as agents of God, serve Him indirectly by serving His devotees. In fact, the teachings of Lord Krishna are especially meant for the guidance of this class of devotees.

Descriptions of the Self in the Bhagavadgita

The Bhagavadgita acknowledges the existence of both God, the Supreme Self, and the individual Selves. It presents Isvara as the omniscient, omnipresent, and omnipotent Lord and Controller of the universe, and the source of all, including all our actions, achievements, births, deaths, and destinies, whose grace is required even to attain liberation. Nature is an integral aspect of Him and works according to His will. The individual Self in each Jiva is but an aspect of Him, but remains a passive witness, enjoying the actions of Nature. It believes in the rebirth of jivas and their delusion and bondage to the cycle of births and deaths because of the triple gunas and desire-ridden actions. It suggests various solutions for their permanent escape from births and rebirths in the mortal world.

The scripture dwells upon various subjects like birth, death, delusion, desires, attachment, departure of the soul from the body, its upward journey to the higher worlds, it rebirth or return journey to the earth to continue its cycle of births and deaths, its relationship with God and how humans can overcome their ignorance and delusion, and attain liberation. It declares that the Self is eternal and indestructible (2.18), which neither slays nor can be slain (2.19). Lord Krishna clearly states that the Self is never born, never dies, and after coming into existence, never ceases to be. It is eternal (nitya), permanent (sasvatah), and very ancient (purana) (2.20). It does not suffer from afflictions and cannot be tainted by modifications.

At the time of death, it does not die, but leaves the body and enters a new body (2.22). Weapons cannot pierce it, fire cannot burn it, water cannot moisten it, and wind cannot dry it (2.23). It is impenetrable, incombustible, all-pervading, stable, and immobile (2.24). It is invisible, imperceptible, and immutable (2.25). We find many such descriptions about the Self in the Bhagavadgita. They all convey the message that the Self is distinct from the body, eternal, indestructible, unchangeable, and is distinct from and above all the tattvas of Nature. It is a small part (amsa) of God only, having all His attributes. However, different schools of Vedanta interpret the same verses from the Bhagavadgita to justify their respective doctrine. They find in it justification for both Dvaita and Advaita philosophies.

The scripture is succinctly aware of the limitations of the human mind in discerning the true nature of the Self or oneself. Therefore, it concurs with the Upanishadic notion that the Self is incomprehensible, unreachable, and indefinable. Speaking of the wondrous nature of the Self, it makes these profound declarations. One looks at it with great surprise, another speaks about it with great surprise, another hears about it with incredulity, and yet another, after hearing about it, knows it not (2.29). In a living being, the Self is superior to everything else. It is the highest. The senses are great, greater than the senses is the mind, greater than the mind is intelligence (buddhi), and greater than the intelligence is the Self (3.42). In these descriptions, the scripture sounds very much like an Upanishad.

The Self residing in the body is referred to as the Lord of the Sacrifices (Adhiyajna). We are told that when Purusha, the Supreme Lord (Adhidaiva), resides in the body as the inner Self, He becomes the Lord of Sacrifice (8.4). These descriptions refer to the internalization of the Vedic sacrificial ritual, Yajna, into a spiritual practice, which happened during the later Vedic period, and the symbolic representation of its various parts and processes analogous to various physiological and biological functions in the body. Thus, the body is the sacrificial pit, food is the sacrifice, the digestive fire is the fire into which the offering is made, the organs are the deities to whom the sacrifice is offered, and prana (life or vital breath) is the fruit of the sacrifice which arises from it. The embodied Self is caught in the modifications of Nature (Prakriti) but remains passive and unchanged. The jiva cannot escape from them without making adequate spiritual effort and seeking divine help, which is earned through divine grace (Isvara prasadam). At the time of death, the bound Self leaves the body and goes to either the immortal world of Brahman or the world of ancestors, depending upon whether the jiva has attained liberation or is still bound to samsara.

According to the Bhagavadgita, what a person remembers at the time of death is equally important, because he verily attains that which he remembers. Whatever a person thinks of at that time, that alone they attain (8.6). Thus, if he departs from the body thinking of God alone, he will undoubtedly attain Him (8.5, 12 &13). If he thinks of worldly things or his relations, he will return to them and live again among them as a mortal being. Therefore, it is important to remember God constantly, even when one is engaged in obligatory duties and worldly matters. Whoever remembers the Supreme Lord only at the time of death is bound to reach His abode and join Him.

Atma and Jiva, Pure Self and embodied Self

In its essential nature, a liberated Self is not different from the embodied Self. Although it is bound to the body, the embodied Self remains immutable and impervious to nature's modifications. Thus, the difference between the two is situational. While the being undergoes transformation and purification, the Self that resides in it does not because it is eternally pure. Whatever changes take place happen to the body or the Field of Prakriti, not to the Self, the Knower of the Field. Just as soot accumulates on a lamp and hinders the light that shines in it, while the light itself is untouched, the impurities and modifications of the body veil the Self, but do not diminish its effulgence. However, because of the modifications and impurities, the Self in the jiva remains bound to the body and keeps transmigration from one birth to another and from one body to another.

The embodied Self is also bound to Nature due to the activities of the jiva, which is subject to modifications, desires, and attachments induced by the gunas. Each jiva has a limited existence and lacks continuity in its present form. Only a minuscule part of its consciousness persists as latent impressions and accumulated karma to the next birth. They act as the seeds for the next life. Thus, ensnaring the jivas in the causative world (samsara) through desires and attachment under the spell of Maya, Nature drags the individual Selves into her plans and becomes responsible for their bondage. The egoistic Self in each jiva, which masquerades as its true self, suffers from the consequences of its actions for this very reason. Through desire-ridden actions, it accumulates sinful karma and keeps the embodied Self bound to samsara.

The individual Self, liberated from the snares of the world, remains eternally free in the realm of Brahman. It is never subjected to Nature again. What it does and in what state it exists as a liberated Self, only the adepts know. According to some, it merges into the Supreme Self and loses its distinction. According to others, it remains as an individual Self in the world of Brahman in the company of other liberated souls and divine beings, enjoying proximity to Him. At the time of the dissolution of the worlds, it may be temporarily withdrawn by Brahman, but it remains immutable. In future creations, it may move even closer to Brahman and play an important role as a divinity or emanation.

Realizing the Self

The Self is a mystery. It is an invisible and intangible aspect of each jiva's consciousness and beingness. Even though it exists in us, we do not feel its presence because it has no connection with our minds and bodies and resides in its distinct dimension beyond the reach of our minds and senses. It is like space, imperceptible and intangible. We cannot feel its presence because we do not look deep enough into ourselves or make sufficient effort to purify ourselves and allow its light to shine through us. Distracted by the world, we do not let our minds and bodies settle into silence, so that the Self can reveal itself. To discern the Self within, even vaguely, we must withdraw our senses, silence our minds, and purify our consciousness so that we can see the reflection of the Self in the tranquility of our being. Just as you cannot see your reflection in murky waters, you cannot see the Self in the depths of your being if your consciousness is filled with impurities. Therefore, to see it clearly, you must transform yourself by cultivating the predominance of sattva and making yourself pure and transparent like an uncontaminated glass that partakes in the nature of the light that passes through it.

The Bhagavadgita declares that deluded people do not perceive their true Selves when they are present in their bodies or when they leave them in the end. Those with the eyes of discernment see them. With intense effort, they find their Selves seated within their bodies, while the imperfect and indiscriminate ones cannot perceive them even with striving (15.10 & 11). The Self is luminous. It is the light of the lights. The same brilliance that illuminates the Sun and the moon also illuminates the jivas as their inmost Self. God is its source (15.12). The Self is also the source of our memory, knowledge, and even their loss (15.15). We are able to know, think, and remember because of the Self that is present in us. Our aims should be to know Him and return to our essential nature.

Self-realization is the ultimate goal. It can be reached by restraining the senses, stabilizing the mind, and transcending the gunas. For that, the body must be conditioned through intense self-purification. As the Bhagavadgita declares (6.19), the mind should be like a lamp in a windless place that does not flicker. When that state is reached, one sees the Self abiding in the Self and remaining satisfied within oneself. In that state, the skillful yogi who is firmly established in himself does not deviate from truth or reality. He does not think of any gain or loss from any action or undertaking, or any sorrow as vexing or troublesome. Lord Krishna says that this disassociation (viyogam) of his mind from sorrow and suffering (dukham) is called yoga, the state of liberation or absolute freedom. This yoga should be practiced with resolve and without despair and dejection (6.23), withdrawing the senses gradually, step by step, with firm resolve, fixing the mind in the Self, and thinking of nothing else (6.25).

Apart from the senses, the triple gunas (modes), namely sattva, rajas, and tamas, play an important role in binding the Self to the body (14.05) and keeping the jivas bound to samsara. Sattva binds them through pleasure; rajas through attachment; and tamas through ignorance. The gunas are responsible for all desire-ridden actions and the modifications that arise from them. It is their natural function to induce beings to engage in desire-ridden actions and seek worldly objects and pleasures for enjoyment so that they serve Nature's essential purpose of keeping the jivas bound to samsara, birth after birth. Yoga aims to subdue the gunas so that the mind and body become free from their influence and stabilize in sameness.

Yoga in this context means the integral yoga, which combines the best practices of karma sannyasa, pursuit of knowledge, renunciation, self-purification, self-control, meditation, and exclusive devotion. Whatever methods one may choose, self-control is the bedrock of all the paths that lead to liberation. When a seer sees that all actions arise from the gunas and he is not in them, he realizes the Self, which is different from them and higher than them, and attains liberation (14.19). Going beyond them, he becomes free from birth, death, aging, and sorrow (14.20). He also becomes equal to all the pairs of opposites (14.24). With devotion to God and serving Him selflessly, he transcends them and qualifies for attaining oneness with Brahman's absolute state (14.26).

Seven Teachings of Bhagavadgita

Every scripture contains some wisdom and a clear message for people who choose to follow it or believe in it. It may have a hidden purpose beneath a revealed one. Its authority may come from different sources, some obvious and some unknown. Its interpretation may change from time to time, while its central message remains constant, bound by tradition and faith. It may represent the collective wisdom of multiple teachers who have seen light on the other side of the phenomenal world or just one enlightened seer who might have transcended human limitations and experienced oneness with universal consciousness. The wisdom contained in any scripture is sacred, reverential, and reliable as a spiritual guide for humanity. However, that wisdom is supreme, which arises directly from God Himself, and comes to us in its purest form without any human fabrication. The Bhagavadgita contains the wisdom of God as spoken by Him in a human form. It contains wisdom that He claims to have revealed to humanity several times whenever order and justice (dharma) declined in the world and evil gained ascendance. It was spoken by Him in the first person, sometimes as Himself in his incarnated form and sometimes as Brahman, without any agency in between. Hence, it is reliable as a valuable source of guidance and ideal for those who seek liberation.

A sacred dialogue

Bhagavadgita is a sacred dialogue, not a monologue, speculative discussion, or debate. It is a conversation between a human being with limited knowledge and God Himself in a human form, in which they mutually appreciate each other's viewpoints and their respective roles as a student eager to learn and assimilate and a teacher intent on teaching transformative wisdom to his student so that he will become His true instrument in the service of Dharma and fulfil the purpose for which he was destined to be born. It is a revelatory dialogue of profound spiritual significance between God and His devotee. It is a two-way interactive communication, not a one-sided oratory, conducted by both participants in their wakeful states, in which mutual love, admiration, faith, and respect are maintained until the end.

As a scripture, Bhagavadgita directly addresses the problem of human suffering as exemplified by Arjuna's sorrow as a human being troubled by his familial bonds and moral precepts. The teaching is a direct response to it. It explores its causes and suggests possible solutions to deliver the bound souls (baddhas) permanently from the control of Nature and the jaws of Death. It encourages believers to perform their obligatory duties as a sacrificial offering to God and not to abandon them even when they are unpleasant or difficult. It explains how they become bound to the world and offers various alternatives to escape from the prison house Nature builds around them, without torturing ourselves with extreme ascetic methods.

Delivered in the middle of a battlefield under extraordinary circumstances and divided into 18 sections, each under the name of a distinct yoga, the scripture contains revelations of God about Himself, His creation, and our roles and responsibilities in it as His numerous manifestations (amsas). It is a book of practical wisdom, which shows us the way to overcome suffering without abandoning our duties and responsibilities. We can divide the teachings of the scripture into four main headings: the individual Self (atman), the Universal Self (Brahman), the relationship between the two, and the liberation of the individual Self.

The purpose of different yogas

Although on a superficial note, the Bhagavadgita seems to favor devotion as the most effective path to liberation, a careful student of the scripture cannot miss the obvious connection among the various paths described in it. The paths of knowledge (jnanayoga), action (karmayoga), renunciation of action (karma-sannyasa-yoga), wisdom (buddhi yoga), and self-absorption (atmasamyama-yoga) are all interrelated. The practice of one contributes to the progress of others. We cannot claim that one path is superior to the others because each has its value in the transformation of our minds and bodies. However, the path of action is considered the most basic because beings cannot exist on Earth without indulging in actions. Besides, our bondage arises primarily from the actions we perform. Karmayoga addresses this problem at the most basic level by suggesting a way to escape from the cycle of karma.

It is normal and natural for humans to perform actions selfishly for their benefit, sometimes at the expense of others, which results in sinful consequences. It is the way of the world. The way of the yogis aspiring for liberation is to perform actions selflessly as offerings to God in the sacrifice of life, which leads to freedom from karma and bondage. The seeds of liberation are sown when we perform actions without desiring their fruit and consecrating them to God. Bhagavadgita assures its followers that when actions are performed selflessly, with detachment and discernment, renouncing their fruit, they do not suffer from their consequences.

However, you cannot practice karmayoga effectively without practicing renunciation. In the context of the Bhagavadgita, true renunciation is not abandoning actions or your duties, but giving up the desire hidden in them and their fruit. This knowledge does not arise on its own. It arises from the study of scriptures, from knowledge concerning the Self and discernment, for which one needs to practice both the yoga of knowledge and the yoga of intelligence (buddhiyoga). The practice of concentration, meditation, and self-absorption (atmasamyama-yoga) also helps one achieve perfection in desireless actions and contemplation of God.

Thus, in an integrated approach, actions, knowledge, detachment, intelligence, self-awareness, devotion, and virtue together enable an embodied soul to escape from the cycle of births of deaths. When a seeker practices these different approaches or yogas for a long time, which may span over several lifetimes, he develops sattva or purity, knowledge, intelligence, and divine qualities that are listed in the Bhagavadgita. With these refinements in his lower self or the ego consciousness, he eventually attains the fourth and the final stage of his spiritual development, which is the practice of exclusive devotion (ananya bhakti) and selfless service to God and His manifestations. In this state, he experiences intense devotion and unconditional love for God and His creation, as he sees Him in every aspect of it. He surrenders to Him and spends his time in His service and contemplation. With his mind and senses fixed in Him, he loses himself in His contemplation, seeing Him everywhere and experiencing oneness with Him. Withdrawing mentally from the external world, he becomes absorbed in His thoughts, aspiring to be in His presence and close to Him always. When his devotion overflows, God reciprocates with His love and liberates Him from the bonds of mortal life forever.

Thus, we can see that the Bhagavadgita does not emphasize a single yoga but a holistic spiritual effort, which encompasses a whole gamut of approaches that are aimed at transforming a devotee both physically and mentally and growing him in the image of God to the extent that the differences between the two become negligible. It places heavy emphasis on physical and mental purity, pursuit of knowledge, discernment, wisdom, self-control, performance of duty, renunciation, and devotion to God. While it does indicate that devotion is the most effective solution to achieving liberation, it also suggests that true devotion arises from perfection in other yogas, especially the yoga of action and knowledge.

The first yoga is meant to purify the body and restrain the organs of action, while the other approach aims to purify the mind and restrain the organs of perception. With senses restrained and mind purified, one can practice concentration, contemplation, and self-absorption and experience oneness with the Self. True devotion, in which all sense of egoism becomes dissolved and only the thought of God remains, arises after years of practice and self-discipline. It is possible only for those who restrain their senses, stabilize their minds, cultivate purity, and perform their obligatory duties without desires, expectations, and attachments.

Only those whose hearts and minds are pure and infused with the love of God can practice true devotion. If you are filled with desires and egoism, you cannot experience true love for God. When desires rule our minds and actions, our devotion to God would be a mere excuse to further our interests. In fact, it is how a vast majority of people delude themselves into believing that they are devoted to God or their religion, whereas in truth they are serving none but themselves. Those who claim themselves as devotees of God should search their hearts to see how sincere they are in their devotion and aspiration. If you are in love with yourself, it will be difficult for you to love God unconditionally and surrender to Him. Until you reach that pristine state of devotion, you have to keep purifying yourself and perfecting your actions with supreme intelligence. This is the goal for every seeker of truth in the initial stages. This becomes obvious when we try to build a coherent strategy using the divergent paths and practices suggested by the Bhagavadgita to achieve liberation and freedom from sorrow.

Different interpretations of the Bhagavadgita

In the past, Bhagavadgita was interpreted differently by different scholars belonging to various philosophical and spiritual traditions (sampradayas). In the scripture itself, Lord Krishna mentions the lineage of teachers who received the knowledge from Him at different times in the long history of the world spanning over several cycles of creation. Ancient scholars and commentators relied upon the knowledge contained in the scripture to support their respective views or refute those with which they disagreed strongly. Sri Shankaracharya (8th-9th century A.D) wrote a commentary on it in support of the Advaita philosophy (nondualism), declaring Brahman to be the only reality and delusion as the main cause of the duality, egoism, and desires, and bondage we experience. Sri Ramanujacharya (11th century A.D) interpreted it in support of the Vishistadvaita philosophy (qualified nondualism), which propagated. He used the scripture to suggest that while God was the only Reality, He was not without attributes. The individual Selves were similar to Him in their essence. Yet, they were not identical, because there was a subtle distinction between the two, which was difficult to discern but equally difficult to ignore. According to him, the relationship between God and the individual souls is like that of an object and its reflection in a mirror. They are the same but also different.

Sri Madhavacharya (11th-12th century AD), a great proponent of the Dvaita philosophy (dualism), wrote a commentary (Gitabhasya) and an interpretation (Gitatatparya) upon it. He argued that God and individual souls were distinct and different. While their essence was the same, they could not be treated as one because they represented two distinct and eternal realities. God was Supreme, and none could equal Him. The individual souls were also eternal, but they depended upon Him. Those who were caught in the phenomenal world had an opportunity to achieve liberation through surrender and devotion to God. Once liberated, they would live in the world of Brahman eternally. In other words, the distinction between God and the souls is permanent and eternal.

Unlike the school of nondualism, the dualistic schools believe that the phenomenal world is also real and that duality exists not only between God and souls but also in every aspect of creation, all the way down to the pairs of opposites. Other scholars who contributed to our knowledge of the Bhagavadgita include Nimbarka (12th century A. D), his disciple Kesavakasmirin, Vallabhacharya (15th century A.D), the proponent of Suddhadvaita (pure non-dualism), B.G. Tilak, Sri Aurobindo, M.K. Gandhi, and in recent times Sri Swami Prabhupada. These scholars and great masters interpreted the Bhagavadgita according to their respective beliefs.

The seven teachings

As we have discussed before, the Bhagavadgita accommodates different and even divergent interpretations. At the same time, it adheres to some fundamental principles consistently that are deeply rooted in the Vedic religion. Its main theme is liberation, for which it provides different alternatives, paths, or yogas that are in many ways complementary. For the spiritually inclined people, it offers the following seven fundamental perspectives or thinking points. They sum up the philosophy of the Bhagavadgita and its core teachings. The following account is written from a modern perspective, but it is based on the same teachings found in the scripture.

1. Beware of the worldly ways

The world in which you live is impermanent and unreal. It is created and maintained by Nature to serve as the source of your bondage, ignorance, suffering, and delusion. You should be careful when you deal with it because, in many ways, it is a prison house for the souls. It draws you in and binds you to things, keeping you engaged, distracted, and disturbed. Whatever escape it offers ultimately leads you into a deeper trap, making your life even more difficult. With each step forward into it, you distance yourself from yourself. With each thread of attachment, you build with it, you increase your enmity with yourself. As you become attached to it deeply, you become your own enemy and delay your liberation. In the end, you are bound to suffer anyway because you cannot hold on to anything here for long, and when you are separated from things, you will experience sorrow, fear, and anxiety.

2. Know that you are a pure Self

Your identity and individuality are temporary constructions built around your name and form. They hide you from yourself and keep you disengaged from your true nature. Your name and form are illusions. In their defense, you spend several lifetimes only to realize in the end that you have been chasing false dreams. You are neither of them. You are an eternal and indestructible Self that can be neither slain nor injured. You are an aspect (amsa) of God, and you will always be so. The body is like a garment. You wear it and discard it over time. When the body dies, you wear another one to continue your existence in another body. Therefore, you should not lose your peace over the impermanence and the modifications to which we are subject. Think of yourself as an infinite being of pure consciousness, with no limits whatsoever, and look at this world and yourself from that perspective. You are here, but you do not really belong to the world. Living here, you have lost your way. You have to find it again to rediscover your true nature and stabilize in it. By practicing the yoga of self-absorption (atma samyama yoga), stretch your mind far into infinity. Enter into that limitless awareness of the Universal Self so that from that eternal perspective, your problems begin to fade away and you look at yourself and this world with wisdom, knowledge, and discernment.

3. Know how you become bound to the world

You are bound to the world. Your involvement with it arises from the activity of your senses due to desires and attachments. They draw you out and involve you with the world. As a result, you become attached to things and experience restlessness, anger, pride, fear, attachment, and the like. Your involvement with the material world due to desires and desire-ridden actions is the source of your suffering. They are, in turn, induced by the triple modes. They delude you into seeking and striving and accepting as true the duality and diversity of the world under the delusion that your happiness arises from having things rather than being yourself. This desire to have transient things and enjoy them is the cause of our suffering. What begins as a simple expedition into a magical world ends up as a servitude of many lifetimes. You become a prisoner inside your own body, while every action you perform prolongs your sentence and delays your release. If you want to be free from the world, you should control your desires by restraining your mind and senses, withdraw into yourself, and look within yourself to know who you are and how you became bound to the world.

4. You must cultivate discernment to see things as they are

The world is not what it appears to be. It is a trap. If you live here ignorantly and negligently, you will be held in shackles. The world binds you to things and deludes you into believing that you can be secure and happy by having them. The spiritually ignorant ones are led into darkness. Those who live here with their eyes half closed suffer enormously. You cannot sleepwalk through this world. You must live here with your eyes wide open, and your mind wide-awake, watching your steps carefully, as if you are lost in a forest that is full of traps and unknown dangers. You must cultivate discriminating wisdom (buddhi) to know the truth from falsehood and avoid making mistakes. You must live here wisely, making your way safely out of death and impermanence, avoiding sin and binding actions. True wisdom comes from knowledge, and true knowledge is the knowledge of the Self. It arises not from perceptual experience but from transcendental experience, which is possible only when one achieves perfection in yoga.

5. Know the true meaning of renunciation

You are responsible for your life, your actions, and your inactions. You are not bound to this world by them, but by your desires and attachments. Whatever you do or avoid doing in your life, out of desire, shapes your destiny. Both action and inaction arise from the gunas. They are equally harmful when you indulge in them with desires. You cannot avoid karma by avoiding actions or your duties. True renunciation is not giving up actions or the world but giving up desires with firm resolve. It may be painful in the beginning, but in the end, it leads to liberation and freedom from death. You must live, but not for yourself, and perform actions as if you are not performing them. It is possible when you perform them selflessly, without desires, not for yourself but for God or some divine cause. You should live here as if you do not exist and do your duty as a sacrificial offering to God. Giving up your personal needs and comforts, you should live here for the sake of God and in His service, like a true servant (Bhagavata). Then you will be free from the consequences of your actions. Your living becomes an offering, a form of continuous worship. Instead of binding you, your actions will free you from their consequences. Therefore, perform your actions without desires and expectations. Live as if you do not exist, you do not matter, and you are no one.

6. Understand your essential nature and what drives it

The underlying causes of our bondage and ignorance are much deeper than we think. They are an integral aspect of our essential nature and so deeply hidden within our beingness that to know them, we have to go all the way to the source of our creation. Our bodies are our prison houses. They are made up of Nature. We cannot escape from their influence easily because they are filled with the gunas, the primary modes that determine our thinking and actions, and thereby our destinies. We are good or bad, wise or foolish, knowledgeable or ignorant, according to the gunas present in us. We act, react, and seek things because of them. We must therefore know what the gunas are and how they bind us through desires and actions. Wise people know it and thereby remain untouched by their actions or the changes that happen within them. We should also do the same. Knowing that the gunas are responsible for our desires, like wise yogis who have stable wisdom (sthithaprajna), we should remain equal to the dualities of life with an unwavering mind and let events of our lives unfold on their own.

7. Worship the highest Supreme God with exclusive devotion

When you live here, you serve many gods in the hope of finding peace and happiness. Propelled by your gunas and desires, you serve your ego's demands, worship your interests and pursuits, and surrender to your whims. The result of this self-love is bondage. When you worship false gods of your own creation, you delude yourself and fall into greater ignorance. Instead of worshipping material things and taking refuge in your shadow self, you should take refuge in your real Self and the Supreme Self, who is all-pervading, eternal, indestructible, and the true liberator of all. He is the cause of everything and the real Doer of all actions. Those who are filled with rajas and tamas worship themselves or ignorance, but those who are filled with sattva worship the highest God. They offer themselves to God. They place themselves at His feet. Symbolically, they become His sacrificial food (bhatka) in the sacrifice of their lives. Therefore, cultivate purity (sattva) so that you can stabilize your mind in the contemplation of God, transcending your self-love, and experience oneness with Him. Restraining your mind and senses and focusing your mind upon Him, offer your thoughts and actions to Him. With surrender and gratitude, prostrate before Him and offer yourself to Him. If you persist in your practice, you will attain knowledge, wisdom, and liberation quickly. When you seek refuge in Him, He assumes full responsibility for your life and guides you safely across the ocean of phenomenal life towards the world of light and delight.

The Triple Modes or Gunas

The gunas are the inherent modes or the primary driving forces of Nature that are present in all animate and inanimate things of creation and are primarily responsible for their natural conditions, states, qualities, characteristics, properties, and behavior. They provide things and beings with primary impetus or drive that determine their modes of action or their behavioral patterns, tendencies, and propensities. Bhagavadgita is not the first or the only scripture to speak about them. The concept of gunas is not particular to the Bhagavadgita. They are mentioned in several other scriptures and acknowledged by many religious and spiritual traditions of India, including Buddhism and Jainism. They all agree that the gunas are forces of Nature that bind beings to particular and predictable behaviors and make it difficult for them to overcome them or improve themselves.

The gunas are Nature's fundamental driving forces that are chiefly responsible for all the modifications that arise in creation. They are the first forces to become active when Nature becomes manifested (sambhuta) from her unmanifested and primal state (asambhuta) to herald the beginning of creation. In creation, they produce diversity by joining the five great elements (earth, air, water, fire, and space) in various permutations and combinations and impart dynamism, movements, and properties to all manifested things and beings.

The gunas are only three in number, whereas the tattvas (primal parts) of Nature are several. The three modes are sattva, rajas, and tamas, distinguished primarily by the results or effects they produce. They are all-pervading and exist in all aspects of creation, both living and non-living, in various degrees of concentration, combination, intensity, and preponderance. Depending upon their relative strengths, beings exist in different states of purity and awareness, ranging from the highest state of self-knowing, pure awareness, and omniscience to the lowest state of inertia, unawareness, delusion, and ignorance. In creation, they produce a diversity of modifications, dualities, desires, individualities, distinctions, habitual modes, attachments, delusions, ignorance, and bondage. According to the Bhagavadgita, Isvara, the Supreme Lord, is both the efficient and material cause of creation. The gunas arise from Him only when His Nature becomes active and manifests His will according to the order and regularity (Rta), and causes and effects that are already inherently present in it. Deluded by the desires arising from the gunas (7.12), the world does not know God, who is beyond all (7.13).

Although God is their ultimate source, He does not reside in them, but they reside in Him only (7.12). In Primordial Nature (Mula Prakriti), they remain inactive and in perfect equilibrium. When they become active, that equilibrium is disturbed, and they produce a diverse range of modifications, states, properties, behaviors, and conditions of existence. In the jivas, they induce desires and attachments and are responsible for their desire-ridden actions, karma, and the resultant bondage and suffering. Bhagavadgita states that induced by gunas, beings indulge in desire-ridden actions and suffer from their consequences. Deluded by their selfish actions, they become bound to samsara, the cycle of births and deaths. All actions arise from the triple gunas, but due to ignorance and egoism, the deluded ones think that they are the doers. The gunas become active for the sake of the Self only because, seated in Nature, He alone is the Witness and the Enjoyer. When the body is engaged in actions, the wise one knows that the gunas in his body are active and he is not their cause. Thereby, he remains detached and indifferent and does not incur karma.

The gunas and their modifications

In the 14th chapter of the Bhagavadgita, we find a very detailed description of the nature of the triple gunas and the types of behavior and characteristics they produce. The scripture also emphasizes that the knowledge of the gunas is supreme and important for liberation and that by knowing it, sages attained perfection in the past when they departed from here. Those who use this knowledge and attain the Supreme Self are not reborn again even at the time of creation, nor do they suffer during the destruction of the world. The gunas become active when Isvara, the Supreme Lord, enters the womb of Nature and places there the seed of His intention or desire. That is the signal for Prakriti to wake up and initiate creation. As she wakes up, the gunas in her become active and help her in producing a diversity of things, names, and forms. They remain active throughout creation and assist Nature in keeping the jivas bound to delusion and bondage and ensuring the orderly progression of creation.

Of the three modes, sattva is illuminating and healthy. It binds the jivas through attachment to excellent pleasures, peace, happiness, and knowledge. Rajas has the nature of passion (ragatmakam). It induces insatiable desires (trishna) and attachments (sanga) to material things and worldly enjoyments, which strengthen egoism, delusion, passions (raga), revulsions (dvesha), and worldliness in vulnerable beings and bind them to samsara. Tamas arises from ignorance (ajnanam). It deludes beings and binds them through negligence, sloth, and sleep. The gunas tend to suppress one another. Sattva prevails by subduing rajas and tamas, rajas by subduing sattva and tamas, and tamas by subduing sattva and rajas. When sattva predominates, knowledge radiates through all the openings in the body; when rajas predominates, avarice in actions, restlessness, and craving manifest; and with the predominance of tamas, darkness, sloth, carelessness, and delusion arise.

The gunas also determine the fate of embodied souls after they depart from here. When sattvic people die, they attain the pure worlds of those who know the highest Self. When rajasic people die, they go to the ancestral world. When they return from there, they are born among those who are attached to actions. When tamasic people die, they take birth in the wombs of the deluded (mudha yonis). Actions arising from the gunas also lead to different ends. Sattvic actions lead to purity, rajasic actions to sorrow, and tamasic actions to ignorance. Sattva leads to knowledge, rajas to greed, pride, envy, etc., and tamas to negligence, delusion, perversion, evil conduct, and ignorance.

Knowledge of the gunas and their influence is important in liberation. When you know that actions arise from the gunas and that the Self is higher than the gunas and is untouched by them, you can transcend them and attain liberation by concentrating on the Self and becoming absorbed in it. As Bhagavadgita states, going beyond the gunas, yogis become free from birth, death, old age, and sorrow (14.20). Those who transcend the gunas become free from both attraction and aversion (14.22) to things and thereby experience equanimity and sameness towards all. Knowing that the gunas are responsible for all disturbances, they become indifferent and firm in their resolve (14.23). The scripture further states that the gunas can be transcended by serving God without distractions and practicing devotion.

Gunas in creation

The three gunas permeate everything in creation. Nothing in the manifested worlds is free from them. When you transcend them, by becoming indifferent to the desires and attachments they induce through detachment and renunciation, you become liberated. Based on their predominance, everything in creation boils down to sattvic, rajasic, or tamasic types (Chapter 18) with distinguishing features. Thus, you can divide things, beings, and actions into three types or variants of the three types since they are always found together in Nature with different intensities of predominance. Actions performed as obligatory duties as a sacrifice to God, without desires and expectations, are sattvic. Actions performed because of selfish and egoistic desires, attachments, and passions are rajasic, and not performing actions because of negligence, carelessness, or sloth, performing them against established practices, or performing those that are not approved by tradition is tamasic (18.7). Renunciation is also of three types. In sattvic renunciation, one renounces the fruit of one's actions; in rajasic renunciation, one gives up actions that are painful or difficult to perform; in tamasic renunciation, one gives up actions because of delusion, falsehood, deception, or willful intention. Sattvic renunciation leads to liberation; rajasic renunciation leads to bondage, suffering, and rebirth; and the tamasic one leads to delusion and painful rebirth. Those who do not practice true renunciation suffer from the consequences of their actions. Bhagavadgita states that unpleasant, pleasant, and mixed are the results of rajasic and tamasic renunciation (18.12).

Knowledge (jnanam), action (karma), and the doer (karta) are declared in the Gita as the totality of action (karma samgraha). These three also arise from the gunas only (18.19), and they too are divided into sattvic, rajasic, and tamasic types. Sattvic knowledge makes one see the Supreme Self universally in everything. Rajasic knowledge subjects one to duality and diversity. Tamasic knowledge leads to tunnel vision, whereby one becomes excessively fixated with minutiae or insignificant aspects, as if it were all, irrespective of their merits or demerits. Sattvic actions are performed without desires as obligatory duties to uphold dharma. Rajasic actions are performed egoistically out of desire and with striving. Tamasic actions are performed out of delusion without due consideration for the relationship, ability, procedure, societal considerations, or the destruction they may cause (18.25). In the same manner, Bhagavadgita distinguishes intelligence (buddhi), firmness (dhriti), happiness (sukham), and the social class (varna) of each person according to the predominance of gunas.

Gunas and the varna system

Justification for the varna system also arises from the gunas. It was probably the reason for its origin in the formative period of the Vedic religion. The system eventually gave way to a more corrupt and rigid caste system based on birth. However, it is not wrong to think of people in terms of their predominant gunas and classify them accordingly. Based on the gunas, people fall into three primary categories: pure, impure, and mixed. However, since the three gunas are always found in beings in different permutations and combinations, the three categories we mentioned may lead to further subclasses and groups. The Vedic system recognized four varnas according to the predominant modes found in humans: Brahmanas (priests), Kshatriyas (warriors), Vaishyas (traders and merchants), and Shudras (workers). Brahmanas with the predominance of sattva are fit for religious and philosophical learning, related obligatory duties, and practices. People with the predominance of rajas, followed by sattva, are well qualified for leadership positions, religious knowledge, and spiritual life. People with the predominance of tamas, followed by sattva, excel in materialistic pursuits such as business, trade, and commerce. Finally, people with the predominance of tamas followed by rajas are better suited for professions involving manual work, sports, and related activities.

Whether Bhagavadgita supports the varna system based on birth or the gunas is not clear. One may find in the scripture support for both arguments. Logically speaking, according to the karma theory, the chances of a sattvic person taking birth in a sattvic family are high. However, we cannot say that all the people in a Brahmana family have the predominance of sattva or that all the people in the family of a lower varna have the predominance of tamas. It is also true in the case of people having the predominance of the other two gunas. Spirituality is not the prerogative of any caste, gender, community, or class to claim superiority. Everyone is born with the spark of God. Everyone is born with a spiritual nature and the potential to realize oneself. Prahlada was born to an Asura but was predominantly pure from birth. Many seers and sages were born in lower varnas but attained fame due to their austerity, purity, knowledge, and wisdom. At the same time, we should also not ignore the importance of self-effort in one's karma and destiny. Family background and birth do not guarantee liberation. They may help, but persistent effort (abhyasam) is vital to one's transformation and liberation. Through practice and discipline, people may acquire sattva and qualify for liberation or acquire higher knowledge even if they are born in adverse conditions. It may not be appropriate to deny them opportunities for spiritual growth.

Lord Krishna affirms very clearly that one should always pursue one's duties according to one's essential nature (as determined by one's gunas) rather than taking the duties of another, even if they are superior (18.47). There is no declaration in the scripture that only sattvic people qualify for liberation. All are qualified to achieve liberation by choosing appropriate methods and yogas according to their essential nature and achieving perfection. Sacrificial and obligatory duties, self-control, and renunciation are suitable for rajasic people. Self-restraint and devotion are suitable for sattvic people. Self-purification and austerities are suitable for tamasic people. Knowledge, discipline, and discernment are vital to all three.

Transcending the gunas

The gunas are a part of primordial Nature. They are indestructible, just as Nature is. However, they can be suppressed by weakening them, or one can become indifferent to the desires and attachments they induce or their influence. When they are active, they bind people one way or another. They keep you engaged with the world and bind you to the body. Even sattva binds people in its way and contributes to their ignorance. Therefore, ideally, one should become indifferent to all three. Liberation is possible only when you become free from their influence or inducement completely. However, for liberation, sattva is the most ideal because it is pure and conducive to the development of divine qualities such as dispassion, detachment, and equanimity, which are essential for liberation. At the same time, sattva alone does not guarantee liberation. Since sattva induces attachment to pleasure, comfort, peace, and happiness, it also produces karma and binds people through desire-ridden actions. Hence, even sattva needs to be suppressed or transcended. The lesson that we learn from the Bhagavadgita is that ultimately, a seeker of liberation must go beyond the gunas by becoming indifferent to them. Through persistent practice (abhyasa) and detachment (vairagya), he must tame his mind, suppress desires and attachments, and transcend his impure lower nature to be the pure Self within himself (14.20).

What are the qualities of a person who has transcended the triple gunas? How does he behave, and how does he actually achieve it? Bhagavadgita states that when a yogi overcomes the three gunas, he does not experience attraction or aversion to illumination, passion, and delusion when they are present or absent (14.22). He remains indifferent and undisturbed, knowing that the gunas are doing their duty (14.23). Alike in pleasure and pain, censure and praise, and honor and dishonor, and free from all dependencies, associations, wants, and needs, he treats equally a piece of gold or a lump of clay. With equanimity and self-control, he remains the same to the desirable and the undesirable, defamation and self-adulation (14.24), honor and dishonor, and friends and foes. Without egoism in performing actions, he transcends all dualities and circumstances (14.25).

One of the important messages of the Bhagavadgita is that the knowledge of the triple gunas is important and relevant to the practice of yoga, purification, and liberation. It is vital for spiritual practice and success in all yogas by all classes of people. The knowledge helps us understand our essential nature (svabhavam), predominant desires, attachments, and proclivities, the impurities that we must overcome, the nature of our actions, and the causes of our bondage. When we realize that the gunas are chiefly responsible for our behavior, thinking, attitudes, habits, and actions, we find solutions to the problem of karma. When we realize that they are obstacles to experience sameness (samatvam), equanimity, contentment (santosham and liberation (mukti), and if we are intent on liberation, we will strive to transcend them. Yogis practice self-purification to transcend the gunas. With their desires and attachments suppressed, their latent impressions burnt away in the fire of detachment and renunciation, their minds and senses withdrawn, resting in themselves, and firmly established in the thoughts of the divine, and their hearts filled with exclusive devotion, they experience bliss and happiness even in their embodied state. Upon departing from their bodies, they attain the Supreme Self.

The Yoga of Sorrow

When Arjuna stood in the middle of the battlefield and saw the two great armies of Pandavas and Kauravas arrayed on both sides, ready to wage a destructive war, he was overwhelmed with negative emotions. When we are confronted with difficult situations and moral dilemmas, emotions invade our minds and fill us with conflicting thoughts. It happened to Arjuna when he was struck by the thought of moral consequences that might arise from the war and his actions in it. He was simultaneously filled with remorse, fear, doubt, and confusion. Thoughts of violence and bloodshed arising from his actions overwhelmed him. He also thought of the consequences arising from the war upon him and his own family. It is very difficult for anyone to view things calmly and weigh the consequences arising from one's actions with a clear mind when confronted with a crisis. We tend to weigh actions in the light of the results they are going to produce and the likely scenarios that emerge from them. Arjuna did the same. He weighed the consequences of the war and its impact upon others and himself. As he thought about it, he was filled with sorrow, fear, and guilt. His knowledge and experience of warfare did not help him at that moment of crisis. They did not soothe his fears or his conscience.

At that moment in his life, he felt that the gains of warfare were far less significant, both morally and socially, than the losses and the destruction that would follow and haunt him forever. He was convinced that he was about to commit a mortal sin by participating in the war and causing the deaths of many of his close relations and great souls to whom he developed an attachment, respect, and reverence. He also felt that the war would leave its mark on his family's name and reputation and lead to its decline. With the death of male members in the family, he reasoned that the women in his family would lose their virtue, resulting in the intermixture of varnas. The thought disturbed him and strengthened his resolve to leave the battlefield. In that fit of confusion, he decided to renounce actions and live an ascetic life, seeking alms from others. He reasoned that it was better to live like a beggar and live on alms than wage war and kill his friends and relations for the sake of fame, valor, and the riches of a kingdom.

The state of sorrow

Arjuna was educated, knowledgeable, and scholarly. He was well-versed in his profession. His ignorance was not of a scholarly type. He studied the scriptures and trained under the best of the teachers. He was skillful in the art of warfare and statecraft. He knew rules and restraints about virtuous living, moral conduct, and his obligatory duties as a warrior and householder. He was also mentally tough and courageous. He fought many wars and won them. He resolved many problems in the past and assisted his brothers greatly in securing victories and overcoming obstacles. However, his intellectual knowledge failed him at the most crucial time in his life. It did not adequately answer his doubts or address his fears and indecision. It did not give him the strength to bear the suffering silently and remain equal to the results of war. It exposed his weaknesses as a human being. The crisis demolished his long-held beliefs about himself and his role as a warrior and householder. It also brought out his vulnerabilities into the open, exposing the most unstable part of his personality hidden behind layers of defenses built by him all along. It showed him that to address the complex issues of human life, one needs to go beyond the mind and the intellect and look for solutions in the realm of the Self. What he lacked was spiritual awareness and his duties and obligations from a spiritual perspective. He needed a different approach, a major shift in his thinking and attitude, which came to him later with the discourse of Lord Krishna.

One cannot blame Arjuna for his lack of conviction at a crucial moment in his life. It happens in many cases. People lose their courage when they need it the most. They become distracted when they are supposed to focus on their goals. They give up when they are expected to persevere. Although Arjuna was a great warrior and highly educated, he was not free from the dualities of life, more specifically from attraction and aversion to things. He also lacked proper knowledge, whereby he assumed that he could avoid sin by avoiding action. His mind was turbulent because of desires and expectations. He personified ordinary human consciousness, with which we are familiar. Although he was well trained in concentration and mental discipline, like most of us, he could not suppress his emotions in front of his close friend and mentor, Lord Krishna, whom he thought was an ordinary human. The same motives, desires, and limitations that assail our minds as we deal with our routine tasks also weighed in his mind and troubled him as he stood on the battlefield, confused, with his beliefs shaken, his fears aggravated, and his intelligence and judgment faltering. In the face of a grave emotional crisis, he spoke the same language that we use when we feel like wanting to escape from the harsh realities of life.

A great warrior, bred on the beliefs and values of his times, Arjuna was intensely religious, morally righteous, socially responsible, ambitious, earthly, and humane. As he laid aside his bow and arrows and sank into the back seat of his chariot, shaken and dejected, there was no pretense in his thoughts or actions. He was neither cynical nor insincere nor vain in his approach. He did not try to evade the problem under some false pretext, hiding his real feelings. His feelings and doubts were genuine, which he expressed truthfully. He truthfully expressed his fear of sin and the bloodshed that might arise from his actions on the battlefield. As a person of great integrity and good human values, his sorrow was genuine, and so was his concern.

Arjuna's sorrow makes sense from a human perspective. We love even those we hate if we see in them a reflection of the ideals and values we cherish. Conditioned by society, we place greater emphasis upon certain social values, even if they are detrimental to the happiness and well-being of the individuals. We respect authority, even if it limits our freedom and opportunities. Arjuna's character and thinking were shaped by the conditions of his time. It would be inappropriate to judge him by today's standards. One cannot criticize him for his arguments about the admixture of castes or his lack of faith in the women of his family. He was but expressing the values and norms of his times and the conditioning to which he was subject.

Knowledge vs. Suffering

Worldly knowledge does not illuminate the suffering mind. It does not reflect the truth adequately. It does not always provide correct solutions to the problems we face in our lives, because it arises from a limited field of experience and does not have the illumination of all-knowing awareness. The knowledge that arises from our interaction with the world, which we hold dearly and in which we take pride, is an ignorant force. It lacks purity of vision, strength, and purpose, which can sustain us through crises. Since it is imperfect and incomplete, it does not suggest permanent solutions but only temporary fixes. Holding us within the walls of perceptual experience and accumulated knowledge of distorted perceptions, it binds us strongly to our habitual thought patterns, mental modifications, desires, and attachments.

Perceptual knowledge arises in the Field of Nature, by the Nature, and for the Nature. It is not a liberating force, but a deluding one. Its purpose is not to set us free but to ensnare us deeply in the phenomena of the world. Its solutions are intended to perpetuate the status quo rather than bring about change. It does not guide us toward light and salvation but into a world of egoism, ignorance, and illusion. Therefore, its source is not light but illusion. Its purpose is not to set us free, but to hold us in bondage, and not to reveal truth but to veil it and show us an alternate reality to keep us deluded and ignorant. Created, nourished, and enriched by the senses, it holds in its perceptions a very limited vision of life, upholding the values that are rooted in our desires and attachments. It does not show us the way but leads us astray, and does not promote divine-centered living but self-centered activity. We cannot say Nature does this deliberately. Nature is inherently programmed to act in this manner, so it happens naturally as cause and effect.

Suffering, the ground reality

Sorrow manifests in our lives in many ways. Our lives are so infused with sorrow that most of the time, we do not even know that we are suffering. For an enlightened person, living itself is suffering. As the Buddha declared, every aspect of living is infused with a shade of sorrow. We may accept suffering, but we cannot deny its existence or its relevance. An embodied self is an imprisoned self. Therefore, it is neither a happy nor an auspicious state. No doubt, for a materialistic person, this may sound very depressing, but, indeed, we are rarely free from suffering or its possibility. Suffering is the underlying theme of our existence, and we spend our whole lives either addressing it or escaping from it. Sorrow does not mean merely crying and shedding tears. They are, but sorrow's most visible and immediate expressions. In real life, it has many shapes, tones, hues, grades, and colors. It arises in many forms, such as agony, despair, anguish, physical pain, sense of separation, sense of loss, helplessness, depression, and the like. Some other manifestations include a crisis of confidence, pangs of failure, self-pity, dejection, depression, mental breakdown, hysteria, self-deception, apathy, indifference, anger, and frustration. These are numerous manifestations of sorrow, which overwhelm our minds and consume our lives.

True freedom arises when we set our minds free from desires, attachment, accumulated knowledge, and conditioning. We are free when we are free from attraction and aversion to things. We experience peace when we break out of the confines of our conditioned minds and our limited knowledge and look at things from a broader perspective that comes with intelligence, learning, purity of intent and purpose, and spiritual awareness. Suffering helps us in this process. As long as we are not willing to go beyond sense gratification and sensory perceptions, and not willing to free our minds from routine thought processes, surface impressions, and habitual reactions and responses, we remain prisoners of our impure minds and worldly desires. Without overwhelming sorrow and suffering and without knowing their causes and lasting solutions, we cannot develop a distaste for worldly life or turn to God or spirituality to find lasting peace. Without suffering from adversity and without learning from difficult and troubling situations fate or circumstances put in our way, we cannot change our habitual thoughts and responses, and unhealthy choices, or think of changing and improving ourselves morally, materially, and spiritually.

Conclusion

Sorrow is a mental state or condition. Hence, in the Bhagavadgita, it is mentioned as Vishada Yoga. It is also one of the most natural states found in living beings. Human life is filled with suffering. Indeed, the lives of all beings are full of suffering. Its essential purpose is to draw humans from worldly life to spiritual life and from the worldly pursuit of Dharma, Artha, and Kama to Moksha, the final liberation. Without suffering, humans will not feel the need to turn to God, spirituality, or liberation. Therefore, Bhagavadgita rightly begins with a chapter on Arjuna's sorrow and with sorrow as the starting point of the deeply spiritual and philosophical discourse that follows, in which Lord Krishna reveals a comprehensive approach to resolve it. It also conveys the truth that God indeed responds to human suffering, especially when it afflicts His pure and exclusive devotees and they look to Him for solutions. It affirms His promise that He will take care of those who dedicate their lives to Him and live for Him.

Sorrow arises from the afflictions and modifications of the mind and body, caused by desires, attachment, desire-ridden actions, and the very nature of the mind, which is fickle and restless. Spirituality helps us understand the underlying causes of our suffering and the right methods and practices to overcome this state and enter the highest yoga of equanimity, stability, peace, and sameness, which leads to the transcendental state of oneness and freedom from suffering and rebirth. There are many pathways to reach this august and supreme state. The Bhagavadgita explains them in the remaining seventeen chapters as different yogas.

The Causes of Suffering

Going through suffering is the first part. Understanding it objectively through observation and analysis is the second part. Resolving it intelligently and permanently, if possible, is the third. In understanding our suffering, we should not only discern the apparent causes but also find their root cause. For that, we must examine it deeply, observe dispassionately as a witness the modifications it induces in our consciousness, and, through study, observation, and discernment, realize how it arises and subsides, evoking in the process diverse reactions and responses. We must become familiar with the thought processes and the physical processes involved in our suffering. We can do it by cultivating self-restraint, detachment, and witness consciousness.. When we witness our suffering in a state of detachment and equanimity, we understand it and resolve it better than when our minds are restless or overwhelmed with emotions and mental turmoil. By observing it dispassionately, we can truly understand it, without being influenced by our desires, likes, and dislikes.

The first part of the scripture, from Chapter One to Chapter Six, mainly discusses this subject with Arjuna, symbolically representing a human being, as the main focus. As I wrote in my Bhagavadgita Simple Translation, "Suffering is usually caused by thoughts of the death of oneself or others, by loss or impermanence, and by the desire to stop or prevent them. Arjuna experienced suffering at the thought of the death of his close relations and the loss of his family's reputation as a result of it. The thought that he would be responsible for it aggravated it. He desired to stop it by withdrawing from the battlefield." However, fear of death is not a deeper cause. It is rather an effect than a cause. The deeper causes are hidden in our essential nature and the way we are created by Nature and subjected to her control through her deluding and controlling force of Maya.

Bhagavadgita suggests that desires and attachments are the primary causes of suffering. They are, in turn, caused by the actions of the senses as they interact repeatedly with the objects of the world. The senses are, in turn, induced by the triple gunas to seek things in which they are predominantly present. When humans engage in desire-ridden actions, they incur sinful karma and suffer from bondage to the cycle of births and deaths. The bondage makes the existence of jivas a continuous and unending state of suffering. The impurities with which the jivas are born, such as ignorance, delusion, egoism, instability, etc., also ensure that the jivas will continue to suffer in samsara until they achieve liberation. Thus, gunas are the hidden causes, desires and desire-ridden actions are the apparent causes, egoism, delusion, etc., are the ancillary causes, and karma and bondage are resultant causes. Behind all these causes is Nature, with Maya, her force, acting as the material or instrumental cause because, without delusion, the jivas do not engage in deluded and desire-ridden actions and suffer from their causes. If we assume that Nature is an integral part of Isvara, the Supreme Lord, and that He is the source of all, then we must infer that He is the efficient and the ultimate cause of all suffering beings experience in the mortal world. He is the source of suffering, as well as the liberator of jivas from that suffering.

From the above, it is apparent that the Bhagavadgita presents a comprehensive array of hierarchical causes that result in suffering with the gunas at the base. Since these causes are hidden and interwoven into Nature's mechanism and jivas' existence, they cannot be resolved without using a complex set of methods and techniques, which is why the scripture offers an integrated approach involving several yogas to resolve them. In the following discussion, we identify some of these causes and their remedy.

Karma and bondage

In Hinduism, karma refers to both action and the consequences it produces. Karma arises from desire-ridden actions. Bondage means bondage to samsara or the cycle of births and deaths. A jiva's accumulated karma leads to its bondage, rebirth, and continuation of its suffering from one birth to another. The cycle can be disrupted and suffering can be resolved only by karma sannyasa, which involves renouncing the desires in actions and the desire for the fruit of such actions. Bhagavadgita suggests that one should offer all actions to God, renouncing desires, and acknowledging Him as the doer and owner of all actions. Actions performed in this manner will not produce karma.

Lord Krishna also hints that, in addition to karma sannyasa, karma can be resolved by earning God's mercy (anugraha) through exclusive devotion. Lord Krishna clearly states that by renouncing actions, no one can escape from karma and samsara. Only by renouncing desires and the desire for the fruit of actions is such an escape possible.

Desires and attachments

Desires and desire-ridden actions are the direct causes of karma, which leads to suffering and rebirth. The consequences of karma can be unpredictable, as it can lead to auspicious or inauspicious rebirths. Attachments perpetuate and strengthen desires, binding the jivas to the world and prolonging their suffering. Desires manifest in the jivas as cravings, attachments, habits, strong likes and dislikes, and attraction and aversion to material things and worldly enjoyments. Because of these and other factors, jivas experience suffering from gain and loss, association and dissociation with dualities such as heat and cold, and with things they like or dislike. Bhagavadgita defines yoga as a state in which we are permanently disassociated from pain and suffering. Gaining what you dislike or losing what you like leads to suffering. Coming into contact with the unpleasant or losing contact with the pleasant also leads to the same. Thus, our suffering arises from the delusion of ownership, from union and separation, from attraction and aversion to things, etc. They are all caused by desires and attachments. As stated before, desires are the apparent or direct causes, but the real culprits are the triple gunas. They are responsible for our desires. They induce desires of various kinds for sense objects, which lead to attraction and aversion to the pairs of opposites as the senses repeatedly interact with them under their influence.

Fate and acts of God

Bhagavadgita recognizes three types of actions from which suffering and bondage may arise: internal factors or one's actions (adhyatmika), external factors or others' actions (bhautika), and supernatural factors such as God or fate. All three may arise from one's actions or karma. Of them, the first can be controlled or mitigated if we know their exact causes. The second type of causes is difficult to control since they also include natural events such as catastrophes, floods, pests, famine, epidemics, etc. Acts of enemies also fall into this category, and they, too, are difficult to mitigate. External causes may also arise from collective karma or the collective actions of several entities. Supernatural factors or acts of God are even more difficult to resolve, especially if they are a part of God's design. The Lord of the Universe may often create problems and difficulties for humans or groups of people to teach them a lesson, reform them, or help them overcome their sinful karma. Some of the suffering arising from it can be mitigated through exclusive devotion or by performing certain rituals prescribed by the scriptures or tradition.

Impurities of the mind and body

Bhagavadgita also mentions some impurities that are responsible for our suffering. However, they cannot strictly be considered causes since they play an ancillary role in human suffering. They are indeed effects arising from the primary causes, which either aggravate suffering or make suffering difficult to resolve. The gunas are responsible for the impurities, especially rajoguna and tamoguna. Sattva also creates impurities by inducing attachments to pleasures and worldly enjoyments. Therefore, the impurities arising from all three gunas must be resolved to attain peace and equanimity. Through these impurities, the gunas control the jivas by inducing them to engage in desire-ridden actions that will result in karma, bondage, and suffering. Bhagavadgita suggests that humans must transcend the triple gunas through self-purification, renouncing desires and attachments, cultivating discernment and equanimity, and practicing self-control and exclusive devotion. Through these practices, when a yogi transcends the gunas and suppresses desires and attachments, he attains freedom from karma (naishkarmya siddhi), which means he will not incur any karma even if he engages in approved or prohibited actions. The following are a few important impurities that perpetuate and prolong human suffering and make liberation a truly arduous process.

Ignorance: Knowledge leads to liberation; ignorance leads to bondage and suffering. In human beings, ignorance can arise in several ways. The Ignorance, which we are specifically mentioning here, is spiritual ignorance, which leads to delusion and duality. According to the Bhagavadgita, it includes ignorance of the individual Self, the Supreme

Self, the means to liberation, and ignorance about our phenomenal existence, the binding nature of actions, and the gunas. Our ignorance arises from the impurities present in our minds and bodies. They veil our consciousness and prevent us from knowing the truth about ourselves. In the state of ignorance, things that do not exist may appear to exist and things that appear to exist may not exist.

Egoism: Ego is a Nature's tattva in the human body, which creates the delusion of being distinct and different from the rest of creation. It is responsible for egoism or the feeling that one is the cause of one's actions and the source of one's achievements, and that one must live for oneself and work for oneself. The attachment to name and form, and worldly things, leads to egoism, atomicity (anavatva), or the feeling of being small and insecure, and selfish desires to perpetuate oneself. Egoistic actions bind you to the world and subject you to the cycle of births and deaths. Egoism is a major obstacle to liberation. It can also be a source of demonic qualities in deluded beings in whom tamas is present predominantly. As the Bhagavadgita states, demonic people are insincere, careless, vain, and deluded. They despise God and engage in sacrifices or worship with ulterior motives due to pride, vanity, or selfish reasons.

Delusion: The mistaken notion that the body is the real Self is the main source of suffering, as it makes people think of themselves, pursue selfish and egoistic desires, ignore their true nature, and experience passions and negative emotions such as lust, fear, anger, pride, greed, envy, etc. Arjuna experienced profound sorrow on the battlefield because of his mistaken notion that he was a physical being and his actions would cause the death and destruction of others. Hence, Lord Krishna revealed to him that the body is like a garment one wears in each birth and discards at the end, while the Self in him or others, which is eternal and indestructible, neither kills nor is killed by anyone.

Duality: Bhagavadgita suggests that our suffering also arises due to the attraction and aversion we experience towards the pairs of opposites or dualities such as heat and cold, pleasure and pain, good and bad, and the like. Attraction and aversion arise from the gunas and crystallize into desire and attachments. They create varied responses in humans and keep the mind restless and unstable. By nature, we tend to seek pleasure and avoid pain. Dissociation from pleasure and association with pain leads to suffering. Dissociation from both pain and pleasure leads to sameness and equanimity. Bhagavadgita points to this ideal and teaches that yogis must overcome dualities and cultivate sameness towards all. Dualities create the illusion that we are free to make our choices and pursue our desires according to our likes and dislikes, and that we can create favorable conditions and control our lives and destinies by making intelligent choices and engaging in skillful actions. The reality is that the dualities are impermanent, and the conditions and circumstances that precipitate them keep changing and are not entirely under our control. Therefore, they make our lives unpredictable and subject us to uncertainty, anxiety, and varied emotions, passions, and mental states. They also prevent us from seeing the underlying unity of all existence or the absolute reality that remains hidden behind the apparent dualities we experience. The duality of the knower and the known, or the subject and object, is a major source of suffering since it fuels desires and attachments and does not let us experience sameness and stability. Yogis must cultivate equanimity and remain equal to all dualities, for without sameness, one cannot attain liberation. Indeed, Bhagavadgita defines sameness as the highest yoga.

Mind's instability: The human mind is fickle by nature. The mind of a worldly person who lacks purity and self-control remains unstable and restless as his senses run in all directions. He cannot control himself or his desires and attachments. As a result, he cannot perform his actions without desires and attachments or experience peace and equanimity. The instability is resolved when a yogi withdraws his mind and senses into himself and establishes them in the Self through concentration and contemplation. Through the persistent practice of detachment and renunciation, he transcends the gunas and attains sameness (samsiddhi) and freedom from karma (naishkarmya siddhi).

Impermanence: The mortal world is impermanent and unstable. Nothing that exists here is permanent, except the embodied Self that resides in the jivas and the Supreme Self who pervades all this. All things that are made up of Nature's tattvas are impermanent and perishable. Death is the lord of the mortal world. No one can escape from Him. Impermanence of the world is chiefly responsible for suffering as we experience gain and loss, and association and disassociation with the things of the world to which we become attached. When we cling to things that we like and are impermanent and unstable, and when we are forced to part with them, we are bound to suffer. Hence, the Bhagavadgita suggests that one should practice detachment and renunciation to control the mind and become indifferent to worldly things and pairs of opposites.

Doership and ownership: Doership is the egoism that one is responsible for one's actions and their results, and ownership is the feeling that one has the right to possess or accumulate things. Both lead to karma and suffering, since we own nothing, and God is the source of all that exists and happens here. These conditions arise from ignorance, delusion, and egoism when people assume responsibility for their actions and ignore God's role in their lives, believing that there is nothing beyond their minds and bodies, and that death is their final salvation. The wise ones, in contrast, relinquish these notions, acknowledging God as their source. As a result, they do not incur karma even when they perform actions. By overcoming their attachment to names and forms, and remaining centered within themselves, they remain uninvolved, indifferent, and at peace when they perform actions, thinking that their bodies are active due to the gunas, and they are not responsible for them.

Lack of discernment: When people engage in indiscriminate actions, they experience suffering and bondage. The knowledge that the body is the not-self and distinct from the Self arises from discernment only when intelligence is purified. Lord Krishna says in the Bhagavadgita that the intelligence of the resolute-minded is one-pointed, but it remains divided and scattered in those who are irresolute. When the mind is afflicted with the desire for material wealth is thereby lost, intelligence does not settle well in that person. It does not help him experience peace and happiness or escape from karma and suffering. Without discerning intelligence, we cannot distinguish between truth and falsehood, or what leads to suffering or freedom from suffering. When we lack discernment, we do not know how to resolve our problems, navigate through our lives, identify the causes of our suffering, or resolve them effectively.

The Purpose of Sorrow

Suffering serves a definitive purpose in our lives. It teaches us life's important lessons and prepares us well for life on earth and the life hereafter in ways that will eventually lead to our liberation. It is a correcting and improving mechanism, just like the fruit of karma that arises from our thoughts and actions. The knowledge and experience we gain out of suffering and the insights we learn in the process awaken us to a new reality and knowledge or awareness of the world and people, and our strengths and vulnerabilities. From that awareness and understanding, we become wiser and tolerant and work for our progress and transformation on the path of liberation and self-awakening. We turn to religion and spirituality mostly due to suffering when we lose faith in ourselves and feel helpless against the forces of adversity. Unless we have suffered enough, we do not realize the futility of worldliness and the need for renunciation. In suffering, we become introspective. We become wiser. We begin to look within. We learn to withdraw from the things that give us pain.

When our hearts are heavy with the tears of sorrow, we become philosophical, even cynical about the world and the strange ways in which it holds our attention and wields its influence. When we are in despair, we look for solutions to lighten our hearts and escape from the burdens of life. Sometimes, when we are not ready, it breaks our spirit and puts us on self-destructive paths; and sometimes, when we are ready for change, it builds our hopes and leads us towards our dreams. The Patient Lord does not grant us liberating and uplifting wisdom until we drink enough poison from the cup of life and open our eyes to the reality of the world and the need to escape from it. Sorrow is thus a divine opportunity that comes to us in the form of providence (daivikam) and a divine blessing (prasadam) to realize the delusion into which we have fallen and the need to recover from it.

It is far-fetched to assume that God always grants us our wishes or gives us whatever we pray for. He shows His love and mercy in mysterious and most unexpected ways, sometimes doing exactly the opposite of what we seek. If we pray for happiness, He may give us pain, and if we seek comfort, He may force us to deal with situations that we tend to avoid habitually. The purpose is to free us from the duality of attraction and aversion in which we become caught and settle with contentment and sameness. It is His way of saving us from our ignorance, impurities, imperfections, and wayward tendencies. Our suffering mitigates greatly when we become equal to all the dualities in life, and with the insights we gain from each suffering in our lives, we move towards that supreme goal.

Suffering arises in our lives from our actions (adhyatmika), the actions of Nature (adhibhautika), and the actions of God or supernatural forces (adhidaivika). In all these, the purpose is the same: to unravel our lives and manifest our destinies according to the actions we perform and the karma we incur, and create opportunities that will help us cultivate divine qualities, virtues, sameness, peace, balance, and equanimity and become better individuals and God's true servants on Earth as upholders of Dharma. We move towards this ideal goal the hard way through suffering, learning from our mistakes and imperfections, and fumbling through ignorance, indiscretion, uncertainty, ambiguity, and delusion. Sorrow wakes us up from our complacent, ignorant, and indulgent ways and opens our eyes to the impermanent and uncertain world in which we are subject to Nature and its modifications.

Thus, suffering is a seemingly negative and critical but truly positive and constructive force of Maya, the precursor of enlightenment, in whose womb the soul prepares itself for its eventual liberation. By revealing the transience and meaninglessness of our existence and exposing our limitations and failures, it nudges us, often harshly and painfully, towards our final goal of liberation. It encourages us to withdraw from the world and its distractions and look within ourselves to find God, believe in Him, depend upon Him, surrender to Him, and seek His help. Sometimes it may not offer God as the solution, but create a center of strength and stability in which we can find our sanctuary and experience peace and equanimity.

Suffering is thus a faithful messenger of truth and a counselor in our spiritual progress. As an instrument of light, it subjects us to transformation, in rather unpleasant and, sometimes, frightening ways. It wakes us up from our illusions to remind us of our essential nature and the true purpose of our lives. A teacher may sometimes use rather harsh methods to instruct his students about the virtues of a divine-centered, virtuous, and spiritual living or practice, so that they can transcend their ignorance and delusion. In the darkness of suffering and depths of sorrow, most of us feel the need to change our lives and cleanse ourselves of the impurities that we accumulate in the course of our existence upon earth. Arjuna did not see the pleasant form of God. He saw a fierce and frightening Deity, Death (Kala) Himself. He saw death and suffering in their most terrible and destructive aspects. In that symbolism is hidden the true meaning and purpose of life, fate, and suffering.

In our lives, too, from time to time, God manifests Himself as suffering. We can learn from the lessons He delivers through the suffering and march towards freedom, or ignore them and face more intense forms of suffering. Unless one is burnt in the fire of sorrow and suffering, spiritual life is but a remote possibility, a distant dream, or a mere intellectual debate or whim. The light of the Self cannot shine in the hearts of those who have not shed tears and learned lessons. Sincere prayers cannot come from the hearts that have not quivered and cried for divine help. The world of God opens not to those whose hearts are not soaked with tears of suffering and cries of pain. Along the paths carved by sorrow, mortal beings go through trials and tribulations into an immortal world that negates what they have previously experienced or understood. In no other way can the human mind be shaken out of the stupor and the delusion into which it habitually descends due to the destructive influence of the impure gunas. Arjuna suffered and, in the process, became wiser. He sought divine help, and God taught him valuable lessons about life and suffering through the Bhagavadgita, which He declared as the secret of all secrets. He revealed His immortal celestial teachings to Arjuna, by knowing which one would attain freedom from suffering here and salvation hereafter.

Therefore, however distasteful it may be, sorrow is not to be despised but looked upon with respect, gratitude and sameness, for it descends from above with a definite purpose, hiding in its bosom a hidden message, the seed of an awakening, or a line of spiritual instruction that can draw us close to the Universal Teacher. Sorrow is the poison that manifests as we start churning the ocean of mortal life to understand its mystery and transience and find the elixir that would make us immortal. Just as the great churning of the ocean of life led to the emergence of the elixir of life (amritam), the churning of the mind in the form of sorrow leads eventually to immortality only.

However, unless we know how to deal with sorrow and respond to it with peace and equanimity, we cannot achieve this sacred and auspicious goal. Even the great gods and the mighty demons had to deal with the poison of suffering as they began churning the ocean of life in search of the elixir that would make them immortal. Lord Siva neutralized the poison by drinking it and holding it in his throat, without letting it either go up into his mind or go down into his heart. In both places, it would have caused great harm and disrupted the very balance of creation and the existence of life, but in His throat, it remained ineffective and harmless and helped the gods and the demons to continue their quest for immortality. From this episode, we learn this lesson: Sometimes, you must swallow pain, but do not let it destroy you mentally or physically. However insufferable it may be, you should not speak about it vainly or worry about it. You must endure the pain with equanimity and let it pass. When suffering strikes, it is a reminder that God's attention is on you, and He has not forsaken you but has set you on a path to self-purification and self-realization.

Resolving Sorrow and Suffering

Sorrow or any feeling of sadness or emotion, which often afflicts our minds, is fleeting, just like all the phenomena in our impermanent world. However, suffering, in one form or another, continues to haunt the mind until one is liberated or develops inner strength and stability to remain equal to all situations and dualities. Suffering does not mean physical or mental pain and suffering only. In spirituality, it has broader implications. Birth is suffering. Living is suffering. Aging is suffering. Loss and gain are suffering. Dying is suffering. Rebirth is suffering. The very existence in samsara or bondage to the cycle of births and deaths itself is suffering. All the modifications that arise in the mind and body are sources of suffering only. Wants, needs, desires, attachments, association with anything, or disassociation from anything, all cause suffering only. Some people suffer from chronic depression that defies a permanent cure. We are speaking here of existential suffering, which is inherent to the lives and survival of all the jivas due to impermanence and association and dissociation with impermanent things.

Since suffering plays a vital role in our lives and comes in many forms, we need a suitable strategy to manage it without being overwhelmed. We must find solutions not only to resolve it but also to ensure our material and spiritual progress without disrupting our lives. As we have discussed before, suffering serves a vital purpose in our lives. It opens our eyes to our imperfections and vulnerabilities. It is a teacher in disguise, which imparts valuable spiritual lessons the hard way so that we can know ourselves, resolve our problems, and deal with our sorrows and suffering, or our emotions and passions, with awareness, wisdom, maturity, and intelligence. In the process of mitigating our suffering and dealing with adversity, we gain the wisdom, patience, and resolve to break out of the confines of our minds, bodies, and the world in which we are held in bondage by Nature. We grow into spiritually enlightened humans with a definitive purpose: to overcome death and rebirth.

Suffering teaches us that we must tread carefully in this world and not become involved with it or develop deep roots. We must view our existence here as temporary and ourselves as travelers in God's miraculous creation. Life itself is a miracle and a wonderful opportunity to experience it. Although suffering is a problem, it should not dampen our spirit to appreciate life, participate in it with enthusiasm, and fulfill our obligations to God and His creation. Suffering in the spiritual sense means suffering from bondage, mortality, impermanence, delusion, egoism, desires, attachments, dualities, mental instability, the opposing forces of attraction and aversion, etc. From this perspective, even having positive feelings such as happiness or joy also denotes suffering because you experience them due to desires and expectations. Besides, since they are fleeting, most likely suffering will arise when they subside. This is the truth. Whatever we may do, suffering is inherent in our very existence, and we can never be separate from it. As long as we are subject to desires and the dualities of life, we are vulnerable to suffering and modifications of our minds.

In this sense, living itself is a continuous state of suffering. Therefore, to believe that somehow we can cure our suffering magically and permanently, without addressing the basic causes, is a pure mistake. We may resolve suffering through other means, but it would be temporary. In some situations, it may even aggravate our suffering in the end. The Bhagavadgita suggests that we can resolve suffering permanently by acquiring knowledge and wisdom, controlling our desires and attachments, and cultivating sameness and equanimity. Until we reach that goal, we should learn to accept our suffering as an inevitable aspect of life and bear with it, without being disturbed by it. We should not abandon actions or escape from our duties and responsibilities in the hope of mitigating our suffering because suffering arises not from actions but from our desires and attachments hidden in them.

The Bhagavadgita is clearly a discourse on resolving human sorrow and suffering. It provides plausible and practical spiritual solutions to resolve it on a lasting basis. At the same time, it acknowledges that suffering is caused by impermanence, changes to our minds and bodies, and the activities of the triple gunas. Since they are inherent to our essential nature, the problem of suffering cannot be resolved easily without addressing the basic cause, which is our propensity to engage in desire-ridden actions due to delusion and egoism. Therefore, it suggests a comprehensive solution consisting of various approaches to resolve it permanently, such as the following.

1. Identify yourself with your inner Self rather than your mind and body. The Self is real. The mind and body wither and fall away. The name and form associated with them are temporary. If you think that you, like others, are a mere mortal and identify with your mind and body, or your physical self, you will suffer from the dualities of union and separation from the objects you seek and enjoy or the relationships you build. You are an immortal Self. If you are centered in it, you transcend your attachment to your mind and body and experience peace and stability. Therefore, always think that you are an immortal Self and live with that conviction.

2. Know the causes of your attachment and resolve them. Your attachments arise from your constant and repeated involvement with things and people. Attachment leads to habitual dependence upon things and to suffering caused by the duality and delusion of union and separation it creates. Desire and passions are at the root of your attachments. If you cultivate detachment and dispassion, you become equal to the pairs of opposites and experience peace and stability.

3. Perform your actions without ownership and doership. Ownership and doership arise out of egoism and the predominance of rajas. They are responsible for our striving and seeking and our bondage to earthly life. God is the true owner of all things in creation. He is the Self of all jivas and the source of all actions and movements. One should therefore renounce all notions of ownership and doership to attain knowledge, discernment, equanimity, sameness, and liberation.

4. Offer your actions to God with devotion as a sacrificial offering. When you surrender to God and offer Him all your actions with devotion and without desiring their fruit, He takes responsibility for your life and actions and all the consequences arising from them. The Bhagavadgita clearly states that God is the Sacrificer, the Sacrificed, and the result of sacrifice. He personifies sacrifices and remains hidden in them as the witness and enjoyer. In the sacrifice of our life, by offering our actions to Him selflessly without desiring their fruit, we can make God the true sacrificer, our actions sacrificial materials, and the results arising from them the fruit of the sacrifices. This way, our actions will not bind us.

5. Acknowledge God as the Supreme Lord of the Universe and the source of all. When you see God's presence everywhere, you will live with the sacred feeling that you are always in His company and under His guidance. Therefore, develop the expansive vision of feeling God's presence in every aspect of creation, seeing Him in all and all in Him, and without wishing to harm, disrespect, or criticize anyone. A skillful yogi neither disturbs anyone nor is disturbed by anyone. In the Bhagavadgita, Lord Krishna says such people are the dearest to Him.

6. Practice constant and continuous contemplation upon God. Whatever one thinks at the time of death, one becomes that. The Bhagavadgita assures that whoever contemplates upon God continuously acquires sattva and experiences peace, equanimity, and sameness. What one remembers at the time of one's death is also important. Those who spend their time thinking of God only remember Him at the time of their death and go to the world of immortals by the sunlit path.

7. Practice self-purification by increasing sattva. The predominance of sattva leads to the purification of the mind and body. With the predominance of sattva and suppression of rajas and tamas, the practice of detachment, meditation, contemplation, and self-absorption becomes easier. The mind becomes free from afflictions and experiences sameness towards the pairs of opposites. However, as the Bhagavadgita states, all gunas induce desires and attachments, and through them, desire-ridden actions and karma that will lead to bondage and suffering. Hence, one must eventually transcend all three gunas and become equal to all dualities.

8. Acquire the right knowledge. With the right knowledge comes the right discrimination and the ability to distinguish the difference between reality and illusion, truth and false, and the Self and the not-self. Right knowledge comes with self-study, practice of yoga, discernment, and the grace of God. With the right knowledge, you realize that the Self is real, immortal, and indestructible and that desires are the root cause of suffering. With that knowledge, you overcome delusion, see the world as a play of God, realize your true purpose, and work for your liberation.

9. Freedom from karma: As long as karma exists, a jiva remains bound to samsara and suffers from births and deaths. Bhagavadgita recommends appropriate yogas to arrest the flow of karma by practicing karma sannyasa, in which one must perform all actions without desires and offer their fruit to God. By transforming all actions into sacrifices and devotional and sacrificial offerings in the sacrifice of life, and by renouncing doership and ownership, one can resolve the problem of karma and attain liberation. There is no rebirth or suffering for those who attain freedom from karma (naishkarmya siddhi) and remain established in sameness, devotion, and contemplation.

Change and impermanence, attachment, desire, delusion, perceptual knowledge, duality, egoism, and impurities of rajas and tamas are some of the underlying causes of human suffering. Our suffering is a modification of Nature. It arises from the activity of the gunas, which are responsible for our desire-ridden actions and our attachment to material things. The knowledge of the Bhagavadgita helps us understand the causes and nature of our suffering. It teaches us how, with that knowledge, we may live in the world without being touched by its impurities. Suffering is a process of self-purification and inner awakening. The wise ones vouch for this. We can use suffering as a teacher to know how we are living and in what direction we are progressing. The cure for suffering is a comprehensive yoga or approach that leads to purity (sattva), obligatory duty (dharma), knowledge (jnanam), discernment (buddhi), and devotion (bhakti). The Bhagavadgita repeatedly returns to these subjects in the long discourse as the means to overcome duality and delusion and achieve liberation.

Symbolism of Arjuna's Sorrow

Symbolically, Arjuna represents an average human being, who is worldly, attached to his family, engages in householder duties, subject to mental and emotional instability, passions, desires, and attachments, strongly opinionated, but at the same time strives to live virtuously, safeguard the honor and reputation of his family, respects elders, understands the difference between sin and virtue, and is eager to fight for a righteous cause even if it is risky and may lead to his demise. Like all other humans, he was part divine and part human, rooted in both knowledge and ignorance, subject to dualities and delusion, and prone to engage in desire-ridden actions in the pursuit of Dharma, Artha, Kama, and Moksha. He was, by nature, a virtuous person, goodhearted, but vulnerable to doubt and confusion in moments of crisis and moral dilemmas. Being a warrior by profession, he was subject to the influence of the gunas, especially sattva and rajas.

He was also a God's devotee with unsteady faith and devotion. His predicament regarding the war and its consequences stemmed essentially from his ego that was firmly conditioned by pragmatism, worldliness, the authority of faith and tradition, his love and respect for his family members, elders, scriptures, and the promise of worldly enjoyment, name and fame through the conquest of a kingdom. His piety was the piety of an ego bred on relative human values and prevailing religious beliefs. His sorrow was the sorrow of a weak-hearted, approval-seeking human who was afraid that his actions would be disapproved by the world and bring harm and infamy to him, his family, and others. His tears were the outpouring of a mind filled with limited knowledge and egoistic beliefs. His depression was the depression of a mind propelled by standard biases and irrational and exaggerated fears. His grief was the grief of a deluded person caught in the snares of worldly life, pining for permanent escape.

Sorrow and depression are the natural expressions of a mind that is overwhelmed with conflicting values and the realization that our actions may lead to death and destruction, and bring misery upon others and ourselves. We stay within the confines of our comfort zones as long as our values and convictions are not challenged and our abilities are not put to the test. We open our eyes to the truths underlying our lives and actions only when we are confronted with our limitations and forced to perform unpleasant actions against our notions of right and wrong, which need not necessarily represent the eternal values enshrined in our scriptures or religions. In the middle of the battlefield, Arjuna was in the same situation. He had to deny a part of himself in order to resolve a serious moral conflict that confronted him, which arose because he decided to participate in a greatly destructive war.

Conflict and confusion are inherent in human life. In the oceanic depths of samsara, each being must navigate from conflict to conflict and confusion to confusion, until they find the raft of wisdom by which they can safely swim towards the other shore. Arjuna was a great warrior and learned scholar, but he was not free from the confusion caused by his egoistic thinking, relative values, and limited knowledge. His acquired beliefs, values, and the accumulated knowledge he gained from the sacred scriptures (smritis) were seriously challenged by the needs of the war and his duty as a warrior and brother to King Dharmaraja, for whom he was obligated to fight. Faced with the predicament of waging the war against his relations and familiar faces on the other side, he had to rethink and relearn the truths about his duty, conduct, and the consequences of the war. He needed new knowledge and awareness, which would absorb his conflicts without seriously disturbing the continuity of his life and actions. His consciousness needed the touch of divine knowledge so that it would attain peace and harmony. Spiritually, he was ready for the dawn of light from above. It came to him in the form of Lord Krishna, his Friend, Philosopher, and the Supreme Self.

Arjuna was an earthly being bound to his traditions and beliefs, with an ego that was caught in its own illusions. The words of Arjuna, therefore, echo the suffering and confusion we face in our lives, and his conflict resembles the innumerable conflicts we experience every day as we deal with our problems, in which we have to compromise our values, beliefs, relationships, and duties. We are not always wise in our actions. When we come under the sway of our emotions or when our reasoning is greatly impaired by fear and anxiety, we falter in our thinking and judgment. Nor can we claim authority over the forces of Nature with our limited knowledge. According to our scriptures, our knowledge is more qualified as ignorance rather than real knowledge. We are subject to many influences and susceptible to bias and perceptual errors. We cannot entirely rely upon our beliefs and conclusions because what we perceive and comprehend as experience is colored by our prejudices, faulty reasoning, selective memory, and mental fatigue rather than truth and the reality of the world itself. Because of the impurities present in our consciousness, there are bound to be errors and mistakes in our awareness, which, unfortunately, we do not easily recognize and do not willingly rectify. This makes our effort of self-transformation a difficult, painful, and arduous task.

The play of ego

The ego is responsible for all the activity arising from the desires that are induced by the gunas. It is responsible for our selfish actions, self-promotion, and self-preservation, and thereby for our karma. Ego is a blind force, which is mostly mechanical, ignorant of the Self, deluded, and predominantly selfish. As an instrument of Nature, it serves its designs and suffers from modifications. By nature, it is bound to the things of the world. This prevents us from seeing transcendental truths with the help of our intelligence and experiencing peace and stability within ourselves. By its actions and attachment, the human ego keeps the embodied Self bound to the world and delays its liberation. It has no illumination of its own. Hence, most of its actions are instinctual, mechanical, and predictable. Hence, it is not difficult to know what the ego stands for and how it plays its due role as an instrument of Maya. We can identify its presence in our consciousness and behavior since it represents the self-sense or the idea of oneself as a limited being, distinct from others and the rest of creation. The following are a few important distinguishing features by which the play of the ego can be discerned within oneself and others.

1. Ego is the individuality and identity we develop since birth due to desires and attachments, whereby we experience duality, division, diversity, and the delusion that the physical self is the real Self.

2. Ego represents a person's impermanent, deconstructible, and

destructible identity or the not-self that thrives on duality, desires, and delusion.
3. Being a part of Nature's tattvas, the ego-self lives and dies with the body and is never liberated. It lacks illumination of its own but takes advantage of the illumination it receives from the Self.
4. The ego assumes ownership and doership of desire-ridden actions, which produce sinful karma. This results in rebirth and bondage of the embodied Self to samsara.
5. Ego remains under the perpetual influence of the gunas and never ceases to be independent of them until it is completely purified and suppressed.
6. Ego can be purified, transformed, and dissolved into the Self through spiritual practices.
7. It is bound to the world through the activity of the senses.
8. It is part of the internal organ and subjects the mind to mental modifications (vrittis).
9. Ego is the outer layer that envelops and conceals the pure nature hidden in all.

The redeeming feature of the ego is that it is amenable to discipline, control, withdrawal, and purification and does not have to remain perpetually ignorant and deluded. At some point in the long journey of a jiva in the mortal world, it may wake up to the reality that it must surrender to God or the divine Self in the body and work for its purification and liberation. It realizes that until it is completely dismantled and rendered ineffective, its suffering will continue. Through the study of the scriptures and cultivating discernment, it learns that it is bound to samsara because of desires and desire-ridden actions and must strive to cultivate detachment, practice renunciation, and escape permanently from its bondage to the cycle of births and deaths. Having realized the impermanence of the world and the causes of karma and suffering, it turns to spiritual practice and works for its liberation.

Knowing the difference between the true self and false self, and between knowledge and delusion, the jiva who has been under the influence of the ego and remained an enemy of himself and an obstacle to his liberation, becomes a friend of himself. Resting his mind in contemplation, practicing exclusive devotion, renouncing all desires and attachments, he eventually dissolves himself in the pure consciousness of the Supreme Self. Even if he fails in his current life, he resumes his practice in the next, since, as the Bhagavadgita states, there is no loss in this effort. One can always return to the path of liberation and start from where one has left in this life or the next. Those who do not do so continue to remain deluded and bound to samsara. The sum of this is that when it is impure and deluded, the ego helps the jiva in its survival and pursuit of worldly goals. When it is purified and transformed, it becomes an instrument of God and helps the jiva in its liberation. Hence, the Bhagavadgita (6.5) declares, "Uplift yourself by yourself; do not debase yourself. Surely, you are your own kin and truly your enemy."

The True Meaning of Renunciation

Renunciation and liberation are common themes in almost all religious traditions that are native to the Indian subcontinent. Renunciant traditions probably existed in India even during the Indus Valley period and before the advent of the Vedic religion. Numerous ascetic traditions existed in ancient India in the post-Vedic and pre-Buddhist times, each with its own set of rules, teachers, theories, and practices. Traces of their teachings and practices, such as karma, rebirth, austerities, contemplation, self-control, celibacy, etc., found their way into Vedism, Jainism, Shaivism, Buddhism, Vaishnavism, and Tantrism. The Rigveda mentions Kesins, the long-haired renunciants who seemed to have practiced breath control and possessed paranormal powers. The ascetics of ancient India were known by several names, such as Sramanas, Parivrajakas, Jinas, Ajivakas, Vratyas, Adishaivas, Pasupathas, etc. The Bhagavatas also belonged to the same category. They worshipped Vishnu and Vasudeva Krishna, engaged in devotional services, practiced image worship, renunciation, and exclusive devotion, and left an indelible mark on Hinduism. Most likely, the Bhagavadgita was their sacred text. Over time, they merged into Vaishnavism.

The Bhagavadgita adds a new meaning and interpretation to the concept of renunciation. The traditional meaning is giving up worldly life, worldly attachments, and the use of fire, and living in seclusion, away from worldly people and the places they frequent. According to the Bhagavadgita, true sannyasa or renunciation is the renunciation of desires but not obligatory duties. It is well reflected in an attitude of selflessness and egolessness, marked by freedom from desires and absence of attachment in performing one's actions. The scripture goes one step further and declares that true renunciation is renunciation of the fruit of one's actions, not the actions themselves. One should not give up one's obligatory duties and responsibilities, but desire for things and expectations arising from them. Although it looks easy, it isn't easy to practice. You can practice true renunciation only when you become indifferent to your gunas by transcending them and accept the pairs of opposites in your life with equanimity and sameness. For a seeker of liberation, renunciation of actions or his obligatory duties is not the goal, but renunciation of desires and attachment to actions (4.20) is. It is by renouncing the desire for the fruit of his actions that a karmayogi becomes a true sannyasi.

The journey of renunciation must begin first in the mind, mentally giving up all notions of individuality, egoism, desires, and attachments. However, renouncing your favorite things mentally is much more difficult. You may wear the robes of an ascetic and give up attachments, but unless you are mentally free from the things of the world, your practice will remain incomplete and imperfect. You extend yourself into the world through your mind, and in the process, you become your mind. You carry it around, always in your thoughts and actions. In your wakeful state, it is an inseparable part of your consciousness. For ordinary people, it is the consciousness itself because they have not yet experienced the reality that exists beyond their minds and senses. Therefore, if you want to practice true renunciation, you must free your mind from attachments by practicing detachment. In true renunciation, inner conflicts and self-doubts do not exist.

In their quest for liberation, the yogis must know where they stand and what they need to do. They should not practice renunciation even for the sake of liberation because doing something with a desire, or an end in mind, defeats the purpose and the spirit of true renunciation. In renunciation, practitioners must give up everything: their thoughts, desires, and opinions, including their desire for liberation. The Bhagavadgita proclaims that a karmayogi, who neither hates nor desires, should be considered a true sannyasi, because it is by overcoming desires that a person transcends the pair of opposites hidden in his passions and emotions (5.03). It also distinguishes between renunciation and sacrifice (tyagam). Renunciation is giving up the desires hidden within actions, whereas sacrifice is giving up the fruit of all actions (18.04).

Lord Krishna says that one should not give up obligatory duties such as sacrificial rituals (yajnas), charity (danam), and austerity (tapas) because they are purifiers whose practice leads to the predominance of sattva (18.06). However, they should be performed by renouncing attachment and desire for their fruit (18.06). Renunciation and actions are interrelated. The yoga of renunciation and the yoga of action both lead to liberation when they are practiced simultaneously. Renunciation without performing desireless actions is futile. Hence, of the two, the yoga of action is said to be superior (5.02).

What you give up in your renunciation is also important. People practice renunciation according to their nature. Sattvic people renounce desires and attachments. Rajasic people renounce pain and fear. Tamasic people renounce action itself (18.07–09). In true renunciation, a yogi transcends all doubts, emotions, and pairs of opposites. He is contended with whatever he gets by chance. Free from envy, he treats both success and failure equally (4.22). He is untouched by sin, just like the lotus leaf by water. Mentally renouncing all actions and self-controlled, he lives in the body untouched by the consequences of his actions (5.13). Those who do not practice true renunciation suffer from the consequences of their actions. Pleasant, unpleasant, and mixed, says Gita, are the results arising from their actions. God Himself practices renunciation in a sattvic manner. He performs actions even though He is complete and He has no desires.

In terms of attitude and approach, a karmayogi is not different from a sannyasi. A karmayogi is a sannyasi in attitude, and a sannyasi is a karmayogi in action when they both practice renunciation of desires. In both cases, action and renunciation are well integrated into their respective disciplines. To be effective in their practice, karmayogis must act and live with the attitude of sannyasis, while sannyasis must perform actions with the attitude of true karmayogis. Both must perform desireless actions, without any expectations, and remain content with whatever fruit has been gained unsought. They should not be troubled by positive or negative gains that accrue from their actions or past karma, nor should they feel elated when they interact with worldly objects or when they are separated from them. They must respond to pain and pleasures alike, and endure their bodily pains and suffering with equanimity and forbearance, knowing the fleeting nature of all mundane experiences and the need to practice restraint and detachment to attain sameness and freedom from karma. They must be free from jealousy, anger, and such passions and afflictions of the mind and remain inwardly detached from the noise and attractions of worldly life. Though they participate in the affairs of the world, they should control their senses and develop the ability to withdraw themselves from the sense objects at will. In this manner, karmayogis must be like sannyasis in theory, and sannyasis must be like karmayogis in practice.

The Bhagavadgita provides a glimpse of how a true sannyasi lives and thinks. In the fifth chapter, we are informed, "Whether in seeing, hearing, touching, smelling, tasting, walking, sleeping, or breathing, while performing actions, a true sannyasi thinks that he is doing nothing at all. And when he is performing his bodily functions, he knows that only his senses are dealing with the sense objects." (5.8-9). Thus, a true sannyasi is but a karmayogi in daily life. A true sannyasi is God centered. His thoughts revolve around God, and he thinks of God as he performs his actions. He performs his obligatory duties with detachment and offers them to God as sacrificial offerings. He is not concerned with the result as he acknowledges God as the real doer and himself as a mere instrument. Despite his lack of interest in ownership, he does not abandon his duties towards himself, his family, and his society. Sattvic in nature, he is compassionate and unconditional in his relationship with others. He regards his life as an offering to God, surrendering himself to Him completely. The impurities of life do not touch him because he is detached, in control of his mind and senses, and free from egoism. Because he renounces doer-ship and acknowledges God as the real doer, he remains untouched by sin.

The Bhagavadgita declares renunciation as the highest form of spiritual discipline because peace follows renunciation immediately (12.12). The attitude of renunciation is well evident in the life and activities of Lord Krishna himself. Though he led a luxurious life, seemingly enjoying the privileges of royalty as the head of a clan, he was inwardly detached. He stood on the side of righteousness and destroyed demons and evil people, with a sense of duty rather than vindictiveness. In the Mahabharata, while the various characters go through the epic narrative displaying tumultuous emotions and passions, Lord Krishna remains calm and composed throughout, even when the Kauravas intend to harm Him. Indeed, in Lord Krishna, we find the perfect blend of a true karmayogi and sannyasi. You, too, can incorporate into your life the spirit of renunciation like Him and exemplify the idea of karma sannyasa by practicing the following.

1. Performing obligatory duties without desires
2. Cultivating discerning intelligence
3. Knowing and identifying yourself as an eternal Self
4. Overcoming desires and attachments
5. Acquiring knowledge and wisdom
6. Cultivating sattva and divine qualities
7. Practicing self-restraint and detachment
8. Offering your actions to God
9. Practicing self-control and exclusive devotion
10. Acknowledging God as the source of all

Indeed, when the ego is completely subdued and the individuality is fully dissolved in the awareness of the Self or the Supreme Lord, the spirit of renunciation automatically manifests in the nondual state of the yogi. He does not perform actions, even when he appears to perform them. In that state of nonduality, he exemplifies inaction in action and action in inaction, remaining free from the impurities of karma and the world.

Symbolic themes from the Bhagavadgita

You may regard the Bhagavadgita, revered as eternal and divine by millions of people, as an indispensable and authoritative source on Hinduism. One does not have to read many scriptures to understand its essential philosophy. By reading the Bhagavadgita a few times with devotion and concentration, you will know its principal teachings better than most people who are Hindus by birth or namesake. After reading the Bhagavadgita and the Mahabharata, one may draw the conclusion or the inference that Lord Krishna was a great social and religious reformer. According to the Puranas, he incarnated in India to restore Dharma when there were internecine wars, chaos, and disorder due to the ascendence of evil and immorality. He was probably born at a time when conflicting opinions of various schools about karma, dharma, yoga, sannyasa, moksha, sacrifice, God, creation, and other important beliefs were prevalent, and Vedic religion was going through a transformation in search of the right methods, solutions, and direction. Lord Krishna defined and reinterpreted the major concepts, beliefs, and practices of the Vedic religion. He also revived the theistic aspect which was missing in the original Vedic tradition by emphasizing the importance of devotional practice and putting God at the center of the Vedanta philosophy at a time when ritualism, atheism, and agnosticism were on the rise even within the Vedic fold.

The dominant philosophy of those times was the Purva Mimansa school, the original Mimansa, which believed in the supremacy of the Vedic sacrifices (yajnas) as the source of all, ignoring God and His role in creation. The Mimansikas even held that the Vedic yajnas offered all solutions to human suffering, and making sacrifices to the gods was just one of the many gifts that flowed from them. In their worldview, the gods did not matter as much as the yajnas, since through them alone, one could obtain boons from the gods. In other words, they were not opposed to householders performing obligatory duties and sacrifices to fulfill their material and spiritual desires in pursuit of Dharma, Artha, Kama, and Moksha, and attain heavenly life and a favorable rebirth. Lord Krishna offered a God-centric philosophy as an alternative, suggesting that obligatory duties were meant to serve God's creation without desires and, through that sacrifice, attain fulfillment and liberation. He suggested that everything happening in our lives is due to God's inviolable will, and even liberation requires His grace or mercy (anugraha).

In presenting his teachings, he reinterpreted the diverse philosophies of the ancient world, such as Samkhya and Yoga, and presented them from a purely theistic perspective as a composite teaching of liberation that could help practicing yogis escape from samsara. The Bhagavadgita is the result of his lifetime effort. Devotees look upon him as a deity, ignoring that he was also a great teacher and social reformer who revived Vedism and poured new life into it by transforming it from a religion of rituals and sacrifices into a religion of profound spirituality. You may consider the scripture a summary of the principles and practices that now constitute the principal features of Hinduism. Vedism, which was the prevailing religion of his time, is now an integral part of Hinduism. Lord Krishna presented it from a spiritual and theistic perspective for the liberation of pure-hearted souls who are ready for it and willing to practice the sacred discipline of a comprehensive yoga that will eventually lead to perfection and complete freedom.

However, the scripture is not intended for religious propaganda or to declare Hinduism or any of its sects or philosophies as superior. The faithful may use it to validate their beliefs, which has been the practice in Hinduism for centuries. It is not meant for ignorant people to take pride in it without knowing or practicing it. Instead, it helps the Lord's devotees know themselves and build a path to the highest heaven, emphasizing duty, devotion, and liberation through self-purification, bringing God into their lives and inspiring them to offer themselves devotionally to Him as a sacrifice. Certainly, it is not meant to attract new followers from other faiths or to confuse them with unfamiliar concepts. If you read the Bhagavadgita, you know why this is important. In the scripture, Lord Krishna Himself explicitly forbids teaching the knowledge to those who are not qualified. He clearly stipulates four rules and suggests that the recipients must meet all four. Satisfying them is indeed a tall order in today's world. Hardly will you find anyone who can measure up to them.

In other words, the Bhagavadgita, unlike the Bible, is not a missionary tool. It is not intended for propaganda or to attract new followers. Its knowledge is not for everyone. It is especially meant for those who are pure-hearted and exclusively devoted to God, who have love and veneration for Lord Krishna, Vishnu, or any deity whom we worship as Isvara, and who are free from doubt and demonic nature. To follow it sincerely and benefit from it, one must become pure like a clean mirror. To understand its precepts, the mind must be open and receptive to divine truths. If you wish to follow it to achieve liberation, you must possess wisdom and a steady mind to discern right from wrong and reality from delusion. Liberation is not easy for everyone and is not meant for everyone. Swami Vivekananda once said, *"You will be nearer to Heaven through football than through the study of the Gita."* What he meant was that if you are not naturally drawn to the pursuit of liberation or feel inspired by the Gita's teachings, you should rather focus on what you are good at to develop your physical and mental strength and spiritual nature, and keep doing it dutifully until you are ready for the journey of liberation. The Bhagavadgita (6.16-17) amply conveys it when it says, *"Yoga is not for the one who eats voraciously, nor for the one who does not eat at all; not for the one who sleeps for too long, nor for the one who remains awake. He who is sensible in his eating and enjoyment, who restrains his mind in actions, (and) whose sleeping and waking are balanced, for him, yoga becomes the destroyer of his sorrows."*

Karmayoga is the first step in our spiritual awakening because action or movement, which is a form of dynamism (chaitanyam), is the essential and inherent function of life. Your journey of liberation begins when you take your duties and actions seriously and perform them not only for yourself or your family but also for God and His creation. In Hinduism, selfishness is considered evil. When you transcend selfishness, by overcoming your desires, attachments, and ego-centric thinking and attitude, and when you begin to think of not only your welfare but also the welfare of others who are a part of God's creation and in whom He resides as their Self, you qualify for liberation. When your actions become offerings, your life takes a new turn. Your mind opens up and you begin to receive divine guidance, first imperceptibly, then clearly, and convincingly. It heralds a journey that brings you closer and closer to God until you reflect His qualities in your nature without obstructions and attain oneness with Him.

The antiquity of the scripture is uncertain. Whatever may be its true origins, the philosophy it contains, at least in parts, may be as old as the earliest Upanishads. Most likely, it attained its current form much later, with revisions and improvements, but its roots are much older and deeper than those of many Hindu scriptures. We may consider it a compendium of the teachings of the Vedas and several ancient philosophies that are now lost or have become integrated into others. While the teachings of Lord Krishna probably existed in a fragmentary form in the Indian subcontinent since the later Vedic period, they might have been brought together as a scripture much later, probably after the death of the Buddha. Based on the similarities in styles, some historians believe that the Bhagavadgita is a "genuine part" of the Mahabharata. As a scripture in its current form, it probably existed since 400 B.C.E. Its ascendance might have been in response to the growing popularity of Buddhism and Jainism, at a time when the Mathura region, the birthplace of Lord Krishna, came under the influence of foreign rulers like the Sakas and the Kushanas and ascetic traditions such as Buddhism and Jainism gained prominence.

The Bhagavadgita is one of the most dissected, discussed, and debated scriptures of Hinduism. Its message is better organized than that of the Upanishads and is more coherent and direct, making it easier to read and understand. It puts greater emphasis on the subject of liberation and self-transformation rather than the cryptic ritual terminology and its associated symbolism found in the earliest Upanishads, such as the Brihadaranyaka and Chandogya Upanishads. It does not deal with the abstract notions of Brahman but His manifestation as Isvara, the Lord and Controller of the Universe, who is responsible for everything and the secret moving power behind all our actions and destinies. Divided into 18 chapters of varying lengths, it contains 700 verses (according to some versions 699), which deal with various subjects such as the Self, the body and the senses, the field of Nature, the Supreme Self, rebirth, gunas or qualities, liberation, devotion, surrender, and so on.

The scripture is a purifier. Those who read its verses regularly find it very inspiring and enlightening. Some of the verses and phrases found in it make it an excellent source of thoughts and ideas for contemplation and meditation, besides offering great insight into the nature of our lives and the means to liberation. If you read it every day, you are bound to feel the difference in your thinking and attitude. If you are in difficulties, you can rely on it to find answers to your vexing problems. By referring to it frequently and consistently, you will gradually gain peace and stability. However, you will not come to the Bhagavadgita and understand its percepts unless you have accumulated sinless karma in the past and earned enough merit. As Lord Krishna told Arjuna in the discourse, there is no loss in this effort. If you have made some effort in the past, it will precipitate ideal conditions in your life at the right time and lead you in the right direction. It may not be appropriate to read the scripture with the expectation of material gains, although the scripture does not prohibit it. However, if you begin reading it occasionally, you will gradually become aware of the importance of overcoming desires and performing actions for the sake of God rather than for yourself.

One must not be misled by the apparent meaning of some of its verses or the archaic phrases they contain, whose true meaning we might have lost. The apparent meaning is just one aspect of it. People may interpret them in various ways, but what you understand from your study is important because it reflects your own spiritual growth and inner transformation. One may tell you that the scripture is about Advaita, Vishistadvaita, or Dvaita, but you must arrive at its truths by your own convictions and feelings in your heart. The scripture offers you ample freedom to interpret its doctrine. Hence, scholars from every school of philosophy found in it enough evidence to justify their arguments. To understand it clearly, you must have the knowledge of important concepts of Hinduism, such as karma, the Self, rebirth, yoga, Nature, gunas, and so on. Some verses of the scripture are also constructed like sutras, where you may have to rely upon your knowledge and imagination to fill in gaps and grasp their meaning. Some verses of the Bhagavadgita are difficult to understand because the meaning and usage of certain words and phrases found in them have been lost or changed over time. You may also find that the chapter titles may not adequately represent the content presented by them. The scripture also contains hidden symbolism. Even a seemingly inconsequential verse may point to some latent meaning, discernible only to a few. Conceived originally as a text within another text (the Mahabharata), it is presented as a conversation between Lord Krishna and Arjuna in the middle of a battlefield.

While on the surface the discourse of the Bhagavadgita may appear as a religious conversation, hidden within its verses are echoes of the main precepts of Hinduism and their symbolic representation, more particularly the Upanishadic doctrines of Vedism about the Self, the Supreme Self, and liberation. It is difficult to say whether this is intentional or coincidental, but the striking examples of symbolism present in the scripture indicate that it has a far deeper spiritual significance than what casual readers might understand perfunctorily.

The title

Bhagavadgita means the song of the glorious Lord (Bhagavat). It is derived from the Sanskrit word, bhaga, the equivalent of 'baga' of Old Persian and 'bog' of Slavic languages, meaning the lord or god [1]. Bhagavan, another derivative word, refers to the Godhead who is endowed with six supreme qualities, namely strength, fame, wealth, knowledge, beauty, and detachment. Bhaga is also the name of one of the twelve solar deities (Adityas) of the Vedic pantheon. He is mentioned in the Vedas as the god of wealth and marriage. Known for his brilliance, he is mentioned in the Rigveda as the god who rewards people according to their merit. Bhaga also means wealth, prosperity, lordship, virtue, pleasure, enjoyment, beauty, dignity, and distinction, which are usually the qualities associated with God or someone in a position of great power and authority, such as a divine king. Bhaga also means radiance or light, often used as an adjective in reference to fire or the sun. Bhaga is another name for Nature or the womb. Bhagavan is its Lord, the giver of the seed of life and consciousness that manifests in the womb of Prakriti.

Bhagavad means glorious, illustrious, powerful, divine, venerable, and holy. Bhagavadgita is therefore a glorious song or a holy song. According to the Vaishnava tradition, the devotees of Krishna are of two types, simple devotees (bhaktas) and servants of devotees. The latter are known as the bhāgavatas, specially chosen or appointed by God to serve His devotees selflessly. The Bhagavadgita is not only a song about duty, devotion, and liberation but also about how one may learn to serve the Lord and His devotees by becoming a true bhāgavata, performing selfless actions in His service, and offering their fruit to Him only. The bhāgavatas exemplify the principles of the yoga of knowledge (jnana), action (karma), devotion (bhakti), and renunciation (sannyasa). They perform actions with surrender, detachment, and devotion without the expectation of a reward or result. They simply obey the instructions of God with humility and submission. You may compare them to the Bodhisattvas of Buddhism, who delay their liberation to render selfless service to humankind out of pure compassion. Bhagavatas were once an ancient religious sect. They became integrated into Vaishnavism subsequently.

We may consider the Bhagavadgita a sacred song of God for the devotees and those who serve God and His devotees selflessly. It is not meant for everyone, but especially for those who have faith, love, and devotion to God and are willing to give up everything and surrender themselves to Him. In the scripture itself, Lord Krishna declares that of all the people, His devotees are dearest to him; however, even among His devotees, He declares that none is dearer to Him than those who spread His teachings among His devotees. Thus, the scripture offers two choices to those who pursue its knowledge: to be a devotee (bhakta) or be a servant of God and his devotees (a Bhagavata).

Kurukshetra

The dialogue between Arjuna and Lord Krishna took place on the battlefield of Kurukshetra, which is also known popularly as a holy land (dharmakshetram). It is holy because it is saturated with the blood of several great warriors (yodhas) and eminent souls (mahatmas) who fought and died while performing their duties as warriors. The location chosen for the occasion was not by chance. The battle was fated to happen by the will of God, and this was clearly stated in the scripture. Lord Krishna purposefully delivered the discourse in the middle of the battlefield, where an epochal war between good and evil forces was destined to happen. Being the Supreme Self and the Knower of past and future, He would have chosen any other place for the purpose. He would have anticipated Arjuna's reaction and given him counseling even before they reached the battlefield, but waited until they arrived there, because Kurukshetra provided a fitting background for the discourse, which was not just about a war but the wars and conflicts that we face and fight every day within ourselves and at various levels. We are pitted against the unrelenting forces of Nature, and we fight battles every day against those forces to survive and succeed. Indeed, in the battlefield of life, we are all warriors. We fight against our worst instincts and desires, against others who envy us or want to defeat us, and against the invisible forces of Maya that want to keep us under their control, bound to mortality and samsara. Bhagavadgita delivers a practical and useful message for everyone who wants to participate in this battle and become a divine warrior in the pursuit of freedom. Symbolically, Kurukshetra represents Maya's Field (kshetra), otherwise known as the body, the earth, Nature, and world itself. These four aspects of our material existence have one thing in common: they are subject to the influence of the gunas and the play of Maya, and they keep the souls in bondage.

The body is a battlefield in which the gunas wage a constant battle for predominance, while the Self remains as the witness, bound to the body. The conflict between the gunas manifests in us as a conflict between good and evil intentions and between pure and impure thoughts. The divine and demonic qualities arise in us because of impurities, for which the gunas are primarily responsible. Sattva represents purity. The mode of rajas represents passions such as pride and lust, and egoistic desires for worldly enjoyments, and tamas represents evil passions, ignorance, darkness, and delusion. One can also see a similar conflict happening in the outside world as the gunas in different jivas propel them into action and seek things that agree with their nature. Life is a hardship because we have to face many obstacles in our struggle for existence. If we are looking for liberation, our struggle increases manifold. If we want to lead pure and austere lives, we must overcome our evil tendencies that assail us. We will succeed only if we conquer our innate tendencies with the firmness of a warrior, the wisdom of an enlightened yogi, the austerity of a karmayogi, and the noble attitude of a person of renunciation. In this battle, the Self is the witness, intelligence is the teacher, and the body is the devotee. In the Bhagavadgita, Lord Krishna Himself described the body as the Field (kshetra) and the Self as the Knower of the Field (kshetrajna). On the path of liberation, the first obstacle that you must surpass is your attachment to your body and your infatuation and dependence upon it for your identity and individuality. To remedy this, you must withdraw from it into your mind and accept yourself as a being of pure consciousness, and focus on purifying and stabilizing it. You must support and promote good thoughts and intentions internally and externally so that eventually you will overcome the demons of your mind and become equal to all the modifications that arise in you. The mind is thus a battlefield, and so also the body, where you must win if liberation is your goal. Therefore, the battlefield has been appropriately selected for the Bhagavadgita discourse to remind the readers that in this great war of their lives, they must fight their spiritual battles both individually and collectively against painful afflictions (kleshas), temptations, evil tendencies, desires, and demonic qualities, with the help of God, faith, and resolve and with the practice of yoga. All wars must be fought and won first in the mind before they can be won in real life.

Krishna and Arjuna

Lord Krishna and Arjuna, the two principal characters of the Bhagavadgita, represent the two fundamental dualities of creation in the microcosm of a living being (jiva) and in the macrocosm of the Universal Being. In the macrocosm, Lord Krishna stands for the Supreme Self and Arjuna for the individual Self, or in popular terms, God and devotee. In the microcosm, Lord Krishna stands for the inner Self or the eternal Self, and Arjuna for the ego-self. Arjuna personifies egoism, worldliness, delusion, and ignorance, while Lord Krishna is the immortal and indestructible Self. One may also compare them to higher nature and lower nature as well as the higher mind, which is guided by knowledge, intelligence, and discernment, and the lower mind, which is guided by ignorance, impulses, emotions, and feelings. The conversation between the two represents the reflection of the transcendental knowledge in the purified citta (consciousness) of a skillful yogi in a state of self-absorption. It is the reflection of the Knower of the Field in the field itself, whereby one overcomes delusion and becomes aware of one's true identity or spiritual nature and the need for liberation. In a state of duality, Lord Krishna is the subject, Arjuna is the object, and the discourse is the connecting link.

Historically, Lord Krishna and Arjuna are referred to as the eternal Being (Narayana) and the primeval being (nara), respectively. They signify the relationship between God and humans. Their relationship is neither one-sided nor unequal, although the deluded may mistakenly believe so. It is one of mutual love, equality, and respect. When humans worship God with exclusive devotion and dedicate their lives to Him, He readily responds to them by showering them with His love and grace. He grants them liberation, providing them with knowledge, helping them in their purification and transformation, and giving them an exalted place in His heart and Abode. In the hierarchy of His creation, His liberated devotees enjoy a higher status than the gods and celestial beings.

The chariot and the Charioteer

The Bhagavadgita discourse took place not only on the battlefield but also in Arjuna's chariot, driven by Lord Krishna, as He agreed to act as his charioteer on the battlefield without supporting any side or fighting. The chariot he drove on this occasion hides a deep symbolism. The discourse begins when Lord Krishna and Arjuna enter the battlefield in a chariot, with Krishna seated and holding the reins and Arjuna either seated or standing with his bow and arrows. When Krishna stops the chariot between the two armies, they both witness Duryodhana discussing with his generals and preparing them for the day's battle. Arjuna watches both armies, his friends, family, and elders, arrayed on both sides. As the specter of war looms, he loses his heart thinking that he would be responsible for the deaths of countless warriors, the people he loved and admired throughout his life. Wouldn't that be a grave sin? Will he ever be forgiven by the gods and ancestors?

This imagery has obvious implications. The battlefield symbolizes life itself. The armies symbolize the countless attachments and relationships we form with the world. The chariot represents the jiva, body, or Field. You, the eternal Self, enter the battlefield of life in a body, the chariot, and witness yourself in conflict with the things and people that matter to you as you pursue your goals and desires. The chariot's two wheels symbolize the wheel of dharma and karma. The spokes in the wheels represent the tattvas in our bodies and the diversity, duality, divisions, and the pairs of opposites that are inherent to our existence. Arjuna represents the embodied Self (jivatma) and Lord Krishna the transcendental Self (paramatma). We may compare the horses to the sense organs and the reins to the limbs of yoga. The overall symbolism of the chariot and its occupants suggests that to win against adverse forces in the battlefield of life, the occupants of the chariot must keep driving it and keep fighting. In the spiritual sense, it means the embodied jiva must keep performing his obligatory duties, restraining his senses, with God as His guide and teacher, and surrendering himself to His will. When God's devotees surrender to Him fully and unconditionally, giving over to Him the reins of their life, He assumes personal responsibility for them and their actions and guides them in the right direction according to their essential nature.

Sanjaya and Dhritarashtra

The Bhagavadgita begins with a question from Dhritarashtra and an answer from Sanjaya. Those who are familiar with the Mahabharata know that Sanjaya was a clairvoyant. When Dhritarashtra, who was born without eyesight, expressed to sage Vyasa his desire to witness the events on the battlefield of Kurukshetra, he sent his disciple, Sanjaya, to act on his behalf and give the king a firsthand account of the war with his clairvoyance. According to his teacher's instruction, Sanjaya narrated not only the 18 chapters of the Bhagavadgita but also the entire war that lasted for 18 days. Dhritarashtra, the blind king, symbolizes the human ego, which is subject to selfishness, ignorance, delusion, and the lack of foresight and discernment. Sanjaya, endowed with his knowledge and supernatural abilities (siddhis), personifies discriminating intelligence (buddhi) or wisdom. Both of them, the ego and intelligence, are a part of the body (Field) and this worldly (apara), in contrast to Lord Krishna and Arjuna, who represent the transcendental reality (para) as the individual Self and the Supreme Self.

In terms of gunas, Dhritarashtra personifies the mode of tamas (darkness), Sanjaya represents rajas (passion), and Arjuna symbolizes sattva (purity), while Lord Krishna, who represents the Supreme Lord, is gunatita (beyond the gunas) since he embodies pure sattva (suddha sattva) that is not a part of Nature. Although Dhritarashtra had intelligence (Sanjaya) serving him as his counselor, he lacked discrimination and, due to his envy and selfishness, allowed his children to fall into evil ways and precipitate the war. He did not try hard to advise them or stop them from acting unjustly towards their cousins, whom he should have treated as his children and given them their due share of the kingdom. His selfishness prevented him from doing that. From the question [2] he posed to Sanjaya, it is clear that he was not at all interested in the dialogue between Arjuna and Lord Krishna. He just wanted to know what was happening on the battlefield and how his sons were preparing to fight. It was by chance that he happened to listen to the discourse of Lord Krishna. However, from his reaction in the last chapter of the scripture, we can discern that the entire discourse, despite its profound spiritual depth, left no mark on Him, although he listened to it until the end from Sanjaya. Even the fact that in the universal form of Lord Krishna, Arjuna saw the dance of Death and all the warriors marching into the fiery jaws of Death, which forebode the imminent death of all his sons, did not seem to have left any impact on him. In contrast, Sanjaya responded differently when Lord Krishna showed his universal form and when he concluded the discourse. He was filled with rapturous joy and devotion. The two characters offered a marked contrast. People often ignore their greatest blessings in life and remain preoccupied with their depressing and egoistic thoughts and concerns. In life, we find many opportunities to learn from our experiences and observations and grow spiritually. We ignore the spiritual masters even if they are in our proximity or when we have numerous opportunities to interact with them and learn from them, because our interests are elsewhere, or we are too busy with our desires and attachments to notice them or listen to them. It was the same with Dhritarashtra. The discourse left no indelible influence upon him. He was fated to ignore it and remain deluded and disconsolate as his sons were all destined to die in the war, leaving him alone with his wife to ponder over the fate that befell them.

Symbolism of the plot

The Bhagavadgita is a revelation. You will find in its 18 chapters divine knowledge coming straight from Lord Krishna, God-incarnate or God in a human body. He did not deliver it in a trance, nor to a devotee who was in a trance. He delivered it in the middle of a battlefield, while everyone was watching them from a little distance. It was not meant for Arjuna alone but for all humans who believed in the eternal Dharma of performing obligatory duties and achieving liberation through spiritual effort. What this means is that Lord Krishna brought the knowledge from the subtle planes into the wakeful consciousness. However, the scripture does not qualify as a revelatory scripture (shruti), a status traditionally enjoyed by the Vedas only. It was also heard (shruti) by Arjuna, Sanjaya, Vyasa, and Dhritarashtra. Still, it is not considered a scripture that was heard. This raises the question of whether one should take the Bhagavadgita as seriously as the Vedas or the Upanishads. The latter definitely fall under shruti since they are a part of the Vedas. If the Bhagavadgita is not as important a scripture as the Upanishads or the Vedas, one wonders why it has been held in such high esteem by the scholars of Hinduism on par with the Vedas, especially the Upanishads, and with other reputed texts such as the Brahmasutras and Yoga Shastras.

Undoubtedly, the scripture occupies an important place in Hindu literature. Along with the Upanishads and Brahmasutras, it is regarded as one of the triple sources of the knowledge of liberation or final departure (Prasthanatraya) in Hinduism. Its greatness lies in the way the narrative is built and structured around four key characters: Lord Krishna, Arjuna, Sanjaya, and Dhritarashtra. Although the scripture is a dialogue between Lord Krishna and Arjuna, it is heard by three people: Sanjaya, Veda Vyasa, and Dhritarashtra. Sage Vyasa, who clairvoyantly heard it through his disciple Sanjaya, later immortalized it by remembering what he heard and incorporating it into the Mahabharata. In other words, technically, it is a memorial text (Smriti), since Veda Vyasa composed it from memory and included it in the Mahabharata. For Arjuna, it was Shruti, since he heard it directly from Lord Krishna, God in human form. Regardless of its classification, the scripture summarizes all the important teachings of the Vedas, especially the sacred knowledge of the Brahmanas, Aranyakas, and Upanishads, which constitute the knowledge part (Jnanakanda).

Symbolism of the participants

As we discussed in the previous sections, four people, Lord Krishna,

Arjuna, Sanjaya, and Dhritarashtra, participated in the Bhagavadgita discourse. Each of them has a symbolic significance in the discourse. For example, symbolically, they represent the four states of consciousness, four levels of knowledge, four methods of validating truth, and four methods in which knowledge is transmitted. Arjuna represents the wakeful state (Vaisvanara); Sanjaya represents the dream state (taijasa); Dhritarashtra represents the deep sleep state (sushupti); and Lord Krishna represents the transcendental state (turiya), which the Upanishads describe as the state of Brahman. Similarly, of the four levels of knowledge, namely ignorance, lower knowledge, higher knowledge, and transcendental knowledge, Dhritarashtra represents ignorance, Arjuna represents lower knowledge or intellectual knowledge, Sanjaya or Vyasa represents higher knowledge, and Lord Krishna represents transcendental knowledge. Ignorance is a state of delusion in which truth is not perceived at all. It is mental and spiritual darkness, in which one fails to discern right from wrong and truth from falsehood. Lower knowledge is the knowledge acquired by study, reason, and observation. It is useful in the performance of obligatory duties and achieving worldly success, but not very useful in achieving liberation unless it is purified and transformed into higher knowledge, which happened in Arjuna's case but not in the case of Dhritarashtra. Higher knowledge is the knowledge of the Self, which arises from inner purification and the practice of yoga. You can use it to pursue liberation, cultivate virtues and discerning wisdom, or engage in self-transformation. It may also give you supernatural powers such as clairvoyance, but by itself, it does not give you transcendental knowledge unless you take refuge in God and earn His grace. For liberation, you must establish your mind in the thoughts of God, practice desireless actions, self-control, and exclusive devotion, until you overcome duality and delusion and stabilize your mind in sameness and equanimity.

These three personalities, who participated in the discourse apart from Lord Krishna, also represent the three of the four methods or approaches (pramanas) by which Hindu philosophers traditionally ascertain or validate truths, namely seeing directly (pratyaksha), inferring or making educated guesses about something based on available facts, circumstantial evidence, or reasoning (anumana), comparing and contrasting with known facts (upamana), and relying upon the testimony of experts or authoritative texts (sabda). Not all traditions in Hinduism recognize these four methods. Some recognize only two or three. Lord Krishna represents the Truth itself. He represents self-knowing and all-knowing awareness. Therefore, he does not require any method to know or arrive at any truth. Arjuna represents pratyaksha or direct seeing. He witnessed and heard the discourse directly from Lord Krishna, besides seeing the universal form of Mahakal, Death, directly with the help of the special vision granted to him by Lord Krishna. Sanjaya represents sabda. Although he was not present at the battlefield personally, he heard the discourse from an authoritative source, Lord Krishna Himself. Dhritarashtra represents inference. Since he was already prejudiced against Lord Krishna and Arjuna and deluded, he drew faulty inferences from what he heard from Sanjaya according to his state of mind, likes, and dislikes. Hence, the discourse did not transform him into a devotee or alter his perspective about the war. Therefore, he remained skeptical about Lord Krishna's divinity and His teachings.

Let us now turn our attention to the manner in which divine knowledge is transmitted to human beings from a divine source like Brahma, Indra, Vishnu, Shiva, or Shakti. Divine knowledge flows to us in four distinct ways: direct, intuitive, indirect, and memorial. In some instances, God appears before certain individuals and speaks to them directly. This is the direct method. In the Bhagavadgita, Arjuna received divine knowledge from Lord Krishna directly in this manner. We may also mention Nandi, Narada, and Uddhava, who received divine knowledge directly from the source. In some cases, knowledge is transmitted through dreams, intuition, or supernatural powers, such as clairvoyance. This is also a direct method, but you do not see God physically. Sanjaya received knowledge in this manner. History is replete with instances where men received divine messages through their psychic powers or in dream states. Many spiritual truths have been rendered into religious verses in this manner. Sanjaya was like the Vedic seers who composed the Vedas by hearing them in their minds. He received the entire Gita intuitively with his mind's eye. In the third method, knowledge comes to us indirectly through scriptures, spiritual masters, and enlightened people. Dhritarashtra received knowledge in this manner. The method was appropriate for him because, by nature, he was ignorant and deluded. His lack of sight symbolically stands for his spiritual blindness. Most people in the world are drawn to spiritual subjects in this manner. The teaching of the Bhagavadgita was finally composed by Vyasa based upon his ability to remember what transpired on the battlefield on that particular day between Lord Krishna and Arjuna. This is intellectual knowledge or the memorial knowledge, which is reflected in the intelligence as knowledge and wisdom.

Lord Krishna represents transcendental knowledge, which does not require any transmission because it is free from the duality of subject and object and the process of knowing. It is an eternal knowledge, which can be neither learned nor acquired, and which can be known within oneself in a state of self-knowing. In the wakeful state, this knowledge can only be inferred but cannot be ascertained through intellectual analysis or empirical proof.

Lastly, we have to remember that the entire conversation took place on the battlefield, where a multitude of people, on both sides, stood with their respective weapons, ready to fight. They had no clue what happened between Lord Krishna and Arjuna. They did not know why the two stood in the middle of the battlefield or what had happened between them. Their minds were seized with the thoughts of war. As they were busy preparing for the fight, their attention was focused on winning against their enemies. Symbolically, the armies of Pandavas and Kauravas represent the world in general. The vast majority of people who are drawn to worldly life do not give much thought to their spiritual liberation. They live in their egoistic, deluded, and ignorant ways, incurring karma. Even if a few great souls try to put sense into their minds, they ignore them and continue their mundane existence. They fail to realize that human birth is a precious gift and a great opportunity to escape from the cycle of births and deaths.

Symbolism of sorrow

The first chapter of the Bhagavadgita is called 'Arjuna Vishada Yoga.[3] Vishada means sorrow or suffering. Vishada yoga denotes the state of sorrow, which is the dominant state of the jivas caught in samsara.

Suffering is universal and ubiquitous in human life and indeed in the lives of all the jivas. We are constantly dogged by numerous problems. There is no exaggeration in the Buddha's observation that birth is suffering, living is suffering, and dying is suffering. As long as we are subject to birth, death, and rebirth, there is no escape from suffering. Our very existence in this world begins with suffering. The Bhagavadgita, therefore, very rightly and symbolically begins with a chapter on Arjuna's sorrow, which symbolically stands for human suffering. The remaining 17 chapters are dedicated to responding to the problem of resolving human sorrow and suffering permanently. God responds to the suffering of His devotees and helps them in different ways to resolve it according to their nature or devotion. In the Bhagavadgita also, Lord Krishna responds to Arjuna's sorrow with compassion, teaching him how to resolve it and fulfill his obligations as a warrior and upholder of God's eternal Dharma.

Starting with Arjuna's sorrowful state of mind, which sets in motion a profound divine response and a message of great philosophical significance, the scripture reveals that suffering is the starting point of our spiritual journey. It opens our eyes to the truths of our existence and the need for our liberation. Arjuna's suffering led him on a spiritual path in which he was given an opportunity to understand the causes of human suffering and find effective solutions for it without escaping from the harsh realities of life or his obligatory duties. He was advised not to renounce his actions, but to give up the desire to perform actions and the desire for their results. It was also revealed to him that actions by themselves are neither sinless nor sinful and that freedom from karma does not arise from giving up actions but from giving up desires. We have already discussed the importance of sorrow and the symbolism of Arjuna's suffering in previous chapters, so there is no need to elaborate further on that here.

Footnotes

1. The modern name "Baghdad," meaning God-given, is derived from the Persian root word "baga" only.
2. In the sacred field of Kurukshetra, O Sanjaya, what are my sons and Pāndavas doing, assembled together and raring to fight?
3. Arjuna's Yoga of Sorrow.

Bhagavadgita in Daily Life

A scripture is useful only when you can relate it to it personally, believe in its source, and use its knowledge and wisdom to resolve your problems and bear with your suffering with equanimity and understanding. The Bhagavadgita contains ageless wisdom with enormous practical value, which you can use to broaden your awareness, purify your consciousness, and nurture compassion and devotion in your heart. The scripture is a manifestation (vibhuti) of Lord Krishna. By studying it sincerely, you enter into a conversation with Him and open your heart to His purifying influence. His message is clear as far as its purpose: it is meant for those who want to escape forever from the bonds of earthly life, which is stifling and limiting for the soul in many ways. It suggests how you must respond to the unpleasant aspects of your life, without ignoring your duty, and remain focused on your liberation, following the essential principles of yoga that lead you towards it. The following messages are gleaned from the Bhagavadgita. They are designed to help those who want to use the scripture's wisdom in their daily lives and transform themselves and their spiritual destinies.

Share your knowledge with others.

Knowledge is central to our liberation. We are stuck here because of ignorance and the belief that our perceptual knowledge and intelligence are reliable. The Bhagavadgita cautions us against this notion. Lord Krishna says that we should not only know the truth ourselves but also help others know it to the extent possible. Teaching the knowledge of the Gita is in itself a source of liberation. He states clearly that those who teach the knowledge of the Bhagavadgita are the dearest to Him. Thereby, He conveys the importance He places on the act of teaching. The purpose of this teaching is not to proselytize but to liberate ignorant people from the cycle of births and deaths. If you decide to teach it, you should do it without any expectation or reward. You do not have to be an expert on the scripture to teach it. You do not have to be a guru. Teach whatever little you know from your study and understanding. Share your knowledge with your family members, especially children, or friends. Participate in discussions and gatherings (satsangs), where the scripture is discussed, and let others know what you know. You may even distribute copies of the scripture for free. However, as Lord Krishna advises, you must teach it only to those who are interested in it and receptive to it. The Gita is very clear about this. It says that you should not teach it to those who do not believe in God, who are disrespectful and envious of Him, and who are by nature violent and impure.

Delve deep into the scripture.

The scripture reveals itself to the extent you probe into it. Your understanding of it grows as you progress on the path and purify your mind and body by increasing the preponderance of sattva. Svadhyaya, or the daily recitation, is helpful in this. By studying it regularly and delving deep into the knowledge of the Bhagavadgita, your insight into the scripture grows. With regular study and increased knowledge, you become stabilized in the awareness of your pure Self and the thoughts of God. It gradually leads to exclusive devotion, which, as the scripture affirms, is necessary to earn divine grace. Your mind opens to the wisdom hidden in the scripture and the mundane aspects of life. Therefore, let the scripture be your source of guidance and inspiration. Study it regularly with dispassion. Read at least a few verses every day. Refer to it whenever you are in doubt. Learn from others the subtle nuances of the text. As you imbibe its knowledge and spirit, you will experience a great transformation in your thinking and attitude, which you may not even notice in the earlier stages. However, as you begin to think about God more frequently, you open your mind to higher knowledge. With regular study and becoming skillful in the practice of yoga, you also earn divine grace and qualify for liberation, as vouched by Lord Krishna Himself in the scripture.

Know what others are saying about it.

If you do not have time to study the scripture, you may improve your knowledge of the scripture by listening to others or attending the discourses and gatherings (satsangs), where the knowledge of the Gita is taught or shared, where Lord Krishna is respected and worshipped, or where knowledgeable people meet and discuss His glories or essential teachings. Nowadays, you have many alternatives to acquire knowledge on the subject from the Internet in your spare time and saturate your mind with spiritual thoughts. Listening helps you practice concentration or active meditation. Besides, it is a good opportunity to remain passive and mindful as you engage in listening, learning, and observing dispassionately, letting go of your thoughts, opinions, ideas, and judgment. Traditionally, hearing (sravanam) the words of God or spiritual teachers is an established spiritual practice in Hinduism, which leads to self-transformation and the flowering of knowledge. While listening, you can also simultaneously practice karma sannyasa with surrender, humility, openness, discernment, detachment, and devotion, and without desires and expectations.

Virtue still matters in life.

Virtue is the foundation of spiritual life. It is the foremost among spiritual aims. It does not arise from Nature or your primitive instincts but from your purity, knowledge, and wisdom. Your humanity is a part of it. It sets you apart as a spiritual person. The Vedas prescribe rules of virtuous conduct, identifying actions that obligatory, optional, and prohibited. By following them, one can develop spirituality and divine nature. Without practicing virtue and righteous actions and cultivating divine qualities, one cannot bring light and wisdom into one's life. In this regard, scriptures such as the Bhagavadgita are helpful as spiritual guides to mold one's character and conduct. Every scripture suggests that desires are the root cause of suffering. By controlling desires, practicing detachment, and enouncing desires in actions and offering them to God as a sacrifice, one can become virtuous. In recent times, the world has grown so complex that the distinction between right and wrong is becoming increasingly blurred. In these difficult times, we must aim to keep our minds clear and know the distinction between truth and falsehood to avoid falling into the trap of stretching the truth and rationalizing our actions for temporary gains. If you believe in God and the afterlife, you must also believe in the importance of virtue and the need for honesty and integrity in your thoughts and actions. The Bhagavadgita helps you realize the importance of practicing moral purity, living virtuously, and serving God and Truth dispassionately.

Be generous and kind.

One should not live selfishly for oneself alone or one's interests, relations, and attachments. It is a self-destructive choice fraught with many dangers. However, most people do live selfishly, without showing any concern for others or their welfare. They do it even after they recognize that they live here temporarily and their desire-ridden actions bear the bitter fruit of sinful karma. One of the lessons we learn from the Bhagavadgita is that we should live selflessly and do our duties not for ourselves but for others. There is a greater joy in transcending our selfishness and helping others. We do it effectively when we realize our oneness with God and the rest of the creation. We can serve God and His creation in many ways. As the name suggests, the scripture is meant for the guidance of the Bhagavatas, the true servants of God. They are dearer to God. You can become a bhagavata by performing selfless actions and helping others in the service of God. When you serve others with compassion and humility, you serve God. By helping others without expectations, you earn His grace and love.

Cultivate divine qualities.

We can progress in whatever direction we want. With hard work and persistence, we can reach any goals we set for ourselves. Our minds manifest our dominant thoughts and desires. We can increase either light or darkness within us through our thinking and actions. Therefore, we must live responsibly, cultivating the right thinking and attitude with the scripture as our guide. If you want to be closer to God, you must embody the qualities that are ascribed to Him. You must reflect godly qualities in your thoughts and actions so that the godliness hidden in you grows in strength and brings about your transformation. If you are pure in your mind and heart, you will reflect the radiance of your pure Self through your words and actions. By cultivating divine qualities, you cultivate nearness to God. With nearness to God in thinking and actions, you improve your chances of attaining oneness with Him and achieving liberation. To be God like in thinking and actions is the highest aim for a spiritual aspirant on the path of liberation. Therefore, express the best and the highest in you in your thoughts and actions, and make your body a temple of God where the gods are nourished constantly by your sacrificial actions.

Seek divine help.

In living your life, you have many choices. What happens to you depends on how you use your free will and freedom, and with what attitude and character. You can spend your whole life seeking and striving egoistically, or you can surrender to God and live your life spiritually as He decides it for you. You can either take the driver's seat on the highway of life or sit in the backseat and allow God to guide you as your charioteer. In all these, you have a choice. You can live for yourself or you can live for God, your divine Self, giving Him the ownership and doership of your actions and possessions. The best way to invite God into your life is to remember Him in whatever you do and attribute all your successes and failures to Him, assuming that He is working through you and using every opportunity in your life to cleanse you and express Himself through you. Although you have the freedom to live as you like or exercise your free will according to your desires, you run the risk of making mistakes, incurring sinful karma, and prolonging your suffering. Since your knowledge is limited, you may not always make the right choices or choose wisely. Even if you try, the deluding forces of Maya will not let you succeed or live in peace. You can deal with this problem by inviting God into your life and making Him your guide and benefactor. Through prayers and applications, you can request Him to resolve your problems and seek guidance.

See the sacred presence of God everywhere.

The Bhagavadgita declares that God is the Creator of all worlds and beings. He is the Creator, Preserver, and Destroyer. He is also the controller of all that He creates and upholds, including the fate and liberation of beings. He manifests here in various forms and pervades the whole world through his subtle essence. No one knows the true extent of His greatness or vastness. There is no end to His manifestations. Even all that exists here represents but a little fragment of Him. One of the first steps to bring God into your life is to acknowledge Him as the source of all. Arjuna saw the universal form of God. We do see it every day, but we are too hardened in our minds to accept this whole creation around us as the universal form of God. However, if you are wise, you can use this knowledge to feel the sacred presence of God everywhere as if you are living inside a huge temple where every form is an aspect of Him or an extension of yourself. You can see His numerous manifestations and treat them with reverence and respect. As the scripture declares, those who know the omnipresence of God worship Him with great devotion. The knowledge gives them an opportunity to stabilize their minds on the numerous forms of God and experience oneness with Him. Whether you find God or yourself in whatever you perceive, eventually, it leads to freedom.

Know what sacrifice and renunciation mean.

The discourse of the Bhagavadgita begins in response to Arjuna's decision to renounce dutiful actions to avoid killing his relations and follow a safer option by living like an ascetic and begging for alms. In life, we do not always have the opportunity to choose our actions. At times, we may have to perform both pleasant and unpleasant actions as situations demand. The Bhagavadgita suggests that we should not run away from these situations, nor should we renounce actions in the name of renunciation simply because they are emotionally taxing. True renunciation is renouncing the ownership, doership, and the desires hidden in our actions, and true sacrifice is giving up the desire for the results of such actions. We can apply these two principles in our lives and perform our duties with detachment to face the suffering arising from unpleasant situations and work for our liberation. By applying these principles, we can live our lives peacefully without being crushed by the weight of our materialistic goals or our desires and attachments.

Know the distinction between the body and the soul.

The Bhagavadgita teaches you an important lesson about your essential nature. It states very clearly that you are not your mind and body, but a divine soul who is caught in the web of Nature and bound to them by circumstances. You must find a way out of this predicament and free yourself from the bonds of Nature through the practice of yoga so that you can live eternally without being bound to Nature or the cycle of births and deaths. Although most of us are aware of our spiritual nature, we do not acknowledge it or reflect it adequately in our thinking and attitude. Frankly, we do not consider ourselves divine souls. If this were not true, people would not be so preoccupied with their physical features or the class distinctions that set us apart. By studying the scripture and assimilating its knowledge, we can bring about a paradigm shift in our awareness, accepting ourselves as divine souls and shifting our attention from the physical to the mental and then to the spiritual.

See the role of God in every aspect of your life.

If God is the source of all, it follows that He is also the source of our lives, actions, and destinies. When we take pride in our achievements and feel depressed about our failures, we not only ignore the role of God but also fail to realize the significance of our actions (karma) and their consequences. In seeking things out of egoism and desires, we also allow our actions to shape our destinies and sow the seeds of our future lives. You must attribute to God both the positive and negative results arising from your actions, and accept them as the work of God and the manifestation of His inviolable will. You must surrender to the events that unfold in your life with equanimity, accepting them as learning opportunities. Most importantly, you must open yourself to life and stop fighting with yourself over your failures and disappointments.

Focus on the effort, not the result.

We are often consumed by the expectations of what we want to accomplish rather than what actions we must perform to meet our obligations. The Bhagavadgita says this is a flawed approach, which leads to suffering, fear, anxiety, and disappointment. If you want peace, you must set aside your expectations and silence your desires. You can have goals, but your attention should primarily be on the effort or on doing the task rather than on its outcome. If you focus on the task, good results will follow automatically. Even if they do not, you will have the satisfaction of knowing that you have done whatever was necessary. We have no control over what may happen or how our actions may turn out, but we can always control our actions and perform them diligently. We can also control our reactions to external or internal events. The Bhagavadgita rightly advises us to perform our actions dutifully without desiring their outcome. When we focus on the results, we feel anxious. When we focus on the tasks, we become attentive and determined. When we focus on the techniques and the processes rather than on the results, our performance improves vastly. We also become confident and show greater willingness to undertake difficult and even unpleasant tasks for the sake of duty.

Be cheerful and content.

Contended people are happier than those who take life seriously and demand too much from it. We enter this world with nothing, but as time goes by, we develop desires and attachments and accumulate things, relationships, thoughts, opinions, and possessions. At some stage, we realize that our lives have become burdensome as the weight of our actions and their consequences begins to bear fruit, and our suffering begins to weigh on our minds. This is when introspection begins and the seeds of our spiritual journey are sown as we search for peace and freedom from sorrow. We realize how we create our identities and our suffering through desires and actions, and how we can transform ourselves to escape from the repetitive patterns that keep us bound to this world. At this stage, many people turn to God or a supernatural power to find answers and solutions to problems they cannot resolve. The Bhagavadgita advises us to lighten up and not take our lives too seriously or selfishly. Instead of becoming attached to things and pursuing them through desire-ridden actions, it says that we should practice renunciation (which means giving up desires) and live like lotus plants in the waters of worldly existence, unencumbered by its burdens. Renunciation does not mean you should give up the joys of life and live a depressingly boring existence. Unfortunately, it is how most people are conditioned to visualize the life of a renunciant. However, that is simply a matter of choice. The purpose of renunciation is to escape from suffering, not to live through it and become its symbol. Renunciation should unburden and lighten those who practice it so that they can live freely without worrying and feeling anxious about their lives or their future. When you practice detachment, you become free from the bouts of depression and mood swings that are consequential to a life of desire-ridden actions. Becoming detached from the mind's natural association with suffering, negative thoughts, and mental instability is the purpose and goal of yoga. This is clearly stated in the Bhagavadgita.

Live spontaneously

The central theme of the Bhagavadgita is to perform obligatory duties without desires and attachments. The scripture is primarily meant for householders who are engaged in performing their obligatory duties and upholding Dharma. Since these duties arise from God's eternal duties, they must be performed as a sacrifice, selflessly and according to the divine law, to do their part in God's creation, and ensure the order and regularity of the world. The purpose of karma sannyasa, which essentially means performing actions without desires and offering the fruit of actions to God, is to ensure that the devotee who practices it lives freely, placing his faith and trust solely in God, without worrying about what may or may not happen. A true karma yogi who practices karma sannyasa remains equal to the dualities and content with his circumstances. He is not disturbed by others or by fate, and does not disturb anyone as he makes peace with the world and remains satisfied within himself. He lives spontaneously as life happens, feeling neither overjoyed nor depressed by what life offers to him. Even if he is often troubled by anxious thoughts, in moments of weakness, he quickly overcomes them and regains his balance by absorbing his mind in contemplation.

Worship the Highest.

Who you worship influences the quality of your life and experiences. You pursue what you worship, and it eventually catches up with you and becomes a part of you and your life. From the Bhagavadgita, we learn that we should not worship material things since it leads to attachment, delusion, and bondage. Some people worship material things, such as name and fame, and become deeply involved with the world. Some worship dark and evil beings, ghosts, spirits, and other beings of sunless worlds. Others worship divinities through sacrifices, seeking their intervention and blessings. This last option is at least better than the other two since it guarantees a good birth in the next life. However, the best option is worshipping the Supreme Self with exclusive devotion. One may worship God in any form, but the most effective way is to worship Him as the Highest Self. Alternatively, you may worship Him as your inner Self (Isvara). Both approaches are recommended in our scriptures, and both are beneficial.

Bibliography

Aurobindo, S. (1995). *Essays on the Gita*. Lotus Press.

Aurobindo, S., & Baran, A. R. (1996). *Bhagavad Gita and Its Message*. Lotus Press.

Aurobindo, S. (1990). *The Secret of the Veda*. Sri Aurobindo Ashram. (Original work published 1914–1920)

Aurobindo, S. (1972). *The Upanishads*. Sri Aurobindo Ashram.

Besant, A., & Das, B. (1905). *The Bhagavad-Gita: With Sanskrit text, free translation into English, a word-for-word translation, and an introduction on Sanskrit grammar*. Theosophical Publishing Society.

Besant, A. W. (2005). *The Bhagavad Gita Or the Lord's Song*. Kessinger Publishing.

Bhawuk, D. P. S. (2011). *Spirituality and Indian Psychology: Lessons from the Bhagavad-Gita*. Springer.

Byrd, C. M. (2007). *The Bhagavad-Gita in Black and White: From Mulatto Pride to Krishna Consciousness*. Backintyme Publishing.

Chakravarti, R. (1967). *Bhagavad-Gita*. Bharatiya Vidya Bhavan.

Chinmayananda, S. (2000). *The Art of Man Making: 114 Short Talks on the Bhagwad Geeta*. All India Chinmaya Yuva Kendra.

Dass, R. (2004). *Paths to God: Living the Bhagavad Gita*. Harmony Books.

Dayananda, S. (2005). *Teaching of the Bhagavadgita*. Vision Books.

Easwaran, E. (2010). *The Bhagavad Gita*. Read How You Want.

Edgerton, F. (1994). *The Bhagavadgita*. Motilal Banarsidass Publishers.

Feuerstein, G. (2003). *The Deeper Dimension of Yoga: Theory and Practice*. Shambhala.

Giri, S. (1991). *Bhagavad Gita: Interpretation of Sriyukteswar*. Sanskrit Classics.

Hawley, J. (2001). *The Bhagavad Gita: A Walkthrough for Westerners*. New World Library.

Judge, W. Q. (1979). *Bhagavad-Gita Combined with Essays on the Gita*. Theosophical University Press.

Kezwer, G. P. (2009). *The Essence of the Bhagavad Gita: Course Manual*. CreateSpace.

Krishnananda, S. (2000). *The Philosophy of the Bhagavadgita*. Divine Life Society.

Krishnaswami, O. R. (2006). *The Bhagavad Gita: The Divine Message*. Lightning Source.

Lasater, J. H. (1999). *Living Your Yoga: Finding the Spiritual in Everyday Life*. Rodmell Press.

Lipner, J. (1996). *Fruits of Our Desiring: Inquiry into the Ethics of the Bhagavad Gita*. Bayeux Arts.

Lipner, J. (1997). *The Bhagavad-Gita for Our Times*. Oxford University Press.

Mahajan, Y. (2002). *Geeta Enlightened*. Motilal Banarsidass Publishers.

Mahesh Yogi, M. (1976). *Bhagavad-Gita*. MIU Press.

Malinar, A. (2009). *The Bhagavadgita: Doctrines and Contexts*. Cambridge University Press.

Mathai, P. S. (1956). *A Christian Approach to the Bhagavadgita*. Y.M.C.A. Publishing House.

Minor, R. (1986). *Modern Indian Interpreters of the Bhagavadgita*. State University of New York Press.

Nicolas, A. de. (2004). *Bhagavad Gita: The Ethics of Decision-Making*. Ibis Press/Nicolas Hays.

Panda, N. C. (2009). *Bhagavad Gita*. DK Printworld Private Limited.

Patton, L. L. (2008). *The Bhagavad Gita*. Penguin.

Prabhupada, S. B. (1989). *Bhagavad-Gita As It Is*. The Bhaktivedanta Book Trust.

Purohit, S., & Burroughs, K. C. (2001). *Bhagavad Gita: Annotated & Explained*. SkyLight Paths Publishing.

Radhakrishnan, S. (2000). *Indian Philosophy: Vol. 1*. Oxford University Press.

Ranade, R. D. (1965). *The Bhagavadgītā as a Philosophy of God-realization*. Bharatiya Vidya Bhavan.

Row, T. S. (1921). *The Philosophy of the Bhagavad-Gita*. Theosophical Publishing House.

Sastri, A. M. (1901). *The Bhagavad-Gita, with the Commentary of Sri Sankaracharya*. G.T.A. Printing Works.

Sharma, A. (1987). *New Essays in the Bhagavadgītā*. Books & Books.

Sinha, P. (1987). *The Gita as It Was: Rediscovering the Original Bhagavadgita*. Open Court.

Telang, K. T. (1990). *The Bhagavadgita*. Atlantic Publishers and Distributors.

Tirtha, S. S. (2007). *Bhagavad Gita for Modern Times*. Sat Yuga Press.

Jayaram, V. (2011). *The Bhagavadgita Complete Translation*. Pure Life Vision LLC.

Jayaram, V. (2024). *Bhagavadgita: Unveiling The Gita's Secrets*. Pure Life Vision LLC.

Book Cover Credits
Front Cover Image: Adobe Stock Asset ID: #575718363
Cover Design by Jayaram V

www.ingramcontent.com/pod-product-compliance
Lightning Source LLC
Chambersburg PA
CBHW040251090526
44586CB00041B/2746